WHEN THE
Bright
MOON RISES

The Awakening of Ancient Memories

Dena Merriam

FIRST EDITION

ISBN 978-0-578-76682-9

Cover Photo: Anjani Lynn White

Book Design: Sacredhandproductions@gmail.com

Cover Design & Art Director: Mary Arose Hines

Interior Book Design & Typesetting: Kendra Adler

Chapter Head Icon Design: "Solluna" by Felipe Sena

Li Bai poems:

"Drinking in Moonlight", "Conversations Among Mountains", "Waking Up Drunk on a Spring Day"

from FIVE TANG POETS translated by David Young, copyright © 1990 Oberlin College Press, FIELD

Translation Series 15

"Seeking Mistress Tengkong," translated by Lily Xiao Hong Lee

"Song for Accompanying Uncle Hua on Xie Tiao's Tower." The Banished Immortal: A Life of Li Bai by Ha

Jin. Pantheon Books, 2019

"Night Thoughts at Tung-Lin Monastery on Lu Mountain", "Ancient Song," "Thoughts in Night Quiet,"

The Selected Poems of Li Po. Translated by David Hinton. A New Directions Book, 1996

Distributed by **SCB Distributors**

DEDICATION

I dedicate this book to the Vedic Rishis and the Daoist Hermits who have shown us the way to realize our immortal nature; to the poet Li Bai who first awakened in me the love for poetry; to Mata Saraswati, the source of all inspiration; and to the people of India and China, that they may draw upon their ancient sacred wisdom to guide their future.

> *What cannot be spoken with words, but that by which words are spoken:*
> *Know that alone to be Brahman, the Spirit:*
> *and not what people here adore.*
>
> *—The Kena Upanishad*

> *The Dao that can be spoken is not the eternal Dao.*
> *The name that can be named is not the eternal name.*
> *Nameless, the beginning of heaven and earth.*
> *Named, the mother of ten thousand things.*
>
> *—Dao De Jing*

> *. . . Heaven's fragrance everywhere pure*
> *emptiness, heaven's music endless,*
>
> *I sit silent. It's still, the entire Buddha-*
> *realm in a hair's-breadth, mind-depths*
>
> *all bottomless clarity, in which vast*
> *kalpas begin and end out of nowhere.*
>
> *—Li Bai, from Night Thoughts*
> *at Tung-Lin Monastery on*
> *L Mountain*

TABLE OF CONTENTS

CHARACTERS

Between Lives

Usha and **Satya**

Vedic India, Brahmavarta (9th Century BCE)

Sundari

Muni Baba, the wise man of Sundari's forest tribe

Dada, Sundari's great-great-grandfather

Prema, Sundari's sister, lost to the Nagas

Arrav, Saivi, and Nityam, Sundari's brothers

Sachit, Brahmin who has taken a vow of celibacy

Sage Gayatri, powerful woman sage with a hermitage

Kapila, grandson of Sage Gayatri

Eastern Han Dynasty (1st-3 rd Century CE)

Chunhua

Wang Wei, Chunhua's husband, a sorcerer

Chunhua's son and daughter

Zhang Daoling, Daoist master, whose ideals formed the basis for the state of Hanning (idyllic Daoist community)

Zhang Lu, grandson of Zhang Daoling

Yeye, Chunhua's grandfather

Yu Yan, disciple of Yeye

Early Tang Empire (7th Century CE)

Meihua
Consort Niu
Consort Biyu

Tang China (8th Century CE)

Lady Zong Shu, called **Shu**
Li Bai, an historical poet
Zong Jing, Shu's brother
Zong Yue, Shu's sister
Shifu, Daoist master Li Tengkong
Ying, nun at Mt. Lushan monastery, Shifu's disciple

INTRODUCTION

A portal opens when the dream world begins to recede, but before the world of outer sense perception assumes control. That is when certain experiences often occur—memories that emerge from their hidden places, messages and visions that travel through inner pathways. It was at this intersection where time and space are suspended that I saw a beautiful young male being of light arise out of the sun; not the physical sun that we see with open eyes, but rather an internal sun. He was not alone. Many beings of his nature came forth as he revealed himself. Then I saw a beautiful young female being of light arise from the moon world; again, it was not the physical moon we see with open eyes. I felt immense bliss emanating from both the male and female forms and I was swept into their joyous world. Intuitively I knew that some celebration was taking place between the worlds of the sun and the moon.

Then, in the vision, I found myself standing in a field, my dear friend from India by my side. The inner world receded and looking up with open eyes, I saw the physical sun and moon—the sun shining in all its brilliance, as I have seen so many times before, and the moon, round in her fullness, faintly visible in the daytime sky. Then I closed my eyes and again entered the inner world of the celestials where this great celebration was taking place. It was a magical sight. Once more opening my eyes, I saw the physical forms of the sun and the moon. Closing them, I again entered the internal worlds hidden behind the bodies we know as sun and moon and experienced the rejoicing between those two worlds.

As I opened and closed my eyes, moving between the outer and inner worlds, I felt confused. Intuitively, I knew there was a union taking place between two celestial beings. It was as if this union had been created to generate more love in our planetary system. I dwelt for some time in this joy as I watched these beings emerge and join together, then in the vision I turned to my friend and asked, "Where is this internal world I see?" He did not respond, but as soon as I posed this question I came back into normal waking consciousness and was left to wonder about what I had seen, but also to bask in the love I had experienced.

A feeling of tremendous upliftment lasted for many weeks, as did my questions as to what I had witnessed, and why. If indeed that celebration had been a celestial marriage, why had I been called there? This question pursued me for months. I had experienced a great outpouring of love that encompassed much of our physical solar system, but it was hard for my rational mind to understand.

When this vision occurred, I had recently returned from Japan, where my organization, the Global Peace Initiative of Women (GPIW), had hosted an interfaith dialogue. My friend from India, the one who was present in my vision, had joined me in Japan for this dialogue. I would see him several weeks later at a gathering GPIW was planning in Thailand for young climate change activists, but I couldn't get through to him now, so I sat alone with my questions, unable to find answers on my own. As I dwelt on the experience, I could not help but feel it was related to memories that had stirred within me several months earlier.

It was now the fall of 2019. In the spring of that year I had been in

Varanasi, India, for the launch of my book *The Untold Story of Sita*. One day before dawn, a swamini friend took me to the ancient Kashi Vishwanath temple, my first time being there without the usual crowds. Much had changed since my last visit. Neighboring housing had been taken down, revealing the long-hidden *shikharas* (towers) of the temple complex. As I stared at one of the shikharas gleaming in the breaking light of dawn, a vague memory came over me. I saw myself as a young forest girl coming out of the jungle, feeling as if I had entered a heavenly realm when I saw temple towers for the first time. Now at the temple, I stood for many minutes with closed eyes, recalling the first sight of the towers rising in the distance as I left behind my life in the forest. In those few minutes I glimpsed an ancient time.

The voice of my companion and the sound of growing crowds soon drew me out of my reverie, but those moments unlocked memories that swept through me for weeks of a life from the time of the early Vedic civilization.

Months after the vision of the celestial marriage, pieces of various memories were beginning to fall into place. I longed for the time when I could seclude myself and go back into this past to understand more fully the relevance of what I was experiencing, if indeed this was a past life recall. Over the years I have experienced many past life memories, so vividly that I have actually felt myself reliving those lives, experiencing again the pain and sorrow, the loss, the joys and loves, all of which can be quite depleting. It is enough to cry over the struggles in one's current life, but to mourn a loss of hundreds or thousands of years ago only adds to one's burden! Yet these experiences brought much learning and insight, and so I was grateful, accepting what came but not seeking more.

When past life memories first began to arise, I was skeptical and took an investigative approach, traveling to places I had recalled, looking for signs, which always came. I was able to sequence numerous lives, which I recorded in my book *My Journey through Time: A Spiritual Memoir of Life, Death and Rebirth*. Several years after the publication of that book, I was in India when memories of an earlier life as a simple servant in ancient India came back to me, and I subsequently recorded those memories in a book *The Untold Story of Sita: An Empowering Tale for Our Time*. The narrative that had emerged was of a much earlier era, and I questioned whether these memories were mine or was I channeling the life of another? As I experienced the life of that humble servant in ancient India, I relived so many of the events, which were as real to me as events in my current life, that I put aside my doubts and accepted what I was seeing.

The process of past life recall has always been the same for me. I am swept inside, as if a vacuum draws me within, and I see scenes, hear dialogues, and become an actor in an internal play. After writing *The Untold Story of Sita*, my experiences of past life recall paused, but I was not sorry because they consume a lot of energy and cause a withdrawal from my current life. I wondered if that was the end, if I was to see no more, but that was not to be the case. Memories of Vedic India flickered in and out of my consciousness as I carried on with my daily life.

Then came the vision of the celestial worlds of the moon and sun, and I wondered if there was any connection. I could not allow my mind to dwell long on these experiences, as I had the responsibility of organizing a conference in Thailand, which was just weeks away. Within a few days of arriving there, to my great surprise, a whole new series of memories emerged, ones that took me back to the Tang Empire in China in the mid-8th century, a time of great cultural flourishing. This brought more confusion. Until this point, I had had little association with Chinese cultural or spiritual traditions, as my whole orientation had been to India.

As the recollections emerged, I found myself in the presence of a poet. One day I uttered his name, Li Bai, and saw myself as this poet's wife, one who has long been forgotten, a poet in her own right struggling to find her own voice. Honestly, I did not know what to make of these recollections that were emerging with such speed and force that I could not but watch and listen.

Looking back at the early years of my current life, I recalled that I started writing poetry at the age of ten. I majored in poetry in college and graduate school, studying the Tang poets and loving the poetry of old China. I abandoned my aspirations to be a published poet only after taking up a serious meditation practice and shifting my devotion to spiritual texts. I understood that my love of poetry came from a previous birth and was not my true calling in this life. Yet as memories of Tang China returned, I found myself getting up in the middle of the night to write poetry about my experiences. After nearly 30 years of poetic silence, the stream of inspiration was flowing once again. I then realized that my connection to poetry was related to the memories that were now emerging, so I planned a retreat in the Himalayas where I could dive deeply into my interior life and see where the path would take me.

Whenever memories of long ago emerge, I look for a sign, nothing dramatic, a small sign that only I might recognize. Such a sign emerged right before I left for India in January 2020. I was walking with a friend down a street by my office, passing a shop that sells modern lamp shades, a shop I have walked by thousands of times. This day as I casually glanced in the window, as I often did, an antique Chinese lamp caught my attention. There had never been anything antique or Chinese in that store, but what called to me was the jade phoenix on the base of the lamp. I stood staring at it, feeling it held some deep personal significance. I immediately went into the shop and bought the lamp. Thinking me quite impulsive, my friend laughed at me for deciding to purchase such an expensive item on first sight before even asking the price, but it was the sign for which I had been waiting. I knew it to be a gift from my long-forgotten husband of old.

∽

The story that I tell in the following pages is the one that emerged during my time of solitude and retreat by the sacred Ganga (Ganges River), and it is one that I fully relived. I experienced again all the trauma, the sadness, the tears, the joy, the love, the transmission of spiritual wisdom—everything that comes along during the soul's journey in a body. I was able to delve into my memories and record what I was seeing and hearing.

This book begins in the place we return to between births on earth. In that place, memories of a very ancient life began to return, memories of a love that had not been fulfilled. After much growth and spiritual development, those two lovers were able to meet again on more equal terms many thousands of years later in Tang China and bring to completion a love story that had its beginnings in a very different era.

Between Lives

I awoke to find myself in an unfamiliar place, very beautiful but unknown to me. Slowly sitting up, I glanced around me. The landscape was vibrant with color—luscious flowering trees, fragrant meadows, forests in the distance. Taking in the scene before me, I noticed many wonderous beings, but they were not at all familiar and I was not fully present. Memories of my last birth on earth clung to me like wet leaves, refusing to let go. I was neither here nor there, but somewhere in between, and yet here I was, aware that I had been released from earthly life. As I was wondering how to proceed, I heard a voice call me, but I looked around and no one was present. The name called was not the one of the earthly body I had left behind, but the name I was known by in this world. Again, I heard my name being called, "Usha."

That is me, I thought, but who is calling me? I knew that I still had the form of my last birth, a woman named Meihua, but hers was an identity I didn't want to keep. It had been a lonely life and I was glad to be free. I wanted to return to the form of Usha. I wanted to find Satya, my companion in this world of light. Then I realized it was he who was calling me, but how to find him? Slowly I stood up and wondered which direction to take, when my feet spontaneously began walking toward the forest in the distance, as if some force was pulling me there. As I walked, I glanced around and became aware of the joy of all the beings passing me. It felt as if a momentous event was soon to happen, but I didn't have that joy within me. I should not be here, I thought, as I have not yet subdued the memories. I need to find Satya. He is the one who helps free me from whatever clings to me from my last birth.

I hurried toward the forest, noticing that many of the beautiful beings were casting caring glances my way, as if gazing at me with sympathy. They must see the sorrow shading my heart, I thought. I felt enclosed in a shadow, a cloak of sadness, and wondered if they could see it. *Of course they can*, I thought to myself. In this world nothing is hidden, but I knew that those feelings of sadness would soon fall away and become like a dream.

I didn't want to reflect on the life of Meihua. I had shut that door and wanted to free myself of that identity. But there had also been times of discovery and joy in that life. It was in the form of Meihua that I had come to appreciate the beauty of poetry, to know its power to uplift the soul. This love for poetry was still with me now. It had not faded away. Some of the poems I had loved the most still sang in my mind. I tried to push them away. The closer I drew to the forest, the greater was my impulse to suppress all thoughts of Meihua's life. I stopped before entering the forest and said quietly to myself, *Meihua, may your thoughts drift away like vaporous clouds, settling somewhere in the far distance so they will no longer disturb me.* As I thought those words, an image of the moon goddess appeared to me, and I hurried to add, *Not that memory. You, I will remember. Don't hide yourself. Don't sink as memories do into the depths of the mind's bottomless sea.*

The forest was quiet when I entered, with no one present. I looked around. It was not a familiar place. Where was I and why was I so drawn to come here? How would I find my way back to Satya? Regardless of its unfamiliarity, there was something very comforting about this place, which was strikingly beautiful. A sacred quietude hovered over the seemingly endless tracts of trees. Amid the gentle swaying of overhanging branches, I could hear the quiet humming of the great sound vibration, subtle and rhythmic, soothing and embracing. "This is a very sacred forest," I murmured to myself. Slowing my pace, I walked deeper into the assembly of trees, looking around at the tall, majestic trunks that reached high toward the sky and allowed only filtered light to peer through.

I walked and walked, enjoying the beauty until I came to a place where soft moss bedded the land, a small enclosure amid the gathering of trees. Sitting down, I thought: *I must find a way to reach Satya.* Entering meditation, I quieted my mind. The restless sea of thoughts became subdued and I drifted into a sweet calm. As I settled down, suddenly a sharp, deep pain arose in the area of my heart and I let out a small cry. It was then that I felt his hands take hold of mine.

"Usha," he quietly said. "I am here."

Opening my eyes, I saw Satya seated directly in front of me. His very presence soothed the pain that had arisen within me. "Usha, you have been drawn to this sacred forest for a purpose," he said gently. When I didn't respond, he continued, "It is the place for reviving memories, ones that are difficult to retrieve."

I looked at him with both confusion and relief. How glad I was to see him, and yet this was not my normal return, not the way it usually was when I departed from a human life. "Satya, I should feel joy having found you. What is this pain that is arising, this searing sensation?"

He sat quietly with closed eyes for a few minutes and then opened them and replied, "Memories of another birth from long ago are awakening in you, and perhaps this awakening is needed now. Do not resist. Allow to arise what seeks to be known. I will guide you."

"I don't want to remember anything more. I have not yet put to rest the memories of Meihua's life." As he placed his hand on my heart, the pain subsided but memory after memory began to overtake me: scenes of another forest, where I had lived so long ago; images of a life during a most peaceful and elevated time on earth, when the first songs and poems burst forth from the ethers. It was then that my love of poetry began, not in the life of Mei-hua, which was only a rediscovery. But that life of long ago was also filled with sorrow, unfulfilled desire, something incomplete that was pursuing me now, something that I had to bring to completion. The thought arose that I must go back in time and see what pain remained from that life. I told myself that I couldn't proceed, journey forward, until that matter had been resolved, but I didn't know what it was that needed completion or why it had taken so long. As these thoughts entered my mind, I looked to Satya for comfort and guidance.

He was deep in meditation. I felt his spirit align with mine so that he could experience my memories. After some time, he spoke. "I will take you back. What was left unfulfilled will be fulfilled in your next birth on earth. If this forest has called you here, then it is the intention for you to remember before entering physical form again, so that you will choose a path that enables you to fulfil your long-suppressed desire. You will have choices to make and the opportunity to bring this matter to completion."

Closing my eyes, I felt myself relax into the sacred sound vibration, becoming one with it, and allowed myself to be carried back into the distant past. I was like a ship without sails on a roiling ocean, surrendering to the waves as they rocked me back and forth, carrying me to wherever I needed to be, to whatever I needed to remember. As I was sinking deeper and deeper into meditation, I heard a thought enter Satya's mind: *Usha, there is a risk in taking you back. Once open, the door of memory may not so easily be shut. We do not know what will emerge. Is this a risk you are willing to take?* I heard my thought respond, *It is.*

At that moment, my heart began to quiver, but I was so deep in the cauldron of memories that there was nothing I could do. The lid had been lifted, the wounds opened, and I felt the scars left from a long-ago birth.

PART 1: VEDIC INDIA

9th Century BCE (Descending Satya Yuga)

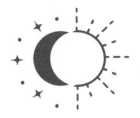

Chapter One

THE MELTING OF THE ICE

T he dense forest that I called home was lush with life. My clan had lived there for many, many centuries, since the ice had melted and the sea had covered our ancestral lands. My ancestors had walked and walked until they came to a place where Muni Baba, a silent sage, was seated in meditation. Our leader at that time said it was this baba who had created the forest for our shelter and food, when the ice melted and the rains came. Our clan leader told us that Muni Baba would protect us in this new home and provide for all of our needs.

This baba spoke to my ancestors through silence. He could exchange thoughts with them without speech, and so he became the silent guide of our clan. Although food in the forest was plentiful, he lived on nothing but whatever light could reach him through a parting in the trees, and on the life energy that he drew from the ether. No one ever saw him take food, and that is one reason why everyone revered him. Generations were born and died, but he stayed, rarely moving from his place among the trees.

In the forests, the trees were tall and wide, so tall that a child could barely see the top branches, and so wide that they provided cover from the rains and the pounding sun for whole families. For centuries after the ice began to melt, the rains came with great frequency, as water was released from its frozen form. The melting fields of ice also gave birth to the rivers, and this is what bred life and allowed the human population to grow. Our elders said this was the reason why the forces of the sky had hurled a giant rock down to earth to break up the ice: so that we could thrive. Even though the melting waters created much disruption, they also birthed new societies as the clans grew in size. My mother led one such clan.

Muni Baba conveyed everything through my *Dada* (grandfather), the great-great-grandfather of my mother, whose wife had once led the clan, and who lived for well over one hundred years. Muni Baba taught our Dada how to make sounds that could activate hidden forces and harmonize with other universal sounds, but for the rest of us he conveyed through Dada a simpler language, not those powerful, secret words. From Muni Baba we learned that sound or vibration was the foundation of everything. He taught us to speak only when necessary and to choose carefully the sounds we would utter, but no one ever heard his voice. He transmitted his knowledge from one mind to another and our Dada was the most receptive, as if their minds were one. Dada's mouth spoke what was in Muni Baba's mind, but I wondered why the baba didn't speak himself.

Muni Baba was still with us when I was born. My mother had taken three husbands and had birthed five children by those husbands. My elder sister and I were of the first husband, who had died unexpectantly. Then came two brothers from the second husband, who had also died, and then another brother from a much younger husband, who didn't die. My sister was going to lead the clan after my mother aged, so she often stayed by my mother's side, learning from her how to guide the clan. She was like a second mother to me, even though she was only two years my elder. That was because my mother was often so busy looking after the clan, tending to the needs of the families, caring for their wellbeing, that it was my sister who looked after me when I was young.

She led me through the forest to magical rock enclosures where beautiful winged creatures lived, creatures so small they would rest on your hand and flicker their light energy in greeting. She led me to other places where the larger creatures roamed, and we delighted in the vast variety of animal life, quietly watching them. She had learned from our mother—who had been taught by Dada, who had learned from Muni Baba—how to speak without words to the creatures, for they had not yet gained the use of spoken language. She communicated with them by catching their mental images. She said they didn't have the ability to grasp the sounds that underlie the universe, sounds that put universal forces into motion. That power, she said, was gifted to humans. It seemed that everything we did was related back to the use of sound and speech to provide for our needs and to maintain the well-being of all around us. My sister had learned what sounds calmed the animals and satisfied their hunger. She had also learned how to maintain the balance in our forest world so that no species would become too plentiful or too sparse.

Dada taught us that what happened in our forest affected worlds far away, as distant as the stars, and that what happened in the skies affected our forest life, and he taught us how to read the messages and understand the language of the star beings. Every night my mother and sister would go with Dada to a clearing where the skies opened up. They would look for signs to see how the movement of the stellar and planetary bodies were affecting our earth, for in every moment the whole universe changes and these movements affect all the many worlds. We are linked by an invisible chain—a chain of love, as my mother used to say. "The stars are our elder guides," she added, "and they help us prepare for the future. It is also true that they are neutral about the information they convey, and it is up to us to use this information wisely."

Even though our clan was made up of many families, we functioned as one large family. Everything we had was shared, and never in all my memory did anyone take more than their portion. This was unthinkable. Never were we to take more than was needed for that one day. My mother once took the whole clan to a small river not far from us where we got our water. She told us that if we stopped the flow of water, the area downstream would dry up and other life forms would die, and we would be responsible. Similarly, if we took more than we needed from the forest, the flow of the life force would slow to a trickle, causing distress in other areas. This is the law of the universe, she said. Every particle is connected to every other, and the one who causes pain is the one who will suffer. The one who treasures and upholds life is the one who will know joy. This was the knowledge inbred in us. Respecting this law is our duty, mother said.

The rhythms of the days and seasons beat in our bodies. We were one with them and sweet contentment filled the air. There was little illness, for the forest foods and water were pure and contained every element our bodies needed. We had medicinal herbs in plenty to correct any imbalance. Death caused sorrow, but it was not a searing sadness because we understood that those souls would reappear, and because we knew that a soul departed only after it had fulfilled its purpose.

On all matters, we turned to Dada for guidance. He seemed to have a storehouse of knowledge, and yet his message was always so simple that anyone could grasp it—to know our place in the universe and to honor the forces that give us life. The children loved his stories. When thunder, lightning, and heavy rains frightened the youngest ones, Dada would calm them by saying *Indra Dev* (the king of the celestial worlds) was sending water to fulfil our needs and to clear the air. The lightning was a great show for us, but the people in our clan began to think of this great power called Indra in rather frightening human terms.

When I sat alone with Dada, he would often say, "The young mind turns the deities into powerful and sometimes scary human-like beings, but that is not the way it is at all."

"Then what are they and where are they, Dada?"

"You will have to find the answers yourself, because they cannot really be expressed in words. The *devas* (gods) can be experienced, but not described. Our human language is very limited, as are our minds, but we can rise above the mind to another level of awareness, as Muni Baba has."

"But he is Muni Baba."

"We can all become like him if we set our will to it." There were many such conversations with Dada, but most often I would stare at him blankly and then scamper off, wondering if I would ever understand his meaning.

In our daily life there was a quiet joy, but few of us could really say that we personally experienced the intensity of joy that shone on the face of Muni Baba. He sat there in a golden beam of light with a slight smile on his face, and we children would peer at him from behind the trees at a distance, sent by our elders to get the blessing of the day but cautioned not to come too close, lest we disturb him.

As I grew older and the clan grew larger, my mother began to divide duties among us, and many believed that this was because a new need had arisen. Previously there had been no need for protection, but the winds were shifting, bringing new elements into the forest, things we couldn't see or understand. For the first time, some of us awakened at night to see shadows lurking behind the trees, and my mother told us that shadow people were moving into the forest seeking to claim it as their own. This was a previously unknown concept to us—claiming territory as one's own.

My mother felt it to be time to take up simple means to keep harm at bay. She called the clan together and said each person should choose a duty that suited his or her skills or desires. My elder sister Prema and two of my brothers were swift of foot and hand and eager to learn means of defense, so they were taught to handle a spear and shoot arrows. The youngest of my brothers loved to uncover forest foods, and he became one of the food gatherers. I had no particular desire, so when my mother asked, "Sundari, what skill do you want to perfect?" I looked at her blankly.

"You make such useful clothing for yourself out of the forest plants and take shells from the nuts to string around your neck," she commented as she fingered the necklace I had crafted. It was true that I loved to gather long grasses, tree bark, and whatever else I could find to weave into wrappings and decorations for my body. "You have a gift for beauty, so let it be your responsibility to help make clothing for the clan and mats to sleep on." Others offered to help keep our encampment clean and prepare the food, and so the duties were divided.

For a number of years, we didn't hear much about the shadow people, but Prema and the others sharpened their spears and learned the art of archery, and I chased any fear from my mind.

When I was about twelve, Prema and I overheard our mother telling Dada that several days ago she had risen especially early, before dawn, and had gone to see the *muni* (silent sage), as she always did first thing after waking.

As she approached, she beheld a most beautiful light form, a female, standing before him. It appeared that she was feeding him her light. As she held out her hand, light poured from her into him. "It was a different kind of light, Dada, unlike sunlight, as if it wasn't meant for human eyes to see," my mother said.

Dada nodded, "That is the light of the celestial world, more refined than physical light." Quickly Prema pulled me down behind some tall brush and placed her finger over her mouth, indicating we should listen quietly. "I suspect that was Shri Devi (the goddess Lakshmi)," he continued. "It is very rare to catch a glimpse of her."

"Shri Devi?" Mother asked in a curious voice. He nodded. "She is so very beautiful. Do you think he is her child?"

"We are all her children," he smiled.

My mother grew thoughtful. "Then it was she who led us here to be under his protection."

"No doubt," he replied.

"She must have intended for me to see her or why would I have arisen and gone there so early?" she mused. "As I stood there, I felt a great warmth and expansion here"—she pointed to the center of her chest.

"That is the heart center, my child, where intuitive knowledge resides," he replied. "Rarely do the *devis* (goddesses) speak through words, as words are insufficient, but no doubt she was blessing you."

My mother paused. After a few minutes she spoke again. "I think her blessing was to prepare me for the future. I have been having dreams, which I have tried to ignore but that seem to foretell an uncertain time ahead. After seeing Shri Devi, the thoughts keep re-occurring that I must pay more careful attention to the changes taking place in the forest, and I must have the courage and wisdom to make some decisions for the clan. Soon, things may shift for us and we may even need to move to another place. If this is so, it will involve upheaval and I will need calmness of mind to see the clan through the times that lie ahead."

Dada was thoughtful, but before he could respond he turned and saw Prema and me hiding. Laughing, he called to us, "If you want to listen, come out and listen in the open." My mother was not pleased by our presence; with a wave of her hand she brushed us away, and we couldn't hear any more.

A day came when one of the clan's children went missing. Those charged with protecting us spread out in every direction, but the girl could not be found. We doubted an animal had eaten her because we knew their habits. They were familiar with us and we with them. We assumed it was the shadow people that had taken her, those we couldn't see but could only feel and sometimes hear. Then, months later, another child went missing.

Prema volunteered to stay awake during the night to see if she could catch sight of those who were stealing our children. Our mother agreed, but I feared for her. If one of them came, would she be able to defend herself, never mind the clan? Prema saw my thoughts as she often did. "Sundari, don't worry. I can protect myself and all of us."

"You have your spear and arrows, but we don't know what weapons they have."

She smiled. "I have another weapon that nobody knows about."

I looked at her in surprise. "What are you keeping from me, Prema?"

Her smile grew larger and she looked around to make sure nobody was nearby. "A *mantra*."

"A mantra?"

She nodded. "Sacred words of great power. Dada taught it to me, but he told me I mustn't share it with anyone. If I misuse it, the power of the mantra will be withdrawn. It allows me to see things beyond the physical world, to see what others can't see, so I will be able to know if the shadow people come here. I will be able to see them. You mustn't say a word, even to Amma (mother)."

"Be careful, Prema. It could be dangerous, if you encounter one of those . . ."

"Don't worry, Sundari. Dada taught me how to use the mantra."

Prema's ability with spears and arrows outshone everyone, so the clan felt safe with her standing watch at night. The months passed and no shadow people came near us. Nobody else went missing and we all attributed it to Prema's astute night guard.

I, however, noticed a change in her behavior. Sometimes she would come with me during the day as I searched the forest for materials to make coverings, but at other times she would take me to the edge of the forest and look below at the vast valley. A dense assortment of trees, different from those of our home, populated the valley, and a misty gaze would come over her as she took in the sight.

"I wonder what is down there," she mused one day.

"We mustn't find out, Prema. Let us go back. I have what I need."

"But I wonder . . ."

"Stop wondering, Prema. Please, let us return. Amma will begin to worry—we have been gone for so long." She stood there in silence for another few minutes. I began to tug at her hand. Finally, she turned to me and smiled. "Okay, let us go."

One day, when it came time for the morning meal, Prema was missing. Since that day by the edge of valley, I had been worried about her; every night before we all went to sleep, I would go to where she stood guard and make sure she was alright. First thing in the morning, I would check on her again. That morning, she had been standing guard as usual and everything had seemed fine, but I had had an uneasy feeling in my stomach. When she didn't appear for the afternoon meal, I became worried. Often she rested in the morning, but never had she failed to show up to eat with us by afternoon.

"Why do things not seem right?" I asked my mother.

"She might still be resting," she replied. "Finish your food and let her be. After we are done, I will go find her."

That turned out not to be necessary. As we were putting away the cooking utensils, Prema appeared. My mother turned to me. "See, you worry needlessly about your sister. She only needed some rest." But I knew something was amiss. Increasingly, Prema was disappearing for hours during the day when she was supposed to be resting, but I had my duties to perform and could not go in search of her. As soon as my mother would become aware of her absence, Prema would reappear.

Then one day, she didn't. I remembered that when I had questioned her about her whereabouts, she had said she was going off to practice the mantra, to make sure she was pronouncing the words properly. This had unsettled my heart. So, when Prema did not appear at all that day, I went to my mother and told her about the mantra.

"I know that Dada taught her sacred words for her protection and the safekeeping of the clan, so she must be okay," my mother replied in an effort to ease my concern, but she wore a worried look and called two of my brothers, who were experts in weapons, to go in search of her. They spent the day scouring the forest, but to no avail, and returned alone when night set in. The next day when Prema still had not returned, the whole clan went in search of her. It was then that I told my mother about Prema's interest in the valley below.

"We have never gone there. Why was she so curious?"

I shook my head. "I don't know, but several times when we reached that point, she would gaze off as if under a spell. Once it took quite some time for her attention to return to me, and there was a strange look in her eyes."

"*Hmmm*. Why haven't you told me this before? It may be that these shadow people can control your mind and lure you away. We don't know anything about them."

"Amma, Prema has a strong mind. Could anyone control it? And she has the mantra. Wouldn't that protect her?"

My mother nodded, but her anxiety was evident. "We will search and search until we find her. We will call those shadow people out of the night darkness to face us. If they have taken my daughter, I will get her back."

Two weeks of searching and still we had no sign of Prema. Dada had been a silent observer of our worries the whole time. Finally he told my mother, "Stop searching. The shadow people didn't take her. She left of her own free will, so you must let her be. It is time for you to take the clan and move from here, for the shadow people will soon become bolder and others will go missing."

"What do you mean, of her own free will?" asked my mother in disbelief. I had never seen my mother shaken, even at the deaths of her husbands, and I started sobbing as this pillar of strength, my mother, the chief of our clan, began to tremble. "She would never do this," insisted my mother. "She would never leave. She is the future head of our clan."

"She had the mantra to protect herself and so no harm could come to her. Of that I am sure," counseled Dada. "Something else must have happened that we don't know about, but the clan cannot stay here. You must put aside your duties as a mother and think of your responsibilities to the clan."

"We can't leave from here without her," I interrupted.

For many months this discussion about our departure took place between Dada and my mother, who continued every day to sent a party in search of Prema. A year passed and then another, two more children went missing, but still I did not give up hope of her return. Then one day Muni Baba left us. His form simply dissolved into sparkling light. Dada saw this as a sign that it was time for us to leave the forest without delay. A few days later I learned that he would not be coming with us.

Determined not to leave without him, I hid behind a boulder in an opening among the trees. I knew the clan would not leave without me. If they could not find me, they would have to stay. It was Dada who discovered my hiding place, and I told him in a firm voice that I would not leave our forest home without him. "Ah, Sundari, this Dada of yours is too old to make the long journey. Forgive me for not accompanying you," he replied in a weary voice. "How I would love to see in person that great river that Muni Baba has shown me in a vision."

"As long as you are alive, Dada, I won't leave you." With a smile, he agreed that the clan would stay for as long as he was there.

Two days later Dada died. At the age of eighteen I had to leave behind the life I had known in the forest.

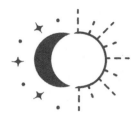

Chapter Two

LEAVING THE FOREST

Before his passing, Dada had shown my mother a vision of our new home and directed her to a settlement, a township really, growing along the banks of a great river, one of the many gifts of the melting ice. He told her that Muni Baba had mentally communicated with some of the *brahmins* (priestly class) there and that they were expecting us. When she asked who the brahmins were, Dada's response startled my mother. He replied, "They are the keepers of the knowledge, the transmitters of wisdom. They will receive you. It is in the best interest of the clan for you to lead them there." My mother responded slowly that she didn't know there was such a group of people who were keepers of the wisdom. "Are they like Muni Baba?" she asked. Dada smiled and replied, "There are few like him."

According to my mother, Dada's death was the second sign she had received, the first being her dreams. She feared that if we did not heed these signs, trouble would follow, but in my small mind, all I could think about was my sister. What if she were to return and we were gone? How would she ever find us? My feelings now seemed not to matter, as the clan began to prepare for our departure.

Dada had given my mother a vague sense of the direction we must take. He told her to follow the flight of the birds who were heading north on the return from their southern sojourn; after a long walk, we were to turn toward the setting sun in the west. He counseled that the forest would provide other signs, so she kept careful watch. We walked during the days and at night we rested on whatever soft spot of forest greenery we could find. Arrav, the oldest of my brothers, had taken Prema's place overseeing the night watch, alternating with my second brother, Saivi, both of whom were skilled in archery. They divided the night between them so each could get some rest.

After many, many weeks of walking, my mother sent a scout ahead, who returned to tell us we were but a day's walk from the great river. Everyone was relieved that the end was in sight.

It was during the second half of the night watch that the thundering of feet broke my sleep. I awoke with a start and found my mother by Arrav's side as they were getting ready to leave our encampment to see what had disturbed our peace. They had heard the pounding noise as well. Anxious for my mother's return, I went to stand by Saivi, who was now on night guard. Many of the clan members had awakened, and we were all on edge. Our peaceful march through the vast forests had come to an end.

Then I saw Arrav running back to us. "Quick," he called. "Bring the medicinal plants. Amma has been hurt."

I froze, but Saivi was able to act. He found Bodhini, the woman in charge of healing, and helped her gather the herbs she had collected during our long walk. They left without providing us with any more information. I calmed myself by thinking perhaps Amma had only twisted her ankle, or had another such mishap, nothing life-threatening. But a short time later they returned, with Arrav carrying my mother in his arms. Turning to me he said, with an attempt at being calm, "She has been shot with a poisonous arrow. Our herbs are not sufficient. Bodhini does not recognize this poison. Sundari, hurry on to the town and get help. Take Nityam with you."

Grabbing my youngest brother by the hand, I left. Dawn was just breaking, enabling the first rays of sun to light our way. The path was straight ahead, with little overgrown brush to slow us down. We ran and walked as fast as we could, knowing how precious time was. Perhaps an hour had passed when I saw a figure approaching us. As he came closer, I made out the form of a young man, dressed simply in a white cloth that covered the lower part of his body. His hair was tied in a knot on top of his head. He was walking quickly and within minutes he was by my side.

"Are you the ones seeking help?" he asked. I nodded. "I have come to help the woman who was wounded. Take me to her."

Swiftly turning around, Nityam and I led him down the sinewy forest path. Within an hour we were back at the encampment, and I led him to where my mother lay by the side of my two other brothers. She was barely conscious. Arrav had withdrawn the arrow and was trying to stop the bleeding, while Bodhini applied the juice from medicinal plants to relieve the pain. The young man who had come asked to be alone with my mother. We all withdrew and sat some distance away, watching as he went into meditation. The whole clan had gathered around Arrav and me, observing this man. He sat upright and completely still with closed eyes, by the side of my wounded mother.

After some time, Bodhini came to me and asked anxiously, "How can he heal her without any plants? I don't think he knows anything about healing."

"Perhaps he is like Muni Baba," I replied. I didn't know why, but I had total confidence that he would bring my mother back to life. "I trust him, Bodhini. Let us watch and see."

The day passed and the young man did not move. My mother's condition remained unchanged. As evening approached, Arrav grew anxious. He called my two other brothers and me to him and asked whether we should try to carry her to the town before darkness engulfed us. My three brothers looked to me for an answer. With Amma stricken and Prema gone, they now regarded me as the one to make such decisions.

"Let me talk to that man first, and then we will decide." I quietly walked over to where my mother lay, hesitant to interrupt the man's meditations but knowing that I had to make a vital decision, one that might mean the difference between life and death for my mother.

I sat down beside my mother, opposite to the man, and for several minutes I vacillated. Internally I called out to her, *Amma, tell me what I should do*. Looking down at her, I saw that her breathing, which had been irregular, was now pulsing in a peaceful rhythm. I saw also that the leaves covering her wound were black with the poison that was oozing from her body. He was lifting the deadly liquid from the limb that had been injured. "He is healing you, Amma. He is bringing you back," I whispered.

Looking up, I saw my brothers seated where I had left them, anxiously awaiting my decision. Returning to them, I said, "He is healing her. Her breathing has stabilized, and the poison is oozing out. I don't know what he is doing, but somehow she is returning to life. Let us wait for him."

Telling everyone in the clan to go rest, I returned to my mother and lay down by her side. Periodically throughout the night I opened my eyes and found that the young man had not moved. He sat there with closed eyes until dawn arrived. I was awake, sitting beside my mother, when I saw her open her eyes and look at him in gratitude. He turned his eyes toward me and smiled. I was too anxious to smile back and so looked away, not knowing what to say to him. I didn't even know his name. As a young woman of eighteen, I was terribly shy in front of this stranger, as I had never before encountered anyone who was not from our clan. The only people I knew were the ones with whom I had grown up.

"May I ask your name?" I inquired, with eyes cast down.

"Sachit," he replied.

"Sachit," I repeated softly. "You have saved my mother. The whole clan will ever be grateful to you."

"You mother will need a few days of rest before she can be moved. Where have you come from?"

"From deep in the forest. It has taken us many weeks to reach here." I replied, still looking down.

"You are now in the region known as *Brahmavarta*. We received word that your clan was coming. There should not have been trouble here."

None of us knew the name of the place to which we were walking. I replied, "We have been heading in the direction of the great river. That is where our elder has sent us."

"May I suggest then that you come with me and bring a few people who can build some huts to prepare for your arrival."

"Will the others be safe here?" I asked.

"I will utter a mantra of protection and they will be safe."

I nodded. "The shadow people . . . were they the ones who did this?"

"Shadow people?" he asked curiously.

"Yes, they have been entering the forest. We have never seen them, but we hear them, and they have taken some of our young people, my sister perhaps also, which is why we are leaving the forest."

He uttered a small laugh. "You mean the *rakshasas* (violent tribes)." I looked directly at him for the first time, with eyes wide open. "They are primitive in their ways but very strong and have developed some magical powers. They believe that eating human flesh enhances their powers, but they cannot counter the effects of the mantras, at least not yet. Your people will be safe here. I am surprised that the rakshasas have come this far. They are invading the forests to the south and east, but should not be in this region. We will have to deal with them now."

I looked at my brothers, wondering if I trusted this man enough to follow him. He had saved my mother but . . . Then my mother grasped my hand and nodded; I knew she was indicating that I should go. I got up and was about to select the people who would accompany me, when Sachit placed his hand on my arm and stopped me, saying, "You have not introduced yourself."

"My name is Sundari," I replied shyly, surprised by his touch. "I am her second daughter, and these are my three younger brothers. My elder sister went missing a year or so ago. My mother is the head of our clan." Nodding, he let go of my arm and I went to gather those few who were skillful with their hands and could quickly erect some shelter for us. We set off with Sachit.

It was only a day's walk. When we came out of the forest and saw what lay before us, I was speechless with awe. Never had I seen such a beautiful sight! I knew I would not soon forget that first impression. Golden towers rose above the plains, sparkling in the sunlight, and I could not stop looking at them. My eyes were so taken with the towers that lined the distance that I hardly took note of the huts arranged harmoniously around courtyards and pathways filled with flowering trees and plants. The shock of such intense sunlight also overwhelmed me. Living in the forest, we were unused to the brightness of such a vast open space. I stood there as if paralyzed, as if I had entered a heavenly realm.

"What is it?" asked Sachit, seeing the amazement on my face.

"What are those golden towers that I see in the distance?"

A look of amusement crossed his face. "They are our temples."

"Temples," I uttered. "They shimmer in the sun like the golden flecks we find in our streams. Were they brought here from another world?"

He laughed. "There is much gold in our rivers and other precious metals. We sprinkle this gold on the homes of our deities."

"I have always wondered where the deities lived," I quietly expressed. "So, they live here."

Again, I saw an amused look come over him. "Come. Let me get you settled so that you can begin building. There are many who will help so that when your mother arrives, she will have a place to stay." I didn't move, and when I noticed his amusement, my shyness returned. *Does he think me ignorant*, I wondered, *because I have not seen such things before?*

In a halting voice, I returned to the demands of the present moment. "I must gather food so that I can feed those who have come with me," I said, recalling what my mother would do if she were here.

He smiled. "No need to gather food, there is plenty here." Quite embarrassed, I followed him as he led us to a place where we could eat. The people were dressed in a very different manner, not using materials from the forest. I wondered what kind of plant material they used, but I dared not show my ignorance. As we walked, I could not help but utter my amazement at the animals that crossed our path, animals I had not seen before. Running ahead to meet a small, white animal who was standing beside some larger ones of the same species, I bent down to hug the little one. When Sachit caught up with me, I asked eagerly, "What do you call these animals?"

He laughed a hearty laugh and replied, "A cow, our most precious animal. She provides us with milk and curd. Most of the families have cows, which live with them as part of their family. They are greatly loved."

"You don't eat them, do you?" I asked timidly.

"Sundari, what a thought! If they are part of our family, how could we eat them?

We care for them as we would a family member." He seemed greatly amused and I could not help but feel self-conscious. Getting up, I resolved to temper my amazement in the future.

It did not take long to erect a few huts in nearby fields, where many of our people could stay until additional living arrangements were made. The others, except for my youngest brother, went back to bring my mother and the rest of the clan, while I stayed in the town to continue the preparations. Sachit returned to his home and duties and I did not see him for several days. Still shy in his presence, I decided to learn more about him. Gathering up whatever courage I had, I found my way to one of the temples to find out his whereabouts. A man standing outside the temple directed me to the temple courtyard where Sachit was preparing for a fire ceremony, called a *yagna*.

Finding me standing there, he looked up and smiled. "What can I do for you, Sundari? Is everything okay?"

I nodded. "May I ask you a question?"

"Here, come sit." He led me to a seat on the ground not far from where the fire ceremony was being prepared. "Do not be shy. Ask what you like. You are now a citizen of Brahmavarta." My eyes were cast down. "Don't be shy, Sundari," he repeated. "You may ask me anything you like."

Lifting my eyes to meet his, I asked, "How did you know to come to us that day when my mother was wounded?"

He smiled. "Is that all you want to know?" I nodded. "My teacher saw in meditation what had happened. He knew that a clan from the forest was coming here to settle. The rakshasas are causing many of the forest clans to leave and we are welcoming them. He saw your mother had been wounded and sent me. It is that simple."

"How did you heal her without any plant medicines?"

"You said you had one question, but you have two." He chuckled, again making me wonder if he was making fun of my ignorance. "That is also quite simple. The power of mantra. The vibrations emitted by sacred sounds have the power to shape and reshape the material world. I used certain sounds to evict the poison from your mother's blood. It had already gone into much of her body by the time I arrived and so it took quite some time to draw it all out. I didn't use outward sounds because too many people were present and these mantras are not to be given without special consent, so I had to utter the mantras almost silently, at a very high octave that the human ear can't pick up. It had the same effect, but it took a bit longer." He paused. "Do you have any other questions?"

I shook my head.

He smiled. "No more questions for now, but I am sure others will arise." I rose to leave. "I will come with some of the elders to greet your mother when she arrives here. I want to give her a proper welcome; after all, she is the head of your clan."

I returned to the hut that had been assigned to my mother and brothers and me, where I continued to make it as comfortable as I could. I gathered soft grasses to make a bed for my mother, and Sachit had sent something I had never seen before made out of a plant that I learned was called karpasa (cotton), softer than the grasses I had gathered. I lay it on top of the bed, admiring its smooth quality. This is what all the people of Brahmavarta wore. He had given me an item made out of that plant to wrap around my body as he said it was more appropriate than the clothing we were used to wearing.

I was determined to learn to reproduce what he had given me so that all our clan members could wear it. But that was for later, after we learned how we were to fit in with this new community. My mother would have to guide us about that.

When my mother arrived, she was much improved. She walked on her own, leaning on the arm of Diyan, a young men of our clan of whom she was very fond. I was at the edge of the town to greet her, and I could see that she was as overwhelmed as I had been by the glittering towers of the temples. There were so many of them, and they seemed like guardians of the settlement. I took my mother by the arm and slowly led her to the hut I had prepared.

"You have arrived safely, Amma," I said quietly. "We will be happy here. The people seem very welcoming."

Once she was settled in the hut, she called me to her and said, "You have truly risen to the occasion, Sundari. I am very proud of you. You have served the clan as Prema would have done. You are every bit as capable."

To me, her words were not ones of encouragement, because I never wanted to take the place of my dear sister. I only wanted her to return, and Amma's words served to remind me of my loss of the sister I had vowed to find.

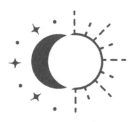

Chapter Three

FINDING PREMA

"Tell me about the man who healed me." My mother and I were sitting in our hut a few days after her arrival. She was still weak from the poison and the long trek to our new home, although she had been carried much of the time after she was wounded.

"Do you not remember him, Amma?" She shook her head. "Well, I think he may be one of those *rishis* (sages) that Dada used to speak of."

"Really?" Her eyes opened wide in surprise. "Why do you say that?"

"He healed you without any medicinal plants, only through the use of mantra, so he must be able to control the vibrations of sound through his mind, as Dada had told us."

"*Hmm*. That doesn't mean he is one of the rishis," she mused. "Prema also knew the use of mantra, and I suspect others here know how to do the same."

"When you see him, Amma, you will notice how his skin radiates light. He looks like a son of *Surya Dev* (sun god)."

She laughed. "His skin looks like that because of his exposure to the sun. Haven't you noticed that the people here are all accustomed to more sun than we are? No, Sundari, I don't think he is a rishi, but I think he is a very good man. He came to welcome me when I first arrived here, but I was not able to thank him properly. I would like to meet him again."

"I will go find him," I hurried to say, but she placed her hand on my arm and stopped me.

"No," she said, "I will send Arrav." There was an awkward moment between us, and I suspected that my all-seeing mother had perceived the seed of attraction that was growing in my heart.

Sachit arrived some hours later with Arrav, and I sat quietly as my mother thanked him and inquired about how to organize the clan. He explained that the society here was divided into different communities, each suiting a separate need. There were those devoted to learning, to reciting the *Vedas* (ancient hymns), and performing the sacred ceremonies, and there were those skilled in weaponry who were also learning how to govern. Those skilled with their hands were making goods and trading them, and those who worked the fields provided food. And then there were those who performed tasks that required the least amount of skill. Each member could choose or be guided as to where they would fit in and how they could best serve the community as a whole. My mother took all this in and said she would consult with every family to help them make decisions. Again and again she expressed her gratitude, which I somehow happily mistook for my mother's tacit approval of my feelings for Sachit.

Sachit rose to leave and I walked him to the door. Lingering there for a moment, he asked if I had met the sacred river yet. I shook my head. "Come, let me take you," he said with enthusiasm. He led me along paths through open fields until we came to a great body of water, far larger than I had ever seen. I was overwhelmed by the sight and asked if that was the sea I had heard so much about from Dada. As he shook his head with an amused smile, I quickly became self-conscious, reminding myself not to show my astonishment. I didn't want him to treat me like a child.

"This, Sundari, is the sacred Sarasvati River. She nurtures our life, caring for our physical needs as well as our spiritual ones. Her lower self manifests as this river, which gives us water to drink and waters the earth so our food can grow. Her higher self has another form, which inspires and transmits great knowledge and creativity. It is this higher self that has given us the sacred hymns that we chant. They have vibrated in the ethers since long ago, but the memory of those words was lost during the great migrations when the ice melted. Sarasvati Devi came to help the rishis reclaim this sacred knowledge. Through her inspiration, many men and women are being trained to preserve what she has taught so the knowledge won't disappear again. A concentrated mind is needed to capture the deeper meaning of these hymns, which describe how the mortal in us can achieve and realize the immortal that also resides in us, how we can retrieve the hidden light within."

I wasn't really listening to his words, as my mind was fully absorbed in the wonderous sight before me. All I wanted to do was touch her water. I ran on ahead with great joy, and I heard Sachit's laughter carried by the wind, but this time I didn't care if he was laughing at my ignorance. As soon as I reached the edge of the river, I lifted the cloth covering me and was about to climb down over the few rocks that stood between her and me, when I heard him call.

"No, Sundari, don't enter. Her current is very strong here. She will carry you away and you will drown." He had caught up with me and had grabbed my arm to restrain me.

"But I want to touch her," I replied eagerly, looking up into his face.

Letting go of me, he said, "Here, take my hand." Extending his hand to me, he helped me climb over the rocks to where the river lapped the edge. Stooping down, he took my hand and dipped it into the water; the coolness sent a tingle through my body. Cupping some water in his hand, he sprinkled it over my head and I felt it dribble down my face. Then he rested his hand for a few moments on the top of my head. As he did, something stirred within me, bringing a sense of joy and expansion. "There, she has now blessed you." I looked up into his face, thinking that this blessing was also confirmation of the feelings growing between us.

Seeing my pleasure at feeling the cool water upon my skin, he said, "Come, I will take you to a shallow part when you can safely enter." He led me along the river to where a pool of water had gathered between some rocks. "You can stand here," he said, "and feel the water."

I looked down but instead of entering, I stood gazing at the image reflected back at me in the water, which had gathered into a still unmoving pool. Never before had I seen my image, and it startled me. Noticing this, he asked in surprise, "Have you never seen your reflection before, Sundari?"

Shaking my head, I ran my fingers along my hair, which fell like many woven ropes down to my waist. I didn't look like the other young girls who lived here, but I had never considered my appearance before, and I could not tear my eyes away. I suddenly realized Sachit was staring at me with such an amused expression.

"I am sorry," I hurried to say in confusion. "I was startled to see my-self."

"Well, what do you think?" he asked in a teasing tone.

"What do I think?" I repeated quietly. Mustering my courage, I asked, "Sachit, how is my appearance? Is it pleasing?"

He laughed. "You have a lovely appearance, Sundari, quite lovely."

When I reached home, I released my hair from its woven form and shook my head, causing my abundant hair to fly in all directions. I must look like a wild woman, I laughed. I was enjoying this newfound freedom, when my mother entered our hut and looked at me questioningly.

"Amma, am I pleasant to look at?" I asked innocently.

Eyeing me suspiciously, she asked, "What has gotten into you, Sundari? Why are you suddenly asking this now?" When I didn't answer but rather looked down sheepishly, she added, "If you are looking for a husband within our clan, we can discuss this."

I shook my head. "It's not that. It's just that I want to look like the other girls here."

"You should be proud of our ways, Sundari," she said as she came over to me and began to weave my hair. "Just because we are settled here, it doesn't mean we should change our ways."

I allowed her to fix my hair again into long braids as I wondered how I could mold myself to become more attractive to Sachit.

A few days later, mid-morning, I found my way to the sacred river. A gentle breeze was blowing, providing relief from the sun, which shone so brightly in the open landscape. Suddenly the sounds of the river and the wind entered my body; untying my hair, I began to twirl as if in a dance. A great sense of freedom came over me as the breezes loosened the cloth wrapped around my waist and my swift movements caused my hair, now un-braided, to sweep with the wind. I could not help but laugh and laugh until I finally fell to the ground. Gazing up into the sun, I said out loud, "I don't know whether you are a god or not, but I do love you, and I feel your love as well. That is enough."

The sound of laughter reached my ear and looking up I saw Sachit standing just a short distance away. Hurrying to my feet, I brushed off my clothing and tightened it around my waist, as I looked at him in dismay. "Are you laughing at me, Sachit?"

"Not at you, with you, Sundari." I wondered how much he had seen.

Had he seen me twirling around like a young child? How embarrassing. "You should not be embarrassed, Sundari," he said gently. "You have a joyful spirit, and I like that very much. You needn't hide it from me." After a few minutes of silence, he took his leave, and I was left to ponder his words, especially his admission that he liked me.

The next months were very busy getting everyone in our clan settled in their new environment. We no longer stayed together as a clan or even as a family. My two eldest brothers were eager to hone their skills in weaponry and so were now staying in a special place where they could receive further training. My youngest brother would wake up at dawn and go to the fields to where the farmers worked. He enjoyed this immensely and I could see how pleased my mother was at the smooth transition, how everyone was finding their place in the new society. A few of the young men and women, those with the quickest and sharpest minds, had decided to engage in strict discipline so they could learn the ceremonies and sacred hymns. One of my childhood friends, Diyan, was drawn to the art of making cloth, and so he moved into that community. Everyone was finding their place, except me.

"Only you and I are undecided," said my mother one day. "But that is okay. Let us be undecided until we find the right place for ourselves. I may go work in the fields with Nityam. The idea of helping the soil create plant life, food for the clan, brings me a deep sense of peace, and I have not known peace since . . . for too long now. Our people have lived so long in the forest that we have forgotten about the life of the soil." Turning to me, she asked, "Sundari, you are so skilled at making clothing and necklaces. Why don't you spend some time with Diyan and learn how to use the new plant material for making clothing?"

I knew what she was implying, and I objected. "Amma, what are you really saying? Do you want me to marry Diyan?" She didn't answer. "Hasn't it been the tradition of our clan that the woman chooses?"

"Yes, and it will be up to you to choose, Sundari, but I hope it will be somebody from our clan who shares our history and practices. You and he were so close when you were children and have been friends for so long and I know he cares for you."

"He is my friend, that is true, but shouldn't a husband be more than that?"

After a few minutes, she asked, "Is there somebody else who interests you? You are nineteen years old, soon to be twenty. You will want a family. With Prema gone, it is your duty . . ." She stopped. Then, dropping all pretense of ignorance, she said firmly, "You must get Sachit out of your mind. He cannot marry, at least not now. Not for a long time."

"What do you mean, Amma?" I asked nervously, not terribly surprised that she had noticed my interest in him.

"I know your sentiments and so I have inquired about him. He has taken what is called a *sankalpa*, a sacred vow, to remain celibate, or unmarried, for a long period of time while he is undergoing his spiritual training. He took this sankalpa before the sacred river in front of his teacher. It cannot be broken. A brahmin cannot break his word." I looked at her in confusion. "It could be ten or twenty years. It all depends on his teacher."

"I don't believe it," I insisted, remembering that day by the river when he had blessed me. "I don't believe it."

"Sundari . . ." she started to speak, but I didn't wait to hear any more.

I ran from the hut and retraced my steps to the spot where I had stood with Sachit some months earlier. "You were my witness," I whispered to the river. "He took my hand and with your water he blessed me, and then a few days later he told me that he liked my appearance." My emotions began to rise, but I had to quickly settle them when I heard someone call my name.

"Sundari, why such a sad expression?" I turned to find Sachit standing nearby, a smile on his face. Quickly I regained my composure, but when I didn't respond, he added, "I know you are missing your sister. I know about her disappearance and I think I can help you find her." His voice was reassuring. In that moment I forgot what my mother had told me about Sachit and was only thinking that he had come to help me once again.

"You can?" I raised a hopeful face to him.

"Meet me here in two days just after dawn and by then I hope I am able to know what happened to your sister."

Eagerly I waited for those days to pass, mistakenly thinking that Sachit would appear with my sister by his side, that he would have rescued her from whomever had abducted her. When he showed up alone two days later, my face must have revealed my disappointment because he hurried to assure me, "I have found her."

"Where is she?" I asked somewhat perplexed.

"Let us find a quiet place to sit." We walked in silence until we found a small gathering of trees where we could stay unnoticed. I was so happy to be with him that I would have been content to walk all day without any words exchanged, and I was so touched that Sachit cared enough about me to help me find Prema. Surely that was a further indication of his feelings.

Finding a secluded spot, he sat down and asked me to sit in front of him. Then he said, "You must promise me, Sundari, that when you see your sister you will not cry out, you will not try to speak to her, you will silently observe. You can only see her through an etheric veil. If you call out, you will disturb her peace of mind. It is for her good that I am asking this. She won't be able to hear you, but you will stir her faded memories of her life with you and your mother. This will create sadness in her that she will not be able to comprehend. She has found a new life and you must let her be. Do you understand?"

I nodded, although I didn't really fathom what he was saying. Why would I not be able to speak with her, embrace her and tell her how much I had missed her? How could she not remember me, her dear, dear sister? It had not been that long since she was gone. Sachit looked at me intently and then instructed me to close my eyes and concentrate at the point between the eyebrows. He entered meditation. I tried to follow his instructions but my anticipation of seeing Prema intruded on my thoughts and a quiet mind was not something I could achieve. He sat there for quite a while. Gradually I began to feel drowsy and lay down in front of him, thinking he would awaken me when he found her.

Then, in my semi-sleep state, I saw her.

There in front me was Prema, looking quite beautiful and dignified, clothed in great finery with glittering jewels in her hair. Beside her was a handsome man who was also dressed very elegantly. She had a young child on her lap, and she was smiling and playing with him. I saw her place the child on the floor and laugh as he wobbled away. Turning to the man beside her, she spoke some words and he smiled, placing his arm around her. It was such a happy family scene and I could feel the love between them, but as I watched them a great need arose in me to make myself known. As this feeling emerged, I saw Prema turn toward me with a questioning look, as if she felt my presence. I had to talk to her so she wouldn't totally forget Amma, or me. I began to call out, but before any sound could escape my lips, I felt Sachit place his hand over my mouth, and in that moment the scene disappeared. I was lying on the ground, coming out of my sleep state, when Sachit emerged from meditation.

"Why did you stop me?" I asked as I rose into a sitting position.

"Did you forget your promise?" His voice was firm.

"Sachit, it was impossible to see her and not call to her. I don't want her to forget me. Why could I not call out to her? Where is that world? I want to go back to see her again."

"Humans normally can't enter the *naga* realm where these semidivine beings, who can assume a human or a serpent form, live. I suspect your sister somehow gained knowledge of a powerful mantra, which enabled her to slip behind the etheric barrier."

"Our grandfather taught her this mantra to protect our clan when the shadow people began to enter the forest. She told me once that if she used it improperly it would be withdrawn."

"Then this is what I suspect happened. Powerful nagas can enter our world, even though we can't enter theirs. A naga prince must have found her, fallen in love, and showed himself to her in a handsome human form. Then she used the mantra to enter his world, thinking she could return whenever she wanted. The mantra had been given for the protection of the clan and not for her personal use, and since she abused its intention it was withdrawn, and she had no power to return. In that realm, our world becomes like a dream, so her memories of you and your mother are very dreamlike. I didn't want you to call out to her because it would disturb her greatly to know that she had loved ones she could not communicate with or reach. Sundari, you didn't keep your promise. A promise is a sacred trust."

I looked down ashamed, but I also thought his request was unreasonable. How could he ask me not to call out to a sister who I dearly loved and had not seen in several years?

"Come, let me take you home," he said abruptly. We didn't speak on the way back and I assumed he was disappointed in me. It wasn't until I got home and he had left that I realized I hadn't even thanked him.

My brief glimpse of Prema served to intensify my feelings of missing her, but also had the unexpected effect of causing me to envy the love she shared with her husband. How happy she seemed. I told my mother what I had discovered about Prema, and she simply nodded and replied, "I knew this. Before he died, Dada told me that she had left willingly to enter the naga world. But why did you ask Sachit to find her? You know, it was a great risk for him to interfere in that realm. Never mind, it is done. Don't bother him anymore with our clan affairs. He is important to this community and has been very kind to us. I will never forget that he saved my life and I don't want to burden him with our matters." Her voice was scolding. Then she added, "Now that you know where your sister is, I don't want her name mentioned again. You are the only daughter I have now."

Her words fell on me like a heavy weight, and I looked at her without responding. How could she banish Prema from her heart? I wanted to tell her that I hadn't asked Sachit. He had volunteered on his own, but she didn't give me a chance to defend myself, and I dared not say a word. Seeing my downcast expression, she added in a cutting tone, "Even though he shows you kindness, don't mistake that for affection, Sundari. He behaves the same to everyone. A brahmin's duty is to spiritually guide and assist all members of the community. It is time now for you to find your place here, to decide which work you want to take up, and who you want to marry." Still I vacillated and my mother's patience was wearing thin. I could not help but think that Sachit's offer to help me find Prema was a sign of his deep affection for me, but I knew now that I had to hide my feelings from Amma.

Some days in the early morning hours, I rose at dawn to gather wild food that grew along the riverbank. Each time, I walked further and further along the river in search of new plants, and one day I reached an area where several brahmins were chanting the hymns that had come to be known as the Vedas, sacred poems that Dada had told us about. The sounds floated through the air like celestial music circling the skies. I slowed my pace but keep walking until a particularly beautiful chanting sound reached my ears. I could not help but pause and sit to listen, with closed eyes. It was the first time I had heard the chanting of those songs, and the sounds of the hymns mingled with the murmur of quiet waves and the humming of wind, lifting me out of my normal awareness. When it was over, I glanced over to the river and saw Sachit standing there, doing pranam—a movement I had learned was a gesture of respect, an honored way of greeting. *So, it is him I heard*, I mused. *This is where he comes to chant in the early morning. This is where I can find him.*

Every early morning thereafter I came to that very spot to listen to Sachit and the enchanting sounds of the hymns. Normally I escaped before he could catch sight of me, but one day I stayed sitting there as I heard him approach. "It is you, Sundari," he chuckled. "I noticed a young woman seated here every morning. Do you come to greet the sacred Saraswati, to hear the hymns, or to see me?"

My face flushed and I didn't respond right away. Finally I said, "I come . . . I come because I love to hear you singing those poems."

"I see." Seating himself beside me, he asked. "You have not yet found a place for yourself in our society, have you?" I shook my head. "I have an idea then. I will speak with your mother about it."

Some days later my mother was called to the temple. When she returned, she told me that Sachit had suggested that I enter the hermitage of Sage

Gayatri, the wife of his teacher, where I could learn to recite the Vedas. "He told me you have great love for the hymns and have been going to the river when the brahmins chant in the morning. Is that true, Sundari?"

I didn't answer her question but rather asked, "If I go to that hermitage, will I be able to see Sachit."

"It is a hermitage for women," she replied coldly. "It is time to make decisions, Sundari." I reflected for a few minutes. Even if I couldn't see Sachit there, I would be able to go to the river where the other brahmins were chanting. I would be part of their community, I reasoned, and so I acquiesced.

A few days later, my mother took me to the hermitage to meet Sage Gayatri, as it was necessary for her to accept me. I was surprised by her striking figure and dynamic presence. As soon as she entered the room, one took note of her presence and could not help but stand and bow one's head to folded hands in deep respect. It was impossible to gauge her age. Her hair was completely white and swept away from her face, piled and tied neatly on top of her head, but there was not even the hint of an age line on her face. Not a single line spread from the corner of her eyes. Her lips were full and also free of any age creases. Her skin was clear and on the fairer side. Except for the color of her hair, she exuded youth. She was dressed in a simple white cloth, as were the other women who were studying under her. I heard her speaking quietly to my mother: "Your daughter wants to come here not to learn the sacred hymns, but to escape from a love."

My mother looked embarrassed. "It was the young brahmin Sachit who suggested that she come study under you."

"Sachit?" she asked. My mother nodded. "He is a student of my husband." She was quiet for quite some time and then replied. "The few women who live here have been with me for a number of years. Many come but most leave after a brief time. Only those who are really serious can withstand the strict discipline. I will accept your daughter and we will soon know if she is meant for this life."

"I am most grateful," replied my mother with a broad smile. Offering pranam, we left. The sage had given a date in the following week for me to enter the hermitage. My mother was exuberant, but I was more cautious. "To be accepted by such a great woman as she is truly an honor," said my mother as we headed back to our hut. "I hope, Sundari, you can fulfill the expectations. You would be the pride of the clan." I didn't respond.

Since I had realized that Prema would never return, I knew that my mother now expected me to someday fill her own position, and this was a burden. Even though the clan had divided into different communities, they still came to my mother about many matters. She remained the guiding voice, and I knew she felt that the training I would receive under Sage Gayatri would make me more than capable of continuing that role, perhaps even extending it beyond the clan.

I had to see Sachit before entering the hermitage, but my mother was now keeping careful watch over me. She rose before dawn to make sure I didn't leave the hut. A few days before I was to begin the training, I made an excuse about the need to get cotton for new clothing and instead hurried to the temple, where I hoped to find Sachit. I was lucky to find him as he was leaving. He was surprised to see me.

He told me how pleased he was that Sage Gayatri had accepted me into the hermitage. "There is no better woman in all of Brahmavarta to teach the deeper meaning of the hymns," he said. I looked at him longingly, thinking: *If this is what it takes to marry you, Sachit, I am willing to do it.* He looked away and said he must get back to his teacher. Pausing for a moment, he turned his eyes back to me. Taking off a beaded necklace that he wore around his neck, he placed it around mine and said, "These are sacred tulsi (holy basil) beads blessed in the River Sarasvati. We often use them to count mantras. I hope it will help you as you undergo training. The training can be long and difficult, Sundari," he said looking intently at me. There was no amusement on his face, as there so often had been when we were together. "Sometimes we are asked to make sacrifices, but they are for the greater good, for the community as well as our own spiritual progress. Try to have the discipline and patience to endure." With those words he turned and walked away.

How long, Sachit, how long must I wait? I watched him disappear from the courtyard where I stood, wondering how I was to bear the separation that lay ahead.

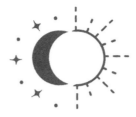

Chapter Four

IN THE HERMITAGE

From the beginning, I could not adapt to the strict discipline of life in the hermitage. I could not wake up in the dark pre-dawn hours to begin the recitations. I could not wait for the appointed hour to eat: when I was hungry, I went outside to forage for food. I could not sit still during the group meditations and would instead lie down and fall asleep. The only hermitage rule I could keep was silence, because no one would speak with me. Sage Gayatri was kind and never spoke a harsh word to me, despite my obvious shortcomings. She ignored my inability to fit in, but the other women soon developed attitudes toward me that made friendship nearly impossible. I compensated by trying to devote extra time to the more servile functions—preparing food, cleaning the utensils, and sweeping the common areas. While performing those duties I could keep my mind on Sachit, hoping that the passing days would bring me closer to him.

After I had been at the hermitage for many months, I overheard a conversation between two of the women students. One of them was questioning why Sage Gayatri allowed the girl from the jungle, meaning me, to stay when she was so ill-suited for hermitage life. The other responded that it was most likely so as not to embarrass her mother, who was the tribal chieftain. "She has no discipline at all," laughed the first woman. "She does not even make an effort."

Although I saw the truth in their words, they stung me, and I hurried from the hermitage to a spot by the river that had become my frequent place of refuge. It was true. Although I loved to hear Sachit chant and speak about the hymns, I had no intention of becoming a knower of the Vedas myself. I was only there for him, to become acceptable so that he would marry me.

Resting myself by the side of the river, I cupped some water in my hand, drew it to my head and eyes, and let it dribble down my face, remembering how Sachit had once blessed me with the water. "Aside from Sachit, Sage Gayatri, and you," I said to the river, "I have no other friends in this new community. But I am content to stay in this hermitage because of you. I can come here to meet you every day, and even when I don't express my feelings, you know what they are. You are the only one who can make me smile these days, and I would much rather sit here by your side than undergo all that training." The water made a gurgling sound and I giggled. "I know you understand, and I know that you are aware of my feelings for Sachit, because you were witness that day when you both blessed me. I only hope that I can one day see your other form, the radiant form he told me about."

I suddenly became aware that I was not alone. Looking around, I saw Sage Gayatri standing just a few feet away. Hurriedly I rose and joined hands in pranam, wondering if she had come to scold me for leaving the hermitage. "*Ammaji* (respected mother), it is you."

"Let us sit together," she said in a reassuring voice as she seated herself on the long grasses that lined the riverbank. "Sundari, do you know why I keep you in the hermitage?" she asked. I shook my head. "It is because of your pure heart, not because of your mother. The other women are learning the hymns, but how many of them come to talk to the great Sarasvati? How many of them feel for her the love that you do? That is why I allow you to stay. True wisdom is a balance between the knowledge of the mind and of the heart. Your heart knowledge is strong, but you must work on cultivating the mind. There are many ways to learn." After a slight pause, she added, "Shall I tell you a story of one of the great women rishis?"

I nodded. "My grandfather used to tell us stories. This is the way he taught us."

"There is a woman rishi named Apala. She is said to be the daughter of the *maharishis* Atri and Anasuya. These two great rishis have already lived for so long. Maharishi Atri is one of the Saptarishis, seven great sages who remain on earth for an entire cycle of time to guide humanity. He has brought forth some of the most complex hymns of the Vedas and a person has to be quite advanced in knowledge to understand their true meaning. Apala is not as well-known as the sons of those two great sages, but she is every bit as wise. When she came of age, a student of her father's wanted to marry her, but he was inspired not so much by love as by the thought of being married to the daughter of the great rishi. Apala knew this, but since he was a beloved student of her father's, she agreed. Some years after the marriage, she developed a terrible skin condition. In fact, she knew this condition had been sent by Indra Dev, but her husband didn't realize that he was being tested. Disgusted at the sight of her diseased skin, he abandoned her." She paused.

"Why did Indra do that!" I exclaimed. "He is a fearsome deva."

She laughed. "Not at all. Actually, Indra is much beloved by the sages for he is the spiritual power that reveals the inner light, that retrieves it from the hidden places. He releases that inner illumination, the light of knowledge that has been overshadowed by darkness, the forces of ignorance. In this role of entering the darkness of our minds to make known the inner light, one of his duties is to test the sages, and he was testing them both. If a sage fears Indra, it is because he fears the tests that will come, but these tests are only meant to strengthen him or her. Anyhow, Sage Apala realized her husband had failed his test; she was not surprised because his love was not very deep, but she was determined to help him.

"One day she was walking in the forest when she came across a Soma plant, which is used to make the drink of immortality, and is beloved by Indra Dev for the intense joy it bestows. One knows that one has achieved immortality when one is able to be always in this state of indescribable joy. It is very rare to find that plant, and instead of keeping it for herself, she decided to offer it to Indra. Plucking the plant, she called out to him and bowing low made the offering. He appeared to her, and in response to her devotion and generosity bestowed on her three boons. Do you know what boons are?"

"Blessings or gifts of the devas?"

"That is how they are perceived, but actually they come as a result of one's spiritual efforts, usually after long years of meditation. In this case, Indra Dev offered these boons to Apala because she had passed two tests and risen above selfish desire. Instead of turning bitter after her husband abandoned her, Apala's love increased; instead of ingesting the Soma plant, she had offered it to Indra. And so, Indra Dev knew the purity of her heart. He told her the first two boons would manifest immediately, but she would have to strive to gain the third boon. Guess what she asked for?"

"To be free of her skin disease?"

"Due to her selfless nature, the first two boons she offered to her father, for his long life and prosperity, that he would always have what he needed, and those wishes were granted immediately. He became young again, and his hair, which was falling out from age, began to grow until it was as thick as it had been in his youth." Sage Gayatri stopped speaking for a few minutes as she gazed out over the river and then turning her eyes back to me, she added, "Since the Saptarishis live for so long, when their bodies ages, they discard the body they had been inhabiting and take a new one. Maharishi Atri doesn't have to do this because of the boon his daughter dedicated to him. His body doesn't age and so he can avoid the problems of discarding one body and taking another." She paused again and then continued with the narrative. "The third boon Sage Apala requested was to help her husband overcome his short-sightedness. But she was going to have to work to gain that. She found a cave where she could enter solitary meditation and she remained there for many years." She paused again.

"How many years?" I asked hesitantly.

Leaning forward, she replied, "Over a thousand." My eyes opened wide. "She encountered difficult struggles, but she persevered because she knew that her husband could not advance spiritually until his heart opened. It is said that Indra Dev pulled her through the eye of the wheel of his chariot."

"How horrible!" I exclaimed as a shudder ran through my body.

"It is a metaphor, dear," she hurried to assure me with a smile. "It means that Indra put her through many tests, but she surmounted them all. Finally, one day she came out of her meditation and returned home, not as an aged woman, but as a very beautiful young lady. Her skin was as clear as a cloudless sky.

"While she had been in meditation, her husband had died and been reborn several times. She knew he was now a young man, so she searched and found him. As soon as he saw her, he fell deeply in love, not with her beauty but with the strength of her spirit, with her spiritual attainment. Her meditations had helped him grow spiritually so he could understand what truly mattered. They married again but this time he loved her deeply, and their marriage provided much benefit to society because they were a model of a perfectly balanced couple, each honoring and respecting the wisdom of the other." After finishing her tale, she fell silent.

"That is a sad story," I said after some thought.

"Why do you say so?"

"She couldn't be with the one she loved for so long, and he had to die and be reborn in order to learn how to love. Why did it have to be like that?"

Sage Gayatri smiled. "We mustn't look at only one life, Sundari. To grow in understanding takes time. Sage Apala didn't mind how long she had to wait. Her only thought was to help her husband grow spiritually. That is true marriage, a true partnership. You should not seek anything less. She could have asked for that boon right away, but she didn't. Why?"

I shook my head, unable to understand the reason.

"Because she realized that the long life and well-being of her father was of more importance than any personal desire. His contribution to humanity is very great and so she first sought his welfare, placing her own needs and those of her husband last. There are many important lessons in the life of Sage Apala, who then went on to bring forth some of the Vedic hymns. From the beginning, Indra Dev saw how it would all unfold. He knew of her selfless nature, that she would ask for her father first. He also knew of Maharishi Atri's importance to the Vedas, so this was part of a greater plan. The gods see far and wide and are not limited to a narrow human vision."

I wrinkled my brow as I pondered the details of her story. Something seemed not right. I was used to the traditions of our clan, which had been led by women as far back as memory could recall. But Apala had gifted her boon to her father, not her mother, why was that? Her mother was also a great sage. Could a woman also be a Saptarishi, I wondered?

"You have question, Sundari. Ask it."

I didn't respond at first but when she pressed me, I hesitantly asked, "are the Saptarishis all men?"

She smiled. "The Saptarishis can be either male or female. In our current cycle of time, they happen to all be men, but there was a time when they were all women. In fact there is an interesting story about that time…" Her voice fell off. I waited eagerly. "That story is a bit complex and may be hard for you to understand." She was quiet and I looked at her questioning-ly. Then she began slowly. "You know of the great cosmic power Rudra or the one we call Mahesha (Lord Shiva) and his female counterpart Uma Ma (Parvati). During the time of union between a deva and a devi, there is an outpouring of love into the created worlds, which affects all living beings. The union of Mahesha and Uma Ma was a particularly powerful time, and a tremendous outburst of love spread throughout the universes. From their union came the birth of a new deva, their son, who is known by many names, one of them being Kartikeya. This took place in the far, far distant past.

It was at this time, eons ago, when a great battle was taking place between the devas, the forces of light and the asuras, the forces of darkness. In this world of duality, there is always this interplay between light and dark-ness, but benevolent cosmic forces work to keep the balance between these polarities. Everything depends on the preservation of this balance. The uni-verses are in a state of expansion; creation in an ongoing process. The asuras are the forces that counter this expansion, and seek to prevent the unfolding of the universes. They are the contracting forces, which, if unimpeded, would lead to total destruction. So this battle between the creative and destructive energies is an on-going one.

"The fiercest of the asuras of that era had received a boon that he could only be destroyed by Mahesha's son, and so as soon as Kartikeya was born, all the asuras came together to find him and to diminish his power—to destroy him really.

"The seven women Saptarishis of that time approached Uma Ma and offered to protect the newborn deva, and so they created a hidden world where he could grow up undiscerned. It was very difficult for them to do this, but by joining together their love and wisdom they managed to create a world encased in a newborn cluster of stars, that even Mahesha and Uma Ma could not discover. And thus this deva was protected until he came of the age when he could assume his cosmic role. At that point the hidden world the women rishis had created became visible. The star family they had birthed to protect the world where this deva resided is now known as the Krttika (Pleiades) star cluster. You can see them in the night sky. The beings who now abide there are highly advanced and have contributed greatly to the development of our earth. Kartikeya is still the protector of the celestial realms."

Sage Gayatri ended her story and noticing my surprised expression, she smiled. I could hardly follow what she was saying. All I could hear was that great women Saptarishis had saved a great deva from destruction, and I was amazed. "Have you heard this story?" she asked.

I shook my head. "My Dada used to speak often about the star beings, and he used to follow the movements of the sky very carefully, but he never mentioned this story. I didn't know that rishis can create stars."

"This story is not known to many because it is such an ancient tale. It was told to me by a woman sage I once knew."

"Where are those women rishis now?"

"The Saptarishis stay on earth for a complete cycle of 25,000 years. In the higher ages they move around openly in society. During darker times, they retreat but continue their work from hidden places. When a new cycle of time begins, a new group of beings assume this role. The Saptarishis of the ancient time I spoke of are no longer the guiding forces of our world. They have moved on to another world, but there will always be those seven, sometimes male and sometimes female, and sometimes a combination, who will guide the world through a cycle of time.

After a few moments of silence, she said rather apologetically, "I had not meant to speak of such lofty matters, which are difficult to comprehend."

With a baffled look, I replied. "I don't think I understand much of what you just told me."

"My purpose in coming to you here was to share the story of the great Sage Apala. What I want you to remember is the sacrifice she made out of love for her husband. Her life story is an example of true love, which involves the giving up of all selfish desire. If you can one day understand this, I will be satisfied."

While I was touched by the story of Sage Apala, I was also perplexed. Why would Apala have stayed in meditation for so long if she truly loved her husband? Why couldn't Indra Dev have brought them together, if he was so benevolent. I dared not confess my confusion, and I tried not to let it show on my face.

She was quiet and then asked, "Would you prefer that instead of meeting with the other women to learn the meaning of the Vedic hymns, you and I meet privately by the river for more stories like this?"

"Ammaji, if you could, but I don't want to trouble you . . ."

"It is no trouble, my dear; it is also a rare opportunity for me to sit by our beloved Sarasvati. One day I will tell you more about her. The next few weeks are busy for me, but when I have time, I will send for you. And, Sundari, you no longer have to attend the early morning recitations." She rose to leave. I also rose and offered pranam. I could not believe my good fortune. Not only was I being excused from recitations, but I would now also have private time with her.

A few weeks later, Sage Gayatri asked that I meet her at the same place after the morning meal. I hurried to the spot full of anticipation. She was not there when I arrived, so I was able to sit by the river and speak to her as I would to a friend. Sometime later Sage Gayatri appeared. Seating herself beside me, she offered pranam to the river by way of greeting. Then she began, "Today I will tell you the story of Urvashi and Puravana from the Rig Veda. This story again involves Indra Dev.

"Sarasvati Devi has a lower self, which is the physical river that we see, and a higher self, the inner river of creativity that brings forth the Vedic poems, music, and so much else. Indra Dev also has a lower and higher manifestation. Indra is considered by most people to be lord of the sky and rains and the *raja* (king) of the heavenly worlds. At a more essential level, he governs the luminous higher mind, the blissful realm of *svarga* (the paradise of the devas) and he comes to test the sages, to help them advance to this elevated realm. It is the higher mind coming to the aid of the lower mind so that it can ascend. In Indra's world, there is a group of heavenly beings called apsaras, who often aid Indra in his testing of the sages, particularly the male sages. These apsaras are beautiful female forms. One famous apsara, called Urvashi, has appeared in a beautiful form to many of the ascetics over the millennia to test their concentration, to see if she can distract them from their meditations. Many sages have failed this test.

"This time, with Indra's consent, she decided to come to earth to experience earthly pleasures and to test one of the chieftains, Puravana, of the lunar tribes. As soon as he saw Urvashi, he fell in love and they married. After four years of happily married life, she realized that earthly pleasures were not nearly as fulfilling as the joys of the celestial world, and so she decided to return to the heavens. She had had enough. Puravana was distraught and pleaded with her to stay, but she was indifferent to his pleas and undeterred in her determination to return to the celestial world. He cried that he would lose his mind and die without her, but she was unperturbed. What was he to do?" Sage Gayatri paused and looked at me.

"It was cruel of her to leave," I commented.

"Not at all. Don't forget, she works on behalf of Indra Dev, who represents the luminous mind, helping humanity reach that state. He wanted

Puravana to grow into his potential, to advance in spiritual understanding, to attain the light-filled mind that exists within all of us, not the lower mind, hankering after sense fulfillment. The only way Puravana could unite again with his beloved Urvashi was to reach for the high place where she resided. She had lowered herself into his world; now he had to reach into hers. But to expand into that high celestial realm, one has to undergo spiritual training, subdue the lower mind with its desires, and elevate the higher qualities. This is what he set out to do."

"Did they eventually unite?"

"His concentration was one pointed: he wanted to reunite with his beloved. After a long time, he was able to attain complete control over his mind, subdue his sense desires, reach that elevated state, and enter the celestial realms. But in the process, his desires changed. He no longer sought marital happiness, but rather the bliss of his true self. His beloved wife had helped him achieve this.

"This is one of the great love stories of the Vedas, but it is difficult to understand its deeper meaning. Some say Urvashi represents the dawn and Puravana represents the sun, and this is a love story between the sun and the dawn, but I disagree. Puravana is said to be the first chieftain of the lunar dynasty, emanating from the subtle worlds of the moon, so I believe this is truly a love story between the energies of the sun and the moon. The seers have much knowledge that they hide within symbols and poetic metaphors; one cannot take at face value the meaning of this multi-layered poetry. There are meanings designed for every stage of human development, and so you can take this story as a simple love story or see a deeper cosmic relationship between the sun and the moon, both vital for life, for every animate being on earth."

"My grandfather used to talk to me about Surya Dev and said we derived from that ancestry. I never understood this. Who is Surya exactly? Is he only the physical sun that we see?"

She smiled. "After hearing these stories, you should understand that everything has a lower and higher manifestation, a physical and non-physical form. Surya is not only lord over our sun but also all the stars, the solar bodies that animate the universe, and not only the physical universe. There are suns in the celestial worlds as well. As Indra's domain is the light-filled mind, so Surya's domain is the illumined or fully awakened consciousness. We humans cannot know Surya through the thinking mind; we must transcend that. We can see the outer manifestation and honor that aspect of Surya, and as we go deeper into our meditative life, we see the subtler aspects of that higher consciousness."

I wasn't following her and had begun to play with the small plants that brushed against my bare feet, so I didn't respond. "I know that you don't understand all that I am saying," she said gently. "But these teachings will sink into your mind and rest there until someday you are able to understand. I had meant only to tell you a love story but could not help but go deeper into the hidden meaning. When you look at the moon and the sun, think of this love story."

I was inspired by my time with Sage Gayatri, but more than that I was deeply touched by her apparent care for me. I began to think that she was looking after me in Sachit's stead, preparing me for the time when I could be with him. She was teaching me how to be a good wife according to the traditions of this new society in Brahmavarta. Why else would she be telling me love stories? Although I didn't understand the deeper meanings to which she referred, I greatly enjoyed her tales as they reminded me so much of Dada.

One day after I had been listening to her chant a hymn and speak about it by the side of the sacred river, she said to me, "Sundari, I think you are coming to understand a little about the Vedas." I nodded slightly. "I must return to the hermitage now and will be away for some weeks, but we will find another time to meet when I am back." Again I nodded and as she rose, I also got up and folded my hands in pranam to her. "You may stay here a little longer and reflect on the hymn." I sat back down again, thinking: *I am so sorry, Ammaji, I am not coming to understand the hymns, but I feel your love and that is enough.* As I sat looking over the river, I allowed my mind to drift off, wondering what Sachit was doing now, what he had experienced in the time I was gone. Was he thinking of me? Was he missing me as I was missing him?

While Sage Gayatri was gone, my mind could fully immerse itself in thoughts of Sachit. He had never actually left my mind, but now I was dreaming of him often. This was both gratifying and disturbing, because it created a yearning that couldn't be satisfied.

Some weeks later, Sage Gayatri returned, and we met again by the banks of the quick-footed river, glimmering in the early morning sun. "The Vedas are as vast as the sky," she began, "and yet we have only a portion of what was given. So much was lost in the migrations during the melting of the ice. While there are many hidden teachings, the essence lies in the power of vibration, of sound. I have told you that there are hidden meanings behind each of the hymns, but actually each sound of the words correlates to a universal force; the rishis know how to use those sounds to activate specific energies. In the vibration of the sounds is secreted the story of how the unmanifest comes into manifestation and how that manifestation can return to the ultimate unmanifest state—the story of descent and ascent." She looked at me to see if I was absorbing what she was teaching, but I stared back at her blankly, too timid to say a word. She spoke of hidden worlds that couldn't be seen, and my limited understanding could not grasp the mysteries, the notion of something being unmanifest, to which she made reference.

"The rishis have developed many mantras for this purpose, but it is critical that these mantras are only known to those who have the purest intentions, who will use the mantras only for the greater good. I know the story of your sister. Your mother relayed it to me. When your sister used a protective mantra for her own purpose, knowledge of that mantra disappeared from her mind. She followed a man she loved into the naga world and, as soon as she got there, she forgot how to invoke the mantra because she had misused it. That is why she couldn't return.

"Your Muni Baba used many mantras to grow and protect the forest life. He also knew the danger of the rakshasas gaining access to the sacred mantras, since they could use them for violent means. They were growing in numbers, as were the human clans, and they had developed special powers to invade the minds of others and gain their knowledge. Muni Baba knew it was time to depart from that area and that is why he made his body disappear. He didn't die though; he appeared somewhere else and instructed your grandfather to ensure that your clan moved to our town. In order to grow our society, many of the clans needed to come out of the forest to participate. It was your grandfather's wish that you and your mother and the whole clan be here, and somehow I believe he had hoped for you to learn the secrets of the Vedas." After sharing this with me, she was quiet.

"I didn't know that you knew Muni Baba, since he never left the forest."

"Oh, he is well known to us, even now. He uses a mantra to travel while his body is stationary. He doesn't need to travel the normal way. I haven't seen him myself, but I know that others here have."

"We all knew that Muni Baba had great powers, but he rarely showed them," I replied fondly as I recalled the image of Baba, who had been such a stabilizing force for our clan. "I have wondered why he didn't destroy those shadow people. I mean rakshasas, since they were taking what was not theirs to take."

"It was not his task to destroy the rakshasas. One of the purposes in their coming deeper into the forest was to push the clans to come out to the rivers. It is only by many clans coming together that we will be able to build a new society. That is the greater plan. I decided to speak to you about this because I know you have felt abandoned by your sister, but it wasn't her wish to leave you. She had no idea that in entering another realm she would not be able to come back."

"Will I never be able to see her again, or communicate with her?" I asked sadly.

"Never is a long time. Don't worry about the future. Keep your mind focused on the task at hand. Even if you don't become a lover of the Vedas, I hope you absorb something of what I am sharing with you . . . for your future."

That was the end of our lesson for that day. I was surprised to hear that she knew of our Muni Baba, because I thought he was known only to our clan, and I was sorry that our lesson had not included a story, as it was her stories that I loved the most.

Some weeks later, I was again called to meet with Sage Gayatri by the river. "Today I will tell you the story of Saci Paulomi. Her story is a very interesting one. She was born as a princess, the daughter of a Danava raja. Do you know who the Danavas are?" I shook my head. "They are one of the *asura* (demon) tribes, meaning that they are generally violent and full of greed, with no moral sense. Yet this daughter of the Danava raja rose to be the wife of Indra Dev, the *rani* (queen) of the heavenly worlds. How can you explain that?"

"Was she very beautiful?"

"They say she was beautiful, but there are many magnificent women in the heavenly realms. She had another quality and she wrote about this in one of the hymns in the Rig Veda (Hymn CLIX). I will chant it for you. Close your eyes and contemplate the meaning."

I closed my eyes and listened as she slowly began to chant, first in gentle tones and then rising with a rush of waves. Her powerful incantations awakened a storm within my spine, like winds surging through me. As I listened, the rhythmic beating of her voice harmonized with the rising of the waves that were sweeping me, but soon began to calm down. When she ended, I was unable to speak at first.

"It is a powerful hymn, isn't it?" she asked after her voice had trailed off.

"What did I just experience, Ammaji?" I asked quietly, in a trembling voice.

"You experienced the shakti, the inner strength and divine feminine energy of the seer. That inner power is within all of us."

"I don't understand."

"Never mind. You will later. What do the words of the hymn mean to you?"

I hadn't paid much attention to the words and so I didn't respond at first. Then she repeated a few lines and asked again.

"I don't know, Ammaji. I guess her words indicate that she is a conqueror, achieving victory over the other wives of Indra Dev. It sounds to me like she is still an asura, using violent means."

She laughed. "Let's look at it. Remember Indra Dev is the light-filled mind, and as his consort, Saci is the female aspect of that shining mind. At the beginning of the hymn, she calls herself a mighty arbitress, meaning she settles disputes and has the final say. Then she goes on to state: 'I am victorious, and my Lord shall be submissive to my will. My sons are slayers of the foe, my daughter is the ruling queen. I am victorious over my Lord; my song of triumph is supreme.' She then says she got rid of all the rival wives, but who are these wives that compete with the power of the higher mind?"

I looked at her blankly and then said, "She is jealous of the other beauties in heaven?"

"Sundari," she smiled, "the other wives are the distractions, those temptations that seek to take away the concentration. She has conquered all the distractions, the lower qualities that associate with the mind, and this higher shining mind now rules supreme. She is in control of all her senses and wandering thoughts; her desires, words, and actions; in control of negative tendencies like selfishness and anger; and has attained the pure light-filled mind. The senses will not control her, but rather they are submissive to her will. Her offspring, her good qualities, are helping her to achieve victory. They are her sons who overcome all distractions and temptations and her daughter, her shakti, is the queen. She calls these distractions her fellow wives, because they are held close by the lower mind, beloved by it, you might say. She is in control now of the higher mind, the light-emitting intelligence. Do you understand?"

Squirming to make myself more comfortable, I turned from her gaze and looked over at the river without answering.

"It doesn't matter if you don't grasp this higher meaning. Your heart enabled you to feel the shakti, the power of the poem. That is enough, and now I will explain what you experienced. The poet uses the vibrations of sound to awaken the shakti, the innate creative power, to conquer the lower mind. You see the physical form of the Sarasvati River, don't you?" I nodded, wondering why she was asking me such an obvious question. "The Vedas speak of seven sacred rivers. Do you know where they are?"

"There are seven rivers like this?" I asked in amazement.

She nodded, "But the Sarasvati is the mother river. I have told you, everything in the Vedas has an outer and inner significance. The physical rivers are sacred because they feed life. Without their waters, we could not live here. But the Vedas are referring to an inner river."

"An inner river?" I asked in amazement.

She nodded. "The river of *prana*, of the life force, which runs in our body through seven sacred channels. That is the true sacred river into which we must dip and purify ourselves every day."

"My grandfather spoke of prana, I remember…I think," I mused.

"The seven sacred rivers are the centers of prana in the body; they flow unimpeded from their resting place at the base of the spine to their destination, in the same way as the outer rivers flow from their source in the mountains to their destination in the sea. When our inner river flows and reaches its destined place at the crown of the head, that is when the higher mind can be realized. The deeper meaning of the Sarasvati is this inner flow of prana. She guides it to its destination here." She pointed to the crown of her head. "This spot is envisioned by the seers as the beautiful lotus on which Devi Sarasvati rests, the single point where all streams gather, the source of all inspiration. Hidden within this lotus are the mysteries of the universe which She reveals."

"That is a lot for me to try to understand," I murmured, as I again looked out over the river wondering how there could be an internal river.

"This hymn can awaken those sacred centers, as it did for you, and it can also serve to strengthen the will. It speaks through the voice of the female creative power, the shakti. I have chanted it so many times when I have been secluded in meditation and have been distracted, and each time I chant this hymn, my higher mind comes forth and slays all the lower tendencies, the co-wives that seek to distract the luminous mind. How many times this hymn has been my lifeline, drawing me deeper into meditation. There is great power in the recitation, in the chanting of the words. I can't emphasize enough, Sundari, how powerful this chant is. Memorize it and use it when in need. This is one of the first hymns the women here in the hermitage chant in the morning, and now perhaps it is time for you to return to the morning recitations."

I nodded. I had been in the hermitage for over a year, and I could see how my time with Sage Gayatri was slowly and subtly changing me, but I hesitated to engage with the other women, who were far superior in their abilities. She must have perceived my hesitation because she added, "Don't compare yourself with anyone else. A teacher's gift is to know how to approach each individual student. There is no one formula for learning. We all grow at our own pace, in our own way, and a true teacher understands this."

I now began to rise early and join the other women with the morning chants. I was not able to memorize the chants as well as they, but I was able to listen and try to discern the deeper meaning of the words. At the same time, my nights were haunted by dreams of Sachit, and the dreams were becoming more sensual. At first, I would kiss him and then I would find myself pulling him down beside me and embracing him. I suspected that Sage Gayatri was aware of my thoughts and so I did my best to push away the sensual images that pursued me. One day she pulled me aside and asked me to join her for a walk by the river. I assumed we would sit at our usual place and she would teach through a story, but this day was different. We walked for quite some time in silence, and then she began.

"There is a great woman ascetic named Sulabha. Of all the women seers, she is perhaps my favorite, and I was fortunate to meet her one time. She has lived for centuries and will live for many centuries more, perhaps millennia, for she is one of those rare maharishis who span the generations.

She is also rare because she does not stay in one place. It is said that she wanders the earth, continually moving from place to place. Before I met her, I had also heard that she does not identify as either male or female but lives fully in the realization of her genderless higher self. But for the sake of serving Indra Dev's function of testing the sages, sometimes she appears as a beautiful young woman. She came one time to test my husband."

This was the first time Sage Gayatri had mentioned her husband to me, and as I knew he was the teacher of Sachit, I paid extra attention to every word she spoke.

She saw my interest and said, "Let's sit by the Sarasvati. It is always good to have her company." We found a comfortable spot to rest ourselves and for a few minutes she was quiet, looking out over the great river. "One day, when I was much younger, an average-looking middle-aged woman ascetic arrived at my husband's hermitage. That was before I had established this hermitage, when I was helping to care for his students. In those days, my husband met with women seers and ascetics and even had a few women students. This ordinary-looking woman was named Sulabha. I would notice that whenever she sat before my husband, he would be mesmerized, unable to tear his eyes away from her. I didn't understand this because she wasn't a beauty, but he seemed entranced every time he saw her. I began to worry what his students would think. His reputation could be damaged.

"Then one day, without my knowing, Sulabha transferred to me a yogic power that gave me the ability to see what my husband was perceiving. He saw her as the most beautiful celestial woman, but he was the only one who saw her this way. I was shocked, and I didn't know what to do. As the days went by, my husband crept closer and closer to her. Then one day I went to him and told him that she must leave, but he refused to send her away, saying she was a great sage. Can you imagine me trying to chase away one of the great seers of our time!" She issued a small laugh and then continued,

"I didn't want to admit it, but I was jealous, and so I had to undergo much introspection. I wasn't jealous of her beauty because I saw her as a rather plain-looking woman, but I was jealous of the hold she had on my husband's attention. I decided that I had to conquer this attachment and so told my husband that I was going off to meditate. Sulabha acted as if nothing was awry. This whole drama took place between my husband and me, and she never said a word to either of us. My husband tried to dissuade me from leaving, but I was undeterred. I went to a remote place and engaged in meditation.

"One day, not long after I had left, I was meditating and had a vision in which I saw that Sulabha was seated before my husband in her beautiful form, and as he was gazing at her admiringly she turned into an old, feeble woman; at that moment he awoke from his illusion. When I opened my eyes, I found her seated beside me in her normal middle-aged appearance. She said that it was Indra Dev who had sent her to test us both, and that because I had not interfered with my husband but had turned inward to overcome my own feelings of jealousy, she would bless me to break all attachment to my husband. She cured me of any jealousy. I stayed in meditation for nearly a year and then returned to my husband. Over the years we have spent far more time apart than together, yet our separations have not diminished the love between us in the slightest, and we don't interfere with each other's work. There is great love but no attachment.

"Since his experience with Sulabha, he has refused to take women students, and rarely meets with women sages. He has a strict discipline for his students, asking them to be *brahmachari* (celibate) for long periods of time to strengthen their will power." She was quiet for a few minutes and then asked, "Do you understand why I am telling you this story?"

Sighing, I nodded, and then asked bashfully, "Ammaji, what is a sankalpa vow and why does one make it?"

"Sachit has told you that he had made a sankalpa?"

I shook my head. "My mother told me, but I didn't believe her. He never said anything about it."

"He should have, because it is a serious matter. Words and thoughts hold great power, especially when there is a strong intention. It is always the intention that brings about the desired result. A sankalpa is a sacred vow often taken in the presence of a holy being, which serves to strengthen the will. Here we do it in the presence of the sacred Sarasvati. By holding to the vow, one's will is reinforced and one's intention realized, and in this way one advances spiritually. On the surface it is a simple process. One takes some water in one's hand, and with closed eyes, invoking the sacred presence, makes the vow and then throws the water back to its source. The power comes not from the outer act but the inner one, the commitment to fulfill all the terms of the vow. It is a form of sacrifice."

"What happens if the vow is broken?" I asked nervously.

"In Sachit's case, it would break his relationship with his teacher, and this would cause him great distress. But it also would be unfortunate for the whole community. Our society looks to the brahmins as examples of spiritual and moral conduct. For him not to fulfil the terms of a vow he has willingly taken would set a very poor example. He was not forced to take the vow; it was his desire to do so. And since it was taken in the presence of a divine form, it also . . . how do I say it . . . well, it would drive a wedge between the divine and the one breaking the vow, hindering one's ability to advance toward that higher awareness.

"I don't interfere with my husband's training of his students, but in this case, I think he was shortsighted and should not have allowed Sachit to take this vow, as I don't think he is ready. Sachit is a rare student with a powerful mind; my husband only sees his potential, not the reality of who he is today. He is the only one among his past and present students who can hear a long hymn but once and be able to memorize it. His memory is re-markable, as is his insight into the deeper meaning of the hymns, but he also has a strong pull toward the senses. He has been blessed by the Sarasvati and her creative stream flows through him, but this can take many forms; this creativity, if not properly guided, will not necessarily lead to higher knowl-edge. One has to have the internal strength and willpower to use her creative energy for spiritual realization, and it is as yet unknown whether Sachit has what is required.

"Many seers and rishis marry, and this could have been the case for Sachit, but because of the story with Sulabha, my husband is stricter than others about this matter. I tell you this so you will understand the serious nature of your attraction to Sachit. If you were able to wait ten, twenty, even thirty years without interfering in his training so that he can develop his inner strength, that would be one thing, but I have no delusions about your ability to endure such a separation. You are a passionate young woman, Sundari, full of the zeal for life, not yet ready to subdue the senses, but one day you will be, and I hope that then you will remember what our seers have taught."

If I had fully understood what she was saying, I would have burst into tears, but internally I believed that my love was greater than any sankalpa and that Sachit and I could endure whatever humiliation would await us from the breaking of a vow.

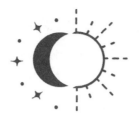

Chapter Five

ENTANGLEMENT

One day, I received word that my brother Arrav was waiting outside the hermitage to see me. I had not seen any of my family in two years and was happy at the news. When I arrived at the entrance, he eagerly received me, reminding me how much I had missed the warmth of the family. After exchanging greetings, he told me that our mother had hurt her back while working in the field and that I was needed at home to care for her. I met this news with mixed feelings. While I was sorry to be leaving Sage Gayatri, I was not sorry to return home where I could go to the temple or down to the river where the brahmins chanted in the early hours and again see Sachit. It had been two long years and in that time my aching for him had greatly increased.

I needed to get Sage Gayatri's permission to leave the hermitage, and I went off to find her. Without much fanfare she nodded and gave her consent. "But before you leave, Sundari, let's sit once more by Sarasvati Devi together, and I will tell you a last story." We walked a short way, until we reached the spot where she had always narrated to me.

"This is a story about a great maharishi named Bharadvaja. Before he achieved such an exalted state, he lived a very austere life, observing strict celibacy for the purpose of gaining the highest hidden wisdom of the Vedas. After praying to Indra Dev for a long life so he could continue his meditations, Indra Dev granted him the years of three life spans, each span being several hundred years. After this time period was up, he still didn't feel he knew the Vedas. Indra Deva appeared to him and asked, 'If I give you another life span, what will you do with it?'

"Immediately Rishi Bharadvaja replied, 'I will continue my life of austerity and celibacy in the effort to penetrate the hidden knowledge of the Vedas.'

"Indra Dev smiled and said, 'Look over there, great sage, at those three hills.' The sage looked at the hills, which were not far away, and watched as Indra went to each hill and took a handful of dirt. Returning, he said to Bharadvaja, 'What you know is comparable to these handfuls of dirt. Those hills are like the vast sea of knowledge contained in the Vedas. What will a fourth life span do for you? It is useless, give up. I will grant you other knowledge.'

"Without taking much time for reflection, the rishi replied, 'I will spend as many lives as necessary to realize the truths contained within the Vedas, no matter how often I need to be reborn,' and in that moment, Indra awakened Bharadvaja's higher mind and he attained realization."

She ended her story and I didn't respond. Finally she asked, "Do you know why I have told you about the great Sage Bharadvaja?"

"You want to teach me that there is no end to learning?"

"That is true, but, more importantly, the lesson is that to gain anything precious, sacrifice is needed. Most people only see the outer form, the sacrificial fire, but the Vedas speak of a different sacrifice, the inner one. Celibacy is one form of sacrifice, not the only one, but this type of renunciation is one path to knowledge, if it is done properly, with the right intention and will. Muni Baba sacrificed speech and sense pleasures, and these are small things to give up in order to gain the ultimate truth, the bliss of the illumined mind. We light the outer fire in the hope that it will kindle the inner flames, the fire of realization, and burn the *samskaras*, the seeds of our past thoughts and actions. That is the true sacrificial fire, and the rishis know this. The ceremonial fire is but a symbol of this inner act. Every outer form has a deeper inner meaning. Never be satisfied with the outer form alone.

"*Agni Dev* (Fire God), who presides over the ceremonial fire, represents the fire of the higher will. When we perform the outer act of lighting a ceremonial fire and invoke Agni Dev, we are invoking this higher will so that we can achieve the inner sacrifice that we ourselves are determined to make. That is why in the ceremonial fire we invoke Agni first. Nothing can be achieved without a strong will. Whenever we invoke a deity, we align ourselves with the quality of that deity. When we invoke Surya Dev, we align our consciousness with the sun, the force from which all light and all life emerges. That is why we invoke Surya Dev every morning, to align our higher self with that energy, that brilliance, the vast intelligence that spreads throughout the universe. We ask that force to illuminate our consciousness in the way it illuminates the dark skies."

Her words perplexed me. In the past Sage Gayatri had spoken to me about an inner river and now she was speaking of an inner fire. This was beyond what I could comprehend.

Sensing my confusion, she paused, and then added with a smile, "I see you are not following me, but no matter. One day you will understand. It does not matter how long it takes. I have confidence that one day you will have this experience yourself. What I want to tell you before you return home is that there is no one path to this knowledge. For Sachit it may be celibacy at this time in his life, and for you it may be something entirely different. Allow him to follow his path, while you search for yours. This is the indication of true love. You must distinguish between passion, sensual desire, and love. If you truly love Sachit, you will help him fulfill his sacred vow by sacrificing your passion."

After falling into silence, she said, "I will leave you to reflect on my words by the Sarasvati, but don't stay too long as your brother is waiting." She began to walk away and then came back. "I am in need of some seclusion and so will be gone for a period of time, but I will see you later on." With those words she walked away.

I sat there numb, not reflecting on her words but trying to suppress the emotions that were swirling inside of me. I was a young woman burning with desire, not for knowledge but for the man I loved. I yearned to bear his children. I could not erase his face from my mind, regardless of whether I was awake or asleep. Prema had been able to follow her heart, why couldn't I? When I saw the joy of love that she and her husband experienced, I wanted the same.

While I greatly admired and respected Sage Gayatri and all the women sages she had spoken of, I was not like them and didn't aspire to be. I was not seeking the knowledge of the Vedas; I was seeking a contented life with the man I loved. Was that so wrong? Sitting there by the Sarasvati River, I only thought of myself, of my needs, and it didn't occur to me to think of what Sachit wanted, despite Sage Gayatri's words. Turning to the river, I implored her to help me fulfil my desires, without thinking that this might not be the best course toward happiness.

After two years in the hermitage, I left Sage Gayatri's care, eager to return to the world. I saw that I had grown in those two years and had become more confident. I was no longer the bashful girl who had emerged from the forest some five years earlier. My mother was happy to see me, although I think she was hoping I would have become more a lover of learning, but scholarship was not in my nature. Soon after my return, I again took up the habit of going down to the river in the early morning hours to listen to the chanting of the Vedic hymns. My main purpose was to see Sachit, but I also drew much pleasure from listening to the poems, as I now was familiar with some of them and they reminded me of my days at the hermitage.

Sachit did not notice me at first, since I remained slightly apart and hidden among the brush as I had done in the past, but with my new sense of confidence I gradually began to show myself and approach him. At first, he was polite, but I noticed a change in him. He wouldn't look directly at me when I greeted him or when he spoke. Rather he would keep his eyes down, and this caused me distress. I had to know what his true feelings were. I decided to take a chance and open my heart to him. I had nothing to lose, and I could not stand to feel his coolness without understanding why.

One day after he had finished his chanting, I came forward and asked him to stay behind for a moment. He motioned to the other brahmins to leave. "Sit with me for a few minutes by the river, Sachit. We have hardly spoken since I left for Sage Gayatri's hermitage. I have changed since then."

"I should not be here with you, Sundari. I am glad you went to her hermitage. I am sure you have much better understanding now of our ways."

"What harm can come from spending a few minutes with me, Sachit? Please stay."

He sat down and I sat beside him in silence. My courage suddenly fled, and then I remembered the words I had spoken to the river before leaving the hermitage. I had asked her to fulfill my desire. Suddenly I burst out, "Sachit, you know my feelings for you. I have to know whether you feel the same." When he didn't respond, I continued, "I missed you terribly while at the hermitage and find it very painful to be . . . to be apart from you." I had been staring into the river, which was as wild today as the emotions coursing through me, but now I turned to face Sachit.

He also turned to look at me and I saw the coldness in his eyes soften into kindness. With a caring expression he said quietly, "You know I have made a sacred vow of celibacy. It is for ten years, and I don't know whether my teacher will ask me to make another vow for another ten years. My life is in his hands. Will you be able to wait that long, Sundari? After the vow is completed . . ."

I didn't let him finish. "Ten years!" I exclaimed. "Why would you do such a thing?" He began to rise, but I pulled him back down.

"I can't have this discussion with you, Sundari, not now. I have made the sankalpa . . . and it will be years before I can think of marriage."

"Why, Sachit, why?" I began to cry.

"Don't, Sundari. After training with Sage Gayatri for two years, are you not able to control your passions?" His voice was gentle but firm.

I don't know what came over me, but I reached out and put my arms around his neck and pulled him down toward me. He didn't resist. We both fell over and before I knew it, he was on top of me. For a moment he rested there, lowering his lips to touch mine, but then he pulled away sharply and stood up. I also got up and cried to him, "Before the sacred Saraswati, I am declaring my love for you, Sachit. It will never change. But I can't wait that long."

"Sundari, don't," he pleaded. "We will both be hurt."

He began to walk away, but I grabbed his leg and clung to it, crying, "Sachit, I want to be with you. I want to have your child. Why is that wrong?"

Pulling away sharply, without a backward glance or another word, he brusquely walked away, leaving me there in tears by the banks of the sacred river, pain searing my heart.

My brother Arrav found me there many hours later. Taking one look at my swollen, red eyes, he asked in dismay, "What happened? Who did this to you?"

"I have done it to myself," I replied quietly. "Arrav, please take me home."

My mother was waiting there. After seeing my tear-stained face, she knew what had happened. She had been worried when she awoke and found me gone, and when I didn't return hours later, she went to find Arrav and asked him to see what had happened. Holding the greatest respect for Sachit, she refused to think he had any blame in the situation, and I also could not accuse him of anything. It was fully my fault.

Later that night, however, when I began to reflect on all of my interactions with Sachit, I wondered if it really was all my doing. The dreams I had been having, could he have had a role in that? The beads he had given me, the many times he had come to see me after our arrival from the forest, and then the moment when he had lowered his lips toward mine—was I imagining his affection? It didn't matter. Only I knew of those little signs, and the last thing I would do was cast any blame on him. I had taken a vow to love him and I would fulfil that vow as he would fulfil his, no matter what was involved.

What I didn't expect, what I could not have predicted, was the humiliation that my mother and I would have to endure. News spread fast that I had thrown myself at the feet of one of the brahmacharis, begging to have his child. The whole clan was distraught, especially since I was in line to be their future leader. My mother, who rarely showed her emotion, spent many nights with tear-stained eyes, hardly speaking with me. I also kept my distance as there was nothing to say. I couldn't excuse myself. Finally, she approached me.

"Sundari, I sent you to learn under the guidance of Sage Gayatri. How could you not have come to see the folly in pursuing this attraction? How could you not understand the need to put the clan first, and set your feelings aside? I told you from the beginning that Sachit was not for you, and yet you persisted. I don't understand this. You have never been one to be so brash. What came over you?"

"I learned many things with Sage Gayatri, but I didn't learn how to undo my love," I replied quietly.

"Love? Can't you distinguish between passion and love? If you loved him, you would help him fulfil his vows, not seek to undermine him, cause him to fail in the eyes of the community."

Hiding my face in my hands, I replied in a choking voice, "Amma, I regret everything, but I can't say that I won't do it again. I seem not to be able to control my feelings. I didn't mean for what happened to happen. I wanted to see him, to talk to him, but in that moment, I couldn't control myself. I need you now to support me. Don't abandon me as you did Prema."

"It was Prema who abandoned us, have you forgotten?" she replied in a cool tone. "I have two willful daughters. How will the clan be guided in the future if you cannot put their interests above your own?"

"I was never meant to lead the clan," I cried out. "That was for Prema and she is gone. Arrav is perfectly capable of leading the clan when you can no longer do so."

"Arrav? It has been the tradition since long back that the eldest daughter leads, and if there is no daughter, it passes to another woman relative. It has always been a woman. If we break with that tradition, I can't think what might happen."

"Why is tradition so important?" I cried.

My mother looked horrified. "Back in the forest, you never questioned me. You never would assume such a tone with me. Where did this willfulness come from?" she asked in a sorrowful tone. "I don't understand it. Do you think yourself fit to be his wife? We don't yet know the ways of this community; how could you be so bold?"

The thought of whether or not I was deserving of Sachit had not even occurred to me. I had just been following my heart.

Events moved rapidly after that. The elders of the community called my mother to meet with them and after several exchanges it was agreed that I would leave the region. I was to be sent away. When my mother told me this news, I could not believe it. I was certain it could not have happened without her consent, so I blamed her for this turn of events. I didn't speak out in my defense. I knew that if I were to stay and by chance saw Sachit, I would call out to him, pursue him in any way I could. I would dream of him at night and find ways to be near him. If he were sent away, that would be a blemish in the sight of all, and he would blame me for that stain on his reputation. So, with much bitterness toward my mother, I accepted my fate.

The night before my departure, I had a dream. In the dream I was standing with Sachit by the sacred Sarasvati. Her waves were wild that day, rushing forward with untamed ebullience. Turning to Sachit, I said with a laugh, "She is like a restless child today."

He smiled and with a glimmer in his eyes replied, "Much like you." Then he asked, "Would you like to see her true form?" I nodded with great earnestness. "Close your eyes, Sundari."

I protested, "If I close my eyes, how will I see her?"

He chuckled and replied, "If you keep your eyes open, how will you see her? She lives in the internal world."

Closing my eyes, I saw only darkness. I was about to open them when a beautiful female form emerged out of the darkness, radiating a light unlike the light of the sun and far more luminous, truly indescribable, and I heard the words gently rising like a subtle echo, "She is Shri Devi's child. I cannot intervene."

In the dream, I opened my eyes and she was gone, but a mist of light lingered over the rushing waters. In total amazement I turned to Sachit, but he was nowhere in sight. I was alone by the river. Then I awoke.

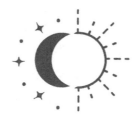

Chapter Six

THE CURSE

A fog settled over me as I left the place I had come to consider my home. Nobody from the clan came to say goodbye except my brothers, who looked at me with saddened eyes. I could not bear to see their disappointment, and so with brief hugs and feigned cheerfulness I told them that surely we would meet again before too long. I had no idea where my maternal uncle was taking me, but I had heard the name Kashi (the old name for Varanasi), a growing town along another very sacred river, the Ganga. It didn't matter much to me where we went. All that mattered was that once more I was being ripped from familiar surroundings and I would perhaps never see my beloved Sachit again. I would have been happy to spend my life by his side, serving him, tending to his needs, supporting him in any way I could, with no aspirations of my own. Why was this being denied me?

Distance had grown between me and my mother and so there were no goodbyes. I had come to think of her as a cold woman, even though Arrav pleaded her case, saying because of her position she was used to putting her personal feelings aside. It was Arrav, not she, who walked me to the waiting boat where we were to meet my uncle. It was Arrav who stood there with tears in his eyes as I climbed into the boat, and it was Arrav who tried to hold onto the boat for some last words before letting me float away. As the boat began to drift into the swift river currents and the reality of the situation hit me, I fell into a desperate silence. My mother was truly shutting me out of her heart, just as she had done to Prema. What was left to me of my mother were her words, "Do you think yourself fit to be his wife?" Those words echoed in my mind for years after, causing me pain upon pain.

I stood up in the boat, realizing that the sadness clinging to me was not only due to the separation from Sachit, my family, the clan, and Sage Gayatri, but it was also because of the separation from the sacred Sarasvati. I had come to love her, and perhaps I would not see her again. How many times her waves had soothed me, her rippling sounds penetrating my heart.

"Sit down, Sundari," called my uncle, as the boat began to sway, and the few people in the boat began to shift back and forth. Sitting back down, I looked at my uncle, who wore a stoic expression on his face. He also was leaving behind the clan he had known since birth, but he was not being sent away. He had volunteered to take me, as he was engaged in the work of making cloth and he knew that in the town of Kashi were cloth makers who excelled in this skill. He was eager to learn from them new ways of using plants to make dyes for the cloth and perhaps someday bring this knowledge back to our clan.

During my childhood I had been close to this uncle because, like me, he had a way with his hands and loved making beautiful objects. I had drifted away from him of late but was somewhat comforted by the fact that it was he and not another clansman who had been put in charge of me. Before we left the forest, my uncle, the youngest brother of my mother, had lost his wife in childbirth and the baby as well. He had not remarried and was hoping that in Kashi he would find a new wife, and a husband for me.

It took weeks to reach Kashi. Had my heart not been so overburdened, I would have enjoyed the journey and the sight of the new town, which was spread along a great river, as wide and wild as the Sarasvati. I wondered if I would grow to love her as much. One of the cloth makers in our town had given my uncle the name of a person to contact when we arrived in Kashi, saying that we would be welcome there. The towns in the whole region were connected by the traveling tradesmen and traders and the brahmins who walked from place to place conducting ritual ceremonies. My uncle had assured me that we would feel as much at home in Kashi as we had in the town by the Sarasvati River, but we would be starting over.

The family that we stayed with upon our arrival was kind enough. They were an elderly couple, who knew all the cloth makers in the community and helped make many introductions. After some weeks, my uncle was able to move us into our own place. Not long after, he found himself a wife, the daughter of one of the cloth makers, and then he began looking for a suitable match for me. I didn't protest. A part of me had withdrawn from life and I cared little for what happened to me. Whether I lived or died didn't seem important. Two years later I married an experienced cloth maker, and I had a family again, all of us living together in a single abode.

Kashi was everything and more than it was said to be. It was larger than the town I had come from, with many markets where trading was the custom. My husband and uncle would go together to the markets for trading, and my husband would trade the cloths he made for food and other items for our household. It was a system that worked well. Soon our home was filled with mats, pottery, metal utensils, and many such things. I never tired of going to the market to see what new crafts had appeared. The streets in the town I had come to call home were wider than in the old town; the homes were larger and made of different materials, and there were beautiful cows wandering everywhere along the streets. Painted walls and carvings decorated the temples. I would have been very happy in Kashi . . . if Sachit had been with me.

Soon after my arrival in Kashi, I began taking walks by the river, the great Ganga, which reminded me very much of the river I had left behind. At times when I went to the river, I remembered Sage Gayatri, and this brought me comfort, but at other times Sachit's face would come to my mind, and this sent waves of pain through my being. Why could I not forget him? I carried with me always the tulsi bead necklace he had given me, wearing it around my neck, and when I was sad, I would run my fingers over the beads. I didn't know any sacred mantras, but I knew the language of the heart, and this is the language I recited as I felt the beads.

The husband my uncle found for me was a kind man and very good at turning plant materials into clothing, and had it not been for Sachit I might have been content with the marriage, but there are some roads taken from which there is no turning back. I had already given my heart away. I had experienced a man who could heal my mother of a poisonous wound by reciting mantras through the day and night, who could take me through different realms to a sister who now lived in another world, and who could cause Sarasvati Devi to appear to me in a dream. How could I be satisfied with anything less? Only I couldn't have him. That was my torment. I was resigned to my unhappiness, but I was also committed to shielding it, burying it deep inside of me. And so, I began married life as a woman in hiding.

Over the next five years I had two daughters, and this drew my attention away from the turmoil of my heart. I applied myself to care for them, and I thought I was perhaps finally beginning to make peace with myself. Several more years passed and then Arrav came to Kashi. I hadn't seen my mother or brothers since the day I left, and I was glad that of all of them, he was the one to come. I didn't realize that he would break open wounds that were festering unhealed. For the first few days of his visit, I had no time alone with him and so the conversation was all pleasantries, with stories about his marriage and son, and his expertise with weaponry. Finally, when we had time alone to speak, he mentioned how sad our mother had been since our parting. "She is getting older now, Sundari, and she wants more than anything to come see you and meet your children. She has grieved for you long enough."

At the mention of our mother, my heart hardened. "Grieved for me? It has taken her a long time," I replied scornfully.

"You must forgive her, Sundari."

"I can't, and I can't see her, Arrav. Please understand."

"Why can't you forget what is passed? You have a husband and two daughters and are happy in your new life."

"Happy? I have made the best of my life that I could, but I would not say that I am happy. I will never forget the look of utter disappointment on our mother's face when I last saw her . . . or the words she spoke to me. How can I forget that? She didn't even come to the boat to say goodbye, showing no consideration for what I was going through. She could have come with me here, even for a brief while to help me get settled. Do you think it is so easy to erase those feelings, to pretend those things didn't happen? I am a mother now, and I know what a mother should and shouldn't do. She sent me away not thinking of my pain . . ."

"It wasn't she who sent you away, Sundari. You must know that. She had no choice, and she has never been one to express her feelings."

"Then who was it, if not her?"

He didn't answer right away, but when I pressed him, he replied quietly, "It was Sachit who sent you away. It was his decision. She had no choice but to comply. He saved her life and she has always felt she owed him a great debt for that. Don't you think it pained her so to have you leave?"

"It was Sachit?" I asked in disbelief.

"Sundari, it has been a long time now. Can't you forget what happened?"

"Sachit. So, it was he who sent me away. I can't believe that." Arrav didn't answer, but when I looked at him and he nodded, I knew it had to be true. Arrav would not make a false statement. "Arrav, for whatever reason, my wounds are still too deep. My feelings for Sachit have not changed, but I am reconciled to the fact that I will have to live without him. I am sorry, but I can't see Amma. I still feel abandoned by her. She did nothing to soothe my heart but only blamed me. Make any excuse you want, but don't let her come."

After Arrav left, I went to sit by the Ganga and reflect on the fact that it was Sachit who was the cause of my separation from those I loved. This was very hard for me to accept and it awakened in me an anger. "He took no responsibility for his part in what took place," I said to the river Ganga. "He led me to believe that he cared, and I know it was not my imagination." This anger did not leave me and for a long while, it accompanied my sadness.

Five more years passed, and in that time, I had a son. The busy-ness of daily life did its part to drown out my sorrows. My growing family had moved out of the house we shared with my uncle and his wife, and we now had our own small home. My husband had gained a reputation in the community, and we were doing quite well, well enough to engage a woman to help with household duties and the children. With the passing of the years, Kashi was also growing, and the beauty of the town was endearing it to me. In the main market, stone buildings now lined the banks of the Ganga, with steps to walk down to her cooling waters and bathe. The temples were bustling with activity, and priests, brahmins, and sages walked the streets, creating a most peaceful and elevated air. I had grown to love Kashi. How could one not? It seemed to us who lived there that our town was the center of the universe, her beauty crowned by the glistening, green Ganga, radiant in the sunlight, soothing under the pattering rains and mysterious beneath the dark night sky.

Over a period of several weeks my husband had been working on one piece of cloth, weaving, dying, and pressing it, and he was nearly ready to take it to the market to exchange for grains. One day I had it in mind to take a boat across the river to the forests to gather wild food. When I left forest life, I did not leave behind my love for this activity—it was a way of merging my mind with the life of the forest. It was a habit I continued to practice whenever I could. Without giving it too much consideration, I grabbed a piece of cloth, not realizing it was that special one that my husband had been working on, and a basket for gathering food, and made my way down to the river. Offering the cloth to a boatman, I asked him to take me across, wait for me, and then bring me back. He was so pleased with the cloth that he eagerly consented.

I had not been to that forest on the other side of the river for many months. My husband discouraged me from going for reasons I couldn't quite understand, and so I was glad that he was away on this day and would not prevent me from enjoying some hours alone among the trees. After we had reached the other shore, I left the boatman, telling him I would return soon, and walked across the sandy riverbank until I reached the forest. Entering, I walked quite a way, deep among the thicket of trees, knowing exactly where to look for food, and I began filling my basket.

The basket was overflowing with plant foods, and I was about to return to the boat when my eye caught a plant I recognized as having a very tasty root when cooked. Bending down I pulled up the wild vegetable and placed it in my basket. As I did, my eyes met those of a large serpent staring at me from inside the brush. It was not a normal serpent as its eyes were large and green and seemed to be staring right at me. For a moment I froze, never having had such a close encounter before with a type of serpent I could not identify. Slowly, I stood up and quietly began walking backward, away from the animal, but with every step I took, it inched forward out of the brush and onto the pathway, keeping its eyes on me. I had no notion what type of serpent it was, whether its venom was deadly or not, but I thought it odd the way it looked at me with piercing eyes. The animals in the forest rarely bothered humans unless they were under threat or hungry, and I was not food for this animal, nor was I threatening it.

During my early life in the forest, I had seen many serpents, but we had lived together peacefully. They never attacked, only hissed when they felt in danger. If I was not posing any danger to this animal, why did it stare at me with such menacing eyes? I began to feel unnerved, and the thought of defending myself entered my mind, but another thought also sneaked into my mental process. It was the nagas who had lured away my sister and I knew that they often appeared in the human world in the guise of serpents. Was this encounter by chance, or was it planned? Was this my opportunity to strike back, to repay the nagas, if this indeed was such a creature, for having taken away my sister?

Quietly placing my basket on the ground, I picked up a large thick stick and held it threateningly toward the animal and in a shaking voice called out, "It was your kind who lured my sister away, a sister I adored. You took her from me, didn't you?" At those words the serpent raised itself high, lifted its hood and began to issue a loud and frightening hiss. "You are not satisfied with taking her. You want me as well," I said, staring at him angrily. At that point, I still did not think of challenging him. "Had your kind not taken her, my life would be different." The serpent inched closer, but I didn't move. I didn't retreat. "I am sure you have loved ones. I should show them what it is like to lose someone dear. I should teach you a lesson and repay your clan for what was done to my family. I will have my revenge." By this time my emotions were rising, and I was becoming increasingly consumed by anger. Inching closer to the creature, I watched as it lifted its hood higher and hissed again in a haunting tone.

I waved the stick before him as he hissed more vehemently, and I knew at that moment the snake was cursing me. Briefly an image of the Ganga flashed through my mind and my spirit called out to her. Then gathering all my strength, I lifted the stick high and brought it crashing down on the serpent's head, hitting it with all my might. It fell over but continued to hiss. Like a mad woman, I smashed the animal again and again until it lay in pieces. After it was over, taking stock at what I had done, I sank to my knees in shock. As I knelt there in disbelief, I saw an image of my sister wavering before me in the air as if behind a thin film. I could barely make out her form, but I could see the look of anguish on her face. Her image lingered in the air for a moment and then was gone.

What had I done? Could I have hurt one of my sister's relatives, a naga who perhaps had come with a message for me? I had never killed an animal before and this alone was enough to shake me, but the thought of perhaps having harmed someone close to Prema was too much to bear. I sat on my knees paralyzed for some time, wondering what on earth I could do to undo what I had done. Finally, I got up and taking hold of my basket of food returned to the boat and the waiting boatman. I tried to calm myself on the ride across the river, but when I saw the tossing waves, I thought perhaps even Ganga was angry at me for breaking the peace of the forest. I had called upon her, but perhaps I had displeased her. "I am sorry, so sorry," I silently appealed to the river. I knew it was a grave matter to kill an animal unless in self-defense, but I couldn't be certain as to whether I had been in danger or not. I had disturbed nature and surely I would have to pay a price. The river current had grown so strong that it was not easy to reach the other side. This is the effect of my anger, I thought. I had sent out ill will, and even the waters were now reacting.

When I arrived home, I found my husband looking for the cloth he had made. "I exchanged it for food," I said quietly, pointing to the basket overflowing with plants, not wanting him to know what truly had happened. He looked at me disapprovingly. "We need grains, not only vegetables."

"I have some wild grains. It will suffice for a while."

I couldn't sleep that night as the memory of striking the serpent haunted me. In the early morning I made my way to one of the temples to see if a brahmin priest could conduct a yagna to ease the curse and find out who that naga was.

"Most of the priests have gone to the Sarasvati River for a big yagna," said the young priest who greeted me.

"Isn't there anyone who can perform a yagna for me? I am in great need." My voice was teary.

"If you explain to me the problem, perhaps I can help." I shook my head, thinking that he was too young to be able to conduct the fire ceremony.

At that moment a man, who appeared to be a few years older than I, stepped into the temple courtyard. "I can perform the yagna," he said gently. "I was not able to go to the Sarasvati as my wife has been ill. Come, tell me why you are seeking to have a yagna performed." He led me into a small room and, after introducing myself, with great emotion in my voice, I explained what had happened. He entered meditation for quite some time. Opening his eyes and casting a compassionate look my way, he said, "I see you have a friend among the brahmins. There has been an intervention."

"An intervention? By whom?" My immediate thought was Sachit. Somehow, he must have known what had happened and had done something to negate the curse.

He smiled, "My grandmother."

Confused, I asked, "Does she know me?"

"She must know you, or why would she have come to your aid? Perhaps you will recognize her name. She is known as Sage Gayatri?"

I was confounded. "She is your grandmother?" He nodded. "I spent two years in her hermitage, but she didn't look old enough to have a grandson your age."

He chuckled. "Someday I will tell you her story, but for now you should know that the naga you killed was a very powerful one, who was threatening the family of a woman named Prema. Is she your sister?"

I nodded. "She was taken to the naga world when she was young and is happily married there."

"Somehow, she knew that this naga, who had been out to destroy her family, was also coming after you, and she tried to stop him. That is why you saw her."

"Then she remembered me?" I asked in surprise. "I thought she had forgotten all about our family."

"In the naga world, our world appears very dreamlike, but something must have startled her out of this state. It must have been the danger to you that awakened her memory. Her sorrow was not over the killing of the naga, but over what he did to you. The battle with this naga was between her family and him, and had nothing to do with you, but he sought to hurt her through you. In killing him, you have done her a great service, but in the process both of you have been cursed. The greater part of the curse fell on her, but you will have to bear it as well. A curse cannot be undone, but it can be alleviated. My grandmother has been able to delay the curse so that it will come to fruition at a most auspicious time, well into the future, when it will bring you both great benefit."

"Is there no way to undo the curse?"

He shook his head. "But we will perform a yagna at dawn tomorrow and appease the naga world so that retribution and violence does not ensue from this, so that the naga's family does not pursue revenge. Remember, the outer fire is a symbol of the inner one, the inner sacrifice, and so you must prepare yourself by abstaining from food tonight and in the morning, and by trying to concentrate your will on the inner vow you will make."

As I got up to leave, I realized that I didn't know his name. I felt a special bond with him as he was the grandson of a woman who I so greatly admired. "You haven't told me your name."

"Kapila," he replied. "My mother named me after the great Sage Kapila, the only son of Maharishi Devahuti," he smiled, "but I have had a very hard time living up to that name."

I left the temple unsure of whether the yagna that I had sought would in any way ease my situation, now that I had received an irrevocable curse.

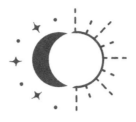

Chapter Seven

THE VOW

Throughout the ceremony, I tried to remember what Sage Gayatri had taught me about the yagna. All I could recall, and as Kapila had reminded me, was that the outer fire was a symbol of some inner fire, but what was that inner fire? What was the meaning of sacrifice? I couldn't remember, and so my mind, instead of being internally focused, was attentive to the outer details of the ceremony—the mantras, the pouring of the ghee, the invocations to Agni Dev. The whole experience was an external one and I knew that I had not fulfilled the greater purpose of the yagna.

When it was over, Sage Kapila, as I called him, said, "The external part is now done, the rest is up to you. Reflect on the deeper meaning of the yagna, and you can always come to ask me any questions, or for my help in any way, but the deeper work must be done by you and you alone. Remember that Agni Dev signifies the higher will, and any sacrifice demands first the invoking of this will, which is strengthened through the process. Nothing can be achieved without a strong will. A curse can also be turned into blessing if the attitude is right because something can be learned from every situation. Remember that, Sundari, with the right attitude a curse can be a cause for growth."

His words did not bring me much comfort. I had hoped the ceremony would be all that was needed because I didn't understand what my part in this process was. I had given up food the night before and the morning of the ceremony. Wasn't that sacrifice enough? If there was something additional for me to do, I didn't know what it might be. I spent days dwelling on the question of what I was called to do, and the thought that Prema might be further threatened by retribution added to my burden. How could I ensure her safety? What could I offer in exchange for her well-being and that of her family? Several times I went down to the Ganga and asked those questions of her, but no answers came. I tried my best to remember all that Sage Gayatri had taught me so many years ago, but my mind was a muddle. The only words that came to me were *will power* and *sacrifice*, and they repeated themselves in my mind over and over again, day and night, but in the process of reflecting on them, my emotions were aroused and I lost the ability to think clearly.

One morning, several weeks after the yagna, I got up early, unable to sleep, and made my way to a deserted spot along the Ganga. Sitting down, I tried to clear my mind of the many emotions fighting their way to the surface. That moment in the forest when I killed the naga had released long pent-up anger—at Sachit and my mother for not defending me and for sending me away, and at the naga for luring my sister into his world. This anger was compounded by my fear that something terrible might happen to Prema and my fear of the curse—all of these feelings were pressing in on me. Then came the conviction that I had to offer up what was most dear to me in order to safeguard Prema and attempt to unravel that which could not be unraveled—the dreaded curse. Sitting there in the darkness behind my closed eyes, the words of Arrav rang in my mind: "It was Sachit who sent you away." Again and again I heard those words. They resounded like thunder and I began to shake.

I remembered the moment by the Sarasvati with Sage Gayatri when my spine tingled with what she called shakti. Calling upon that energy again, I rose in a near-hypnotic state, and tearing the tulsi bead necklace from around my neck, I held it in one hand and with the other took some water from the Ganga and cried into the winds that were sweeping the waves, "With you as my witness, Sacred Ganga, I vow not to meet Sachit again for ten thousand years. Let that be my offering for the safeguarding of my sister. Let that be my offering to appease my anger at him for sending me away." Throwing the water back into the Ganga, I whispered to her in as firm a voice as I could muster, "This is the sankalpa that I make today." Then I hurled the tulsi beads as far as I could into the rushing waters and watched my most precious possession drift away.

There is a sorrow too deep for tears, wells of anguish that rise up, and this was the sorrow that engulfed me as I sank back onto the ground, wondering what on earth I had done. What had moved me to make such a drastic vow that would determine not only my future, but also the future of the one I loved? Was it a moment of anger and fear, or was I moved by some inner need? Whatever the cause, an emptiness sank in that was worse than the pain of separation from Sachit. I sat on the bank of the Ganga in a daze, lifted out of awareness of time and place. Years could have passed, and I wouldn't have noticed. Thoughts of my family, my children at home, were in some distant place, very far from my mind. I don't think I would have come out of that state had she not found me.

I heard a woman call my name. I didn't respond. She called again and this time I slowly turned my head. Sage Gayatri was standing a few feet away, but instead of rising to greet her, I let my head sink onto my folded knees. She came to sit beside me, but neither of us spoke for quite some time. Finally, I lifted my head and looked at her. "Ammaji, what have I done? I have destroyed any chance of happiness for far into the future, into a future I cannot imagine without him."

"No, my dear, that is not what you have done. You have opened the door to a greater happiness. You have taken a vow, a difficult one, and I will help you fulfill it, but I will also submerge the memory of what you have done so you can live with peace in your heart. I sense the quiet workings of Indra Dev here, who is coming to help you awaken."

"Can I withdraw my words, Ammaji?" I asked pleadingly.

She shook her head. "Words do not fade away. They vibrate in the ethers until it is time for them to manifest in the physical world. But surely there was a deeper cause for this vow of yours, one you do not know."

"I am so tired, Ammaji, so tired of struggling against this love I have for him."

"One should not try to suppress love, Sundari, but to expand it. Come, lie down beside me while I chant the sacred hymns." With a pounding heart, I lay down next to her and closed my eyes while she chanted. I don't know for how long she chanted because I fell asleep, and when I awoke, she was still chanting. The sun was near the horizon.

I looked up and saw her. "Ammaji, what are you doing here? How did you get here? I must have fallen asleep by the river . . ." My voice trailed off as I tried to recall what had happened before I had fallen asleep.

"You don't remember?"

I shook my head. Instinctively, as I so often did, I reached to touch my tulsi bead necklace, but it wasn't around my neck as it always was. I started to look around, wondering how it could have fallen from my neck.

"You gave your precious tulsi beads to the River Ganga as an offering," she said very quietly. "You gave what was dearest to your heart. That is your sacrifice, your yagna."

I looked out into the river. "I gave her my tulsi beads . . ." I murmured, confused. "I don't remember." Sage Gayatri nodded. I sighed and said, "I will miss them. They were the only thing I had from Sachit and they helped me feel that he was near."

"You gave them for your sister."

"For Prema?"

She nodded. "Do you remember the yagna Kapila performed?"

"Yes, that was many weeks ago."

"To appease the naga world, you sacrificed your tulsi beads. That showed great strength of will, Sundari."

A slight smile crossed my face. "You taught me that, about the inner sacrifice. Now I don't feel so badly about losing them."

"You haven't lost the beads, Sundari. You gave them for safekeeping to the sacred Ganga. She will keep them for you, as she will hold the love that is in your heart."

I was thoughtful, but her words helped to ease my sense of loss. "It is getting late, Ammaji, and my husband will worry if I don't return home, but I can't bear to leave you, and you haven't told me why you have come. Are you here to visit your grandson?"

"Never mind that. I am here to tell you that I visited your sister."

"You went to the naga world?"

She nodded. "She was distraught after the incident in the forest with the naga. I felt her distress and so I appeared to her one day after Kapila had performed the yagna, and I did a ceremony with her. Your sister is very wise. I didn't need to explain much to her, but I told her what had happened in your life. After some reflection she asked me if I would bring her eldest daughter, who is now sixteen, to live in the human world with her mother, your mother, so that she can one day lead the clan. I have done that. It was her daughter's desire to do so. She is now with your mother and she someday will fulfil your mother's wishes. She is different from you and your sister, not so willful," she said with a wry smile, "and very glad to have met her grandmother and uncles. She will do well with them.

"But," she grew quiet for a moment and then continued in a gentle voice, "Prema's daughter will not be able to return to the naga world, and so her mother will not see her again. That is a sacrifice Prema made, to give her eldest daughter to her mother for the sake of the clan."

"Prema did that? What a sacrifice she has made," I murmured. "I am not surprised. That is how she always has been, thinking of other people. I am sure she has felt guilty all these years for being away from us."

"She didn't remember for a long time. Her family and the life in the forest were like a dream to her, but when the naga threatened you, it jolted her out of her dream state, and she remembered. She tried to appear to you but couldn't. She could have asked me to bring her to her mother or to you, but she didn't. She asked to have her daughter brought. I wanted you to know that your sister is safe. There is no need to worry any more about retribution."

"Did Prema have any message for me?" I asked hopefully.

"She has great love for you and said you should not feel sad over your separation because you and she will surely be together in a future life, and you will be with your loved one in the future as well."

"Yes, I will be with her and with Sachit again. It brings me some comfort to know that."

"The yagna has done its work, as have I. And so, I leave you now. Go home, Sundari, and care for your family."

She began to walk away but I called out to her: "Ammaji." She turned to look at me. I hesitated to ask my question, but I couldn't let her leave without inquiring. Yet I dared not ask.

"What is it, Sundari?"

I had to know the answer. After much hesitation I finally asked in a shaky voice, "Was it really Sachit who sent me away?"

She shook her head. "It was his teacher, my husband, but Sachit was the one who had to give this command to your mother. Your mother did not protest because she has a keen sense of duty and would not disobey the command of an elder, let alone someone as respected as my husband." She was quiet for a few moments and then added, "In fact, Sachit tried to prevent your departure. He offered to go into solitude for many years so you would not have to leave, but my husband would not be swayed from his decision. Sachit became quite sad after that, blaming himself, but time heals all wounds and now he is fine."

"Do you think then . . . do you think Sachit remembers me, ever thinks of me?"

She smiled and replied, "No doubt. You have found a place in all of our hearts." With those words she turned and walked away.

Interlude: The Celestial World

A slight tremor shook my body and jolted me out of my meditation and reminiscence. The memory of the vow I had taken by the river awakened all the emotions that Sundari had experienced. A sob escaped my lips. What had caused me to take such a drastic action? I was still feeling the pain of that moment when I heard my name being called, not the name of Sundari, but of Usha.

Opening my eyes, I realized I was no longer by the river. I was seated in the beautiful celestial forest with Satya in front of me. I was confused. What had I experienced? It was a whole lifetime I had seen, and in many ways, it seemed like a peaceful and harmonious time on earth, without conflict and violence. There had been so much devotion to learning the inspired poetry of the time. Life seemed simpler and more joyful, except for the part about that man who Sundari had vowed not to see again for so long, who had hurt her so deeply. But I didn't see the ending. I didn't know how that life had finished, and I wanted to see it come to completion. I knew there was more, something else of great significance to me. Turning to Satya, I said, "Help me go back, Satya. I want to see the end of that life. There is something else I need to remember." I closed my eyes but couldn't return to that time. No images would emerge. I couldn't get back.

"Usha, now is not the time for you to see that ending."

"Was that really me, Satya?" I asked, still confused as I opened my eyes. He nodded. "I hardly recognize myself in that girl. She was impulsive, the way she threw herself at the feet of that man, with no self-respect, no inhibitions."

"She came from a different world where nothing was hidden. There were no inhibitions, but society was beginning to change."

"She had the rare opportunity to learn from that great woman sage, but she didn't appreciate what was offered. I would not have turned away such a gift."

"That was long ago, Usha. In the intervening time you have had many experiences and learned much. You have grown and have become very different, but there are elements of Sundari still within you," he replied with a slight smile. "When you decreed that you would not meet Sachit for such a long period of time, there was an underlying purpose that you were not conscious of, but your higher self was well aware."

"What do you mean?"

"You wanted to meet him on an equal footing. You had idealized and elevated him in your mind because he had achieved great mental powers. You didn't see his weaknesses, his pride and desire to be recognized, which pursued him in successive incarnations. Through many lifetimes you both have been battered down by life experience but have gained much valuable knowledge. Now you will meet again, only you will not be subjected to your passions. You will be in control."

"Satya, so much time has passed, so much time. How many places I have been, how many bodies I have inhabited . . ." I murmured.

"You have taken many earthly bodies and traveled far," he replied gently. "But what seems like a long period of time is just the flicker of an eye."

"And yet the love has survived? I wonder how this is possible."

"You will meet him again and you will know."

"Satya, I am wary of meeting him. Why unlock feelings that have been put to rest?"

"The feelings have only been subdued, not resolved, not truly put to rest. It is inevitable that they will emerge again, and now is the most auspicious time. In your recent births you have not experienced that type of human love, but you have not overcome the desire for it. The conditions are now ripe for you to experience that love in a very deep way."

Still I hesitated. "Do I have a choice in this matter?"

"There is always a choice."

"Then I don't have to go?"

"You don't have to take this birth. It is only by your design, after all. It was you, yourself, who decreed it. However, the conjunction of forces is right at this time, the stars are aligned to provide the best outcome, to fulfill what has not yet come to fruition. And the choice is made by the higher self, not by the one swayed by fears and self-doubt. Do you not trust yourself?"

"I don't know why this resistance. I suppose I am afraid of being hurt again," I said quietly.

"If there is some weakness that causes you to feel hurt, better to face it."

Slowly I rose and walked along the idling stream that sang a quiet song. Seating myself, I looked at the water. The memory of taking the sankalpa would not go away. I had spoken with such force, in a time when words held great meaning and power, when they could not be revoked. I had hurled into the ethers vibrations that would come back, and now was that moment of return. I had been angry at him, thinking he was responsible for sending me away, but I had been mistaken. I had misjudged him, and I wondered whose love was truly greater, his or mine. He had asked me to wait for him, but I could not. With my limited understanding, a wait of ten or twenty years had seemed like an eternity. And then I had made him wait ten thousand years. How could I face him?

I had been selfish in my thinking, but my spirit had been young and immature, caring only for my own desires. If I were to see him again, and my love were to be renewed, I would not be so self-focused and would put his needs above my own, but suppose he rejected me, no longer felt love for me. How would I cope with that? So much time had passed, so many experiences, would he remember me? Would he still have feelings? Must I undergo more pain on account of that man?

Satya came to sit beside me and said quietly, "You are giving this too much thought, Usha. He will not have any cognizance of your past relationship, but he will be drawn to you because there is an unfinished matter between the two of you. You have the strength to address anything that comes your way, and you will not be overshadowed by him."

"Satya, why have I not remembered that birth until now? Did Sage Gayatri really suppress my memory of the vow I had taken?"

He nodded. "It was not time for you to remember."

"There are other reasons for me to take birth so soon, aren't there, Satya?"

He nodded. "There is a great cultural flourishing. Your creative side will find expression in this life. The Vedas inspired in you a love for poetry, and in your last birth this love was reawakened; now it will find greater fulfillment. It is not only for Sachit that you are taking birth. Your path is separate from his, but there are times of intersection. One has to experience human love, its joys and its limitations, in order to transcend it, to expand that love so it is not limited to only one, to know that love is not an emotion but a state of being."

'To transcend human love," I repeated. "You are right, Satya, I have not experienced human love in a long time, and the yearning is still there."

"He will fulfill it for you."

"Have ten thousand years passed, then?"

"Not quite. The time has been somewhat shortened. Someone has taken those years for you." He looked away so as not to give out any more information.

"Who would do that for me and why?"

"I cannot say more."

I looked out into the distance between the trees, which stood close together but spaced far enough apart that each had its own distinct presence, one not overshadowing another. "That's how I want to be," I whispered, "not overshadowed, not at the mercy of anyone, free and independent." I had not fully forgotten my last birth as Meihua, where I had been denied the outer freedom but gained an inner one, and this I didn't want to lose. "I will meet him in a different way," I whispered again.

I saw the blueprint of the life I was to take. It would again be in China, where I had recently come from. I would pick up where Meihua left off, and I would complete what Sundari had begun. I felt myself being pulled, drawn into a heavier realm, adopting the density of the atomic world. It was a confinement, a process of assuming limitations, narrowing of perception, and losing the vastness of this light-filled world.

I looked at Satya, his smiling eyes so loving and gentle, the one who had become . . . I could not find the words to express who he was to me. The love we shared was truly a transcendent one—if only I wouldn't forget him as I always did when I entered physicality. If only I could remember, then I could endure whatever came my way. His image became fainter and fainter, as did the scene before me, and I felt myself die into the beginnings of another human form.

PART 2: TANG CHINA

8th Century CE

Chapter Eight

MEETING LI BAI

I was born into an aristocratic family, the granddaughter of a prominent government official, a chancellor in the Tang court, but due to misuse of public funds and accusations of bribery, he was executed, and my family fell into ill repute, losing much of its wealth and good name. My father claimed that my grandfather had been falsely accused, the victim of court intrigue and jealousy, but few seemed to believe this defense and we were not very welcome among the elite in our society. Family name meant a lot, and the missteps of one member tarnished the reputation of the entire family. I was not conscious of any of this during the early years of childhood. A detachment from worldly affairs and a love of poetry seemed to have followed me into this life. I had a thirst for knowledge and learning and paid little attention to matters of money or status; in this regard, I was quite different from the rest of my family.

I grew up in the province of Henan, outside a city called Kaifeng, which had been an ancient capital and had many historic sites. It was a lovely city with many markets and parks, taverns and restaurants. Although my family had lost much of its wealth, we had managed to hold on to a few restaurants and wineries and these sustained us. Despite my family's troubles, the reign of Emperor Xuanzong brought stability, peace, and prosperity to our world, ending a time of turbulence. It was an era of cultural achievement, when education and the arts were greatly valued. Many court officials were known for their writing and appreciation of poetry and music. The emperor himself was an accomplished composer. Women held a key place in our society, both in the cultural world and at court, or so it seemed.

Although I was indifferent to the fallen position of my family, my parents were very conscious of our recent history and determined to restore our name and position. My younger sister Zong Yue was ambitious. Intent on our family regaining its status in society, and refusing to abandon our aristocratic heritage, she was drawn to people of high status and to finery of every sort. Her desire for silks and ornaments knew no limit. There could not have been sisters more unlike each other. My younger brother Zong Jing was somewhere in between. He admired great intellectual achievement and desired to restore the family name, but he had a disdain for political affairs and wanted as little to do with government matters as possible.

What distinguished me most from my siblings was my yearning for a life fully devoted to Daoism. During these years of the Tang Empire, Daoism was the prevailing religious philosophy, and even in court life there were many prominent Daoist figures, but for me it was not only a philosophy but also a way of life that infused every aspect of my being. I learned early on that I could not discuss this with any family member as they were all intent on outer gains, not inner ones. In our society many prominent people claimed an affinity with Daoism, yet listening to my parents speak of court affairs, I found such intrigue, hypocrisy, petty jealousy, and quest for power that I wondered how these court officials could claim any knowledge of the Dao.

Keeping my thoughts to myself, I shared little of the poetry I had been writing since an early age, and so I lived a rather enclosed and private life during my childhood, choosing not to engage with the world around me.

A change was forced on me in my later teens when I became of marriageable age. Conversations about me began to circulate through our family. "What aristocratic family would allow their son to marry into a family of our ill repute?" complained my father one day after seeking the counsel of one of his relatives.

"I am not interested in marriage, at least not now," I assured him. Known to have an independent streak, I suspected that my words would not ease his concern, but it was true. I was determined not to marry unless I found a man as committed to Daoism as I was.

"Will you be a courtesan then?" teased my sister. I shot her a disapproving glance.

"You will get married," my father insisted, "but will that man restore our family name and wealth? I worry, Shu, what kind of man you will find who will accept us."

We had been discussing this over tea, and I brusquely rose to leave the room. This discussion was cropping up with greater frequency, in fact, every time our family came together for a meal or for tea. It seemed my parents thought of nothing else. A few days later my father again brought up the subject.

"I am only nineteen. Can you allow me a few more years of a peaceful life before I have to think of this? You know I would never marry a man not of my own choosing."

My father sighed. "I don't expect that many will come around, considering our family situation. You may not have much choice."

"She might have more options if she would dress herself up a bit, and not have such an austere look about her. She is embarrassing all of us," inserted my sister coldly.

"Yue!" my mother replied curtly. "Your sister is a very pretty young woman, no matter how she dresses, even without elaborate clothing."

"Would you all please stop talking about me as if I were . . . as if I were some object!" With those words, I angrily left the room. Shutting myself away, I took out a scroll of Daoist poetry and tried in vain to concentrate, but tears overcame me. Would I truly spend my life alone? My family had not the slightest interest in knowing what was in my heart. I had committed to myself that I wouldn't marry purely for the sake of marriage, not for financial stability or status; I would only marry one who shared my spiritual aspirations. But what if that person did not exist? My family would not look kindly on me entering a Daoist convent, but perhaps I would have no other option. I would much prefer that to marriage with an unsuitable man.

My parents paid no heed to my pleas to end the marriage discussion. At another family meal, my father asked my brother to seek out some of his aristocratic friends. "Speak to them about your sister," he asked. "Tell them how pretty she is."

"You are talking about me this way when I am sitting right here," I protested. "I don't need Jing to help me find a husband."

"Your father is only trying to be helpful, dear," inserted my mother. "Why can't you meet some of his friends?"

"I know his friends, the kind he spends time with. All they do is get drunk and spin tales."

"That's not fair." My brother rushed to defend himself. "My friends are respectable enough." Jing, in fact, was my only ally. He was usually the one who sided with me, but these days he was spending more time out of the house than in, secretly meeting friends who were engaged in bouts of drinking, many of them far older than he.

"I don't mean to insult your friends, Jing. I just wish this conversation would end once and for all. Would it be such a tragedy if I didn't marry?"

"It would be," claimed Yue. "What woman can be happy without a husband? A husband fulfills her needs."

"A number of our royal women have become Daoist nuns, including the emperor's sister, so why can't I?" I curtly replied, getting up to retreat to my room once again.

"Shu, you haven't eaten," called my mother.

"I will fast today," I replied. Fasting was one of the Daoist practices that I tried to engage in at least once a month, having read that it helps with *inner cultivation* (Daoist meditation). After a while Jing came to my room. With pleading eyes, I asked, "Jing, you are the only one who seems to care about what I want. Can you get them to stop talking of marriage for me?"

He nodded. "I will do my best. It seems our parents have expectations that you will find someone to restore our family name and position."

"That will never be me. I can't sacrifice myself to fulfil those expectations. Perhaps Yue will." He laughed. "Jing, sometimes I think I was born into the wrong family."

"Can there be such a mistake?" he asked.

"I suppose not. It's not very Daoist to think that way. Everything has a purpose, even though we may not understand the purpose."

The years passed and conversations about finding a suitable husband for me did not stop. My father continued to enquire among his large group of acquaintances and the search for a husband with an official position began. After meeting several completely unsuitable prospects, I began to think marriage was not an option for me. Then one day my father brought home the son of an acquaintance, a young man who had just received a minor government appointment. Seeing the expectation on my father's face, I could not help but give this young man a chance, and so I allowed some form of courtship to proceed. He had an interest in poetry and this was a definite point in his favor. We admired some of the same poets and this was something we could speak about.

I was beginning to think that this was the best I could do, to find a man who shared some of my creative aspirations, and I was at the point of acquiescing when I had a frightening dream, a nightmare that caused me to awaken in a fearful sweat. Although I didn't remember the details of the dream, it seemed to convey a message, a clear warning about the marriage. I lay awake for the rest of the night, knowing that come morning I would have to end the courtship, no matter the consequences.

The conversation the next morning turned to me, and my mother asked how the courtship was progressing. I sighed before answering and then said solemnly, "I am afraid I have to break it off today." My parents shot each other an anxious glance and then my mother asked the reason. I couldn't give one but as I tried to think of an excuse, I burst into tears and ran to my room. I heard my mother ask my brother to follow and find the reason. When Jing entered my room, I couldn't look at him. How could I explain that my feelings were due to a dream, which I couldn't quite remember, but which clearly conveyed a warning.

"Has something happened between the two of you?" asked my brother. "You seemed to be getting along."

"Jing, should I settle for a man I don't love? Is that what I am required to do?" I replied between tears. "There is nothing wrong with him, it is just that he is not for me. I don't know if I will ever find the one who is for me, but I am willing to be alone if he does not appear. I will end the affair when he comes today."

"What will you tell him?"

"That I am not ready for marriage? No, I can't say that, I am no longer so young and if I am not ready now, when will I ever be?"

"I will handle our parents. Don't worry about them, but you must think about how to end the courtship without hurting the reputation of the family. That will mean a lot to our parents."

Later that day when the young man showed up, I politely told him that although I valued our friendship, I did not feel we were fated for marriage. He accepted this. That evening when the family gathered for the meal, I stood up and with a firmness and conviction I did not know I had, said, "If marriage or the search for a husband is brought up one more time, I will leave this house and enter a Daoist nunnery." A stunned silence filled the air. My family members looked at one another in shock and I withdrew to my room. As I lay in bed that night, I realized that if not for that frightening dream, I would have entered a marriage that would have left me lonelier than I now was. How grateful I was for that intervention, but from whom and why had it come?

That ended the conversation about marriage, at least in my presence, and I was no longer the subject of the evening talk. Rather, my parents now turned on my brother: how to get him to pass the exams and be granted an official position in the government. Knowing my family history, I thought there was a slim chance that this would happen, and it was also out of character for my brother, who was more drawn to the poets, painters, and intellectuals of our town than the government officials. After spending evenings with them, he would often return home late at night more than a little tipsy. When I scolded him about this, he would reply that wine was the drink of immortality. My parents frowned on his behavior, but actually I understood him and sympathized. How else was he to escape their expectations?

One day Yue came to me in a sour mood. "You are the most selfish sister!" she exclaimed.

I looked at her baffled. We didn't have a close relationship, but there was cordial sisterly feeling between us. "What have I done or not done now?" I asked.

"By refusing to marry, you are robbing our family and me of the chance to restore our status," she pouted.

"What makes you think any aristocrat will marry either one of us, with a disgraced grandfather who was executed?"

"You are accomplished, educated, a poet. How many such women are there? And . . . and quite pretty." Her voice quieted as she spoke those last words, as if they were difficult to utter.

"Oh, so now I am pretty, without all the frills, without a painted face and decorations for my hair. I take that as a great compliment, Yue." I smiled. Putting my arm around her, I added, "Yue, marriage is a serious matter. Think about it, spending every day with another person, planning one's life, sharing intimate feelings. Its purpose is not to advance one's status or wealth but to find someone who can complement you. I would be happy to marry if I found such a man, but I don't expect that it will be possible. But if status is so important to you, I will do everything I can to help our father find such a man for you."

She sighed. "I see the life that our acquaintances have, and I want the same. I want fine clothing and jewels for my hair. I want a husband who can give me that. Is that so wrong?"

I shook my head. "It is not wrong, Yue. It's that I don't believe those things bring happiness. Wait a few years and see if the aristocratic life still calls to you."

The years passed and nothing much changed in our household. As I was now in my mid-twenties, I assumed my parents had given up on the idea of a marriage for me, although every now and then my father would bring home a man in the hope that I might show interest, but I sadly disappointed him again and again.

Jing was staying out later and later, often until dawn. I arose early, at the first crack of sunlight, since the house was quiet then; it was the best time to engage in Daoist cultivation practices and to attempt to write poetry, although I didn't consider myself successful in either field. I had nobody to teach me how to practice cultivation, so I mostly sat there in the dark, struggling with my thoughts. I had little life experience to inform my poetry, which I regarded as childish verse. I would stare at the blank paper, struggle to find some words, and when nothing came, I would pick up the poems of the poets I admired most and hope they would inspire me.

Jing and I were like two ships passing in the night, he retiring while I was awakening, and I was often the one to greet him when he arrived home inebriated. I would make him a hot drink and see his wobbly figure off to bed. He would sleep most of the morning and rise around noon. On occasion he would bring home a friend who was too intoxicated to make it back to his own house. I would arrange the guest room and try my best to keep their condition, and the late hour of Jing's arrival, from my parents.

One day I said to him, "Jing, I can get away with defying our parent's expectations, but how will you manage? I can live here the rest of my life, but you are a man and that will not be acceptable. You will have to find some occupation, especially if you are to marry."

"Are you now starting in with me?" he asked painfully.

"I'm sorry, but I am concerned about you. The expectations for you are even greater than for me."

"I'm still young. I know the time will come when I will have to think more seriously about my life, but right now I am enjoying the company of the artists and scholars I meet. They are far more interesting than government officials!"

I laughed. "You and I belong in that creative world. I seem to have escaped our parents' concern for the moment, but I don't expect that will last long. I may be destined for the nunnery, and I would not mind that at all. At least I will learn some Daoist practices."

"I don't think that is your future," he replied with a smile. "Somehow I feel another fate lies in store for you, my dear sister." Jing did not understand my interest in Daoism, but he cared deeply for me and that was enough. We didn't judge each other. I didn't judge his love for drink, and he didn't judge my preoccupations.

About a year later, Jing arrived home one morning before dawn with a friend who was as intoxicated as he was. When I saw the two of them struggling through the doorway, laughing and swaying, I smiled. Then holding my finger to my lips, I reminded Jing that he must be quiet, or he would awaken the whole household.

"I have a warm drink ready for you and your friend, and I will quickly go prepare the guest room." I helped the two of them to the seating area and brought them the drinks, which would help sober them up. Then I guided his friend to the guest room. It was well after noon before the two of them reappeared. I had put aside some food from the noon meal. The household was busy, my parents were out doing errands, with only my sister around. When she saw the two of them, she cast a look of disdain at Jing and began to chastise him.

"Hush, don't you see we have a guest," I whispered to her, embarrassed by her harshness. In a huff she left the room. She had no patience for Jing's drinking and found him to be as useless as I was in terms of helping our family advance.

As I began to serve the food, I felt Jing's friend gazing at me strangely, but I kept my face turned away so as not to catch his eye. Something about his presence intimidated me and I dared not look at him, so I did not take note of his appearance. He spoke little, and after the meal he got up to leave, thanking Jing for his hospitality. Then he turned to me and I couldn't resist lifting my gaze to him. It was only then that I noticed his tall frame and piercing eyes, which shone like pointed lights. I had never seen such eyes. His strong facial features bore the hint of some central Asian ancestry. I couldn't tell his age, but streaks of grey in his hair revealed that he had acquired the knowledge of years. He was an attractive and imposing figure with a dynamic presence. Embarrassed, I cast my eyes down. Neither of us said a word and with a deep bow he took his leave.

Once he was gone, I asked Jing who his friend was. "I have never seen such a man before. You have never brought him here." I was familiar with many of Jing's friends, but this man was a new face, and quite a bit older than Jing and the others I had met.

"That man, he is the poet Li Bai," he replied simply.

"Jing, stop teasing me. Do you take me to be so naïve that I would believe that?" I admired many contemporary poets, but Li Bai was among my favorites. I loved his irreverent and rebellious tone, which often subtly revealed the iniquities of the ruling class and the suffering of the common people, but his poems were also always laced with mystical images and the combination deeply inspired me.

"It's true."

"Jing! Stop teasing me."

"Shu, why don't you believe me? I met him a few years ago while in Luoyang and invited him then to visit me. When I heard he was here, I met him for a drink. After we had many, many jugs of wine, I found out that the rooms at the nearby inns were all taken, so I brought him here for the night." I still looked at him in disbelief. "Don't believe me if you don't want to, but he is the poet."

My eyes shot wide open and for a moment I couldn't speak. Slowly it sunk in that Jing was telling the truth. I had such admiration for Li Bai's poetry that I read everything I could find by him. "Why didn't you introduce him properly? I would have given him a more respectful greeting," I replied regretfully.

"What would you have done differently, Shu? Li Bai is a modest and humble man. He has been through a lot in his life."

"I fear I made a fool of myself," I mumbled.

"Don't worry. I will invite him back."

"No, don't. Yes, do. I don't know . . ."

Jing laughed. "I have never seen you so perturbed by a man." Hitting him on his arm, I withdrew to my room to quiet my emotions. If Jing did invite him back, how would I behave? What would I say to him?

Three days later Jing brought Li Bai home again, but this time it was not in the early dawn and they were not inebriated. They showed up as we were about to take our evening meal and Jing invited him to stay. I was so nervous that I could hardly look at him or speak and so sat there quietly listening to their conversation. I found Li Bai to be a man of great wit, sharp intelligence, and a quick tongue. The banter between him and my brother was both intriguing and amusing.

Having enjoyed quite a bit of wine, my brother was in a jovial mood and at such times he never refrained from teasing me. "My sister Shu is not usually so shy," he explained with a smile. "She is very good with words. I think I may have told you that she is a poet."

"Jing," I exclaimed, casting him a look of displeasure, but that did not stop him.

"And a devoted Daoist." I was horrified that he would speak thus of me while I was sitting right there.

"Oh," commented Li Bai, turning to look at me.

I looked at Jing firmly and replied, "Writing poetry does not make one a poet, and reading books on Daoism does not make one a true Daoist."

"Lady Zong, you are so right," Bai replied thoughtfully. "Many people write poetry but don't have the sensibility of a poet, and there are those who don't write but whose very life is poetry itself. And then on occasion there is one with both the skills and the sensibility, and they are often much misunderstood. I imagine it is the same with Daoism, for Daoism is a way of life more than a philosophy, do you agree?"

I nodded and turned to him. "One may know the principles of Daoism, but truly living the Dao is another matter. I think it is very rare to find such a person."

"This conversation is not for me," interrupted my brother. "Why don't the two of you go off and discuss the Dao."

Li Bai laughed and then said, "I would like that very much, Lady Zong." My parents entered soon after and that ended the conversation.

After he left, I turned to Jing and said, "How I envy that you can be friends with such a man, that you can have the pleasure of his company." There was nobody with whom I could discuss my religious interests, and for many years now this had left me feeling quite alone and isolated. Books were my only companions, and I yearned for a friend who shared my spiritual interests.

Jing laughed. "You are making him into more than he is. Li Bai is the most accessible of friends, and he mingles with all sorts, the highs and lows of society. He doesn't distinguish. What I enjoy about him is his knowledge. He seems to know a great deal about everything. I have yet to find a topic about which he can't give lengthy discourses."

A few days later Li Bai came to our home mid-afternoon. Jing had gone out and as soon as Li Bai arrived, I informed him that Jing was not expected home for a few hours.

"I didn't come to see Jing today," he said. "I came to ask if you would join me for a walk in the forest. I have arranged for a carriage to take us out of the town, if you agree." It was an offer I couldn't refuse. The forest was one of my favorite places, one of the only places that I felt truly free, and yet rarely did I find anyone to accompany me. I quickly prepared.

We rode to the forest mostly in silence, not an awkward one but a comfortable quietude. I didn't feel the need to speak and neither did he. As we began to walk through the many families of trees, I breathed out in relief. I had always felt more at home among trees than among people. Li Bai found a soft spot of moss where we could sit. I lay back against a tree trunk and looked up at the leafy canopy. "I think I once lived in a forest; not one like this, but a wild jungle, bustling with life. I am sure I did, and that is why the forest always calls to me," I murmured. "I feel I once understood the language of the trees, heard the unsung songs that reach the heart but not the ears. Vaguely do I remember such a life, before the concept of self-importance, of superiority, invaded the human mind. There was beauty in that simplicity, but I suppose it was for a purpose that we had to leave the forest behind."

I looked over and saw him feeding bits of grass to a few birds that had gathered around him. "Those birds are not afraid of you. They have come to you freely," I noted in surprise. He nodded. "How do you manage that?" As I spoke, a few more birds came to his hand to nibble small bits of various items he had picked up from the ground. I had risen from my leaning position and bent over to touch one of the birds, but it shyly withdrew. "Why are they afraid of me, but not of you?"

He smiled. "When I was young, a few years younger than you . . ." He looked at me with his piercing eyes and I cast my face down. His mention of my youth embarrassed me, but he appeared not to notice and continued, ". . . I went to Changping Mountain, where I met a hermit named Zhao Rui. He lived in a cave with his family and was an accomplished Daoist. He taught me some basic alchemy and how to commune with animals, particularly the birds. They would flock to him. He lived among the animal and plant life as one of them. He is the only man I have known who truly lived the Daoist principle of harmony with the natural world. Although he lived away from society, I learned from him that even in our divisive and complex world, we can lead simple lives. Isn't that what Daoism teaches?"

I nodded. "But it was easier to live in the Dao before the thinking rational mind took control."

"The thinking mind has its role," smiled Li Bai. "It would be impossible to maneuver through the world today without it."

"I am not adept at maneuvering through this world. I would rather withdraw from it, like your friend Zhao Rui," I replied quietly.

"Although Zhao Rui was a hermit, living in a cave, he closely followed political matters and had strong opinions about governance. He encouraged me to seek an official position."

"Why would he do that if he himself chose the life of a hermit?"

"Why not? Daoist principles should be applied to government as well as to all other aspects of life. Isn't our task to learn to be in the world but not attached to it?"

"I think that is very hard to do."

"For many years an official position eluded my grasp. Finally, I gained a position at court, but found it so full of intrigue and corruption that I resigned after two years. What I have not given up is my desire to influence the direction of our country."

"You have great influence through your poetry."

"I don't know if that is enough. Lady Zong . . ."

"Please call me Shu."

"I have something to ask you."

"Please ask."

"A few years ago, while drinking, I was inspired to write a poem on the wall of a tavern not far from here." He looked at me with a twinkle in his eye. "There is a rumor that some aristocratic lady bought that wall to preserve the poem. Was that lady you?"

I smiled, embarrassed. "Jing told you? That is not exactly the story. He had taken me to the tavern to show me the poem because he knows how much I admire your poetry. There were some wild youth there, quite inebriated, and one of them wanted to paint a landscape over your poem. I was horrified and so went to the tavern owner and said I would pay him to leave your poem on the wall. I begged him not to let anyone deface it."

"I've been looking for that lady to find out what moved her to take such an action."

"The poem was beautiful, and it should have been preserved, but that was not the reason," I replied modestly. "It wasn't the words alone. To me, poetry is never only about the words, but also about the inspiration behind the words."

"Your brother has told me about your love for poetry, but I suspect there is much about you that he doesn't know or hasn't told me."

"Perhaps he has told you the quality in me that my family decries the most?" He shook his head and I let out a small laugh. "I have always had an independent spirit and I know that has been difficult for them. For so many years now, they have talked of nothing but finding a suitable man for me to marry. Finally, I told them that if they mentioned marriage to me again, I would straightaway become a Daoist nun. It must be difficult to have such a daughter. I sympathize with them." As soon as the words were out of my mouth, I wanted to retract them. Why had I raised the issue of marriage, I wondered, blushing from embarrassment.

"Then you have decided not to marry?" he asked.

"I have not decided that, but I have determined that I will not marry anyone who does not share my aspirations. We must complement each other fully, and I know how rare that is to find."

"What are your aspirations?"

I was quiet for a few minutes, as no one had ever asked me this question before. Finally, I replied, "I love reading and writing poetry, but that is not my deepest desire. I don't even have the words to describe what it is, but what I aspire to.... what my aspiration is...... is to live in perfect harmony with the Dao." My voice had grown quiet and thoughtful as I spoke those words, as if I was speaking as much to myself as to him. Then I added, "but for that I will need a master to teach me, and I have no idea how to find such a master."

He was silent for a moment, then responded, "Not long ago I was inducted into a Daoist society. The training was very difficult, many days of kneeling in the sun without food. Most of the other aspirants gave up, but

I managed to stay until the end, and so I am now officially a Daoist. Is that also what you seek?"

I shook my head. "I have no interest in such societies, but if you successfully completed that training, you must have a very strong will," I replied in admiration. "I have heard it is very difficult." I was quiet and looked off into the distance before continuing. "What I am seeking, I suppose, is a teacher who truly lives in the Dao, like your friend Zhao Rui, although I want no part in political life." I had heard my parents speak about some of the Daoist societies. By joining one, you gained many social benefits: you were exempt from paying taxes and could avoid being attacked by government officials. This was not the Daoism I was seeking.

Neither of us spoke for a while, and then he mused, "My life is like a river, endlessly flowing, stopping at no particular place, and yet passing through all places, touching life, but remaining aloof from it. Poetry is the force that drives me forward, that enables me to connect with the life of the people. I see and I observe, yet in some way I take no part in what I witness." I looked at him curiously as he described the Li Bai I had heard about, the creative genius who wandered from place to place without stopping for long.

"Don't you ever want to stand still?"

"It is not a matter of what I want; it is simply the way my life is. I don't know you well at all, but I pride myself on being able to read character, and I can tell that you are like a mountain, firm in your own being, with no need to travel the outer world because all your wandering takes place internally. Even though we have only recently met, I understand that about you."

I looked at him in amazement. This was our first real conversation, yet he seemed to know much about me. "My brother must have told you, but my brother doesn't know . . ."

"Your brother has told me very little, but I feel that I know you. I feel that I have been searching for you for a long time, a very long time."

His last words made me feel uncomfortable, so I stood up and said that we must be headed back. Once alone in the room, I wondered why I had acted so abruptly. I enjoyed his company, being in his presence, so why had I cut short our outing?

Li Bai called on me frequently. We went for long walks, often to the forest, as he now knew of my love for forest life. My family soon began to notice that his visits were to me, not Jing. My brother was under much pressure: he'd been forced to give up his night outings and take a more serious approach to his future. One night as we finished the evening meal, my mother commented on Li Bai's visits. "He knows you are busy, Jing, why does he keep coming here?"

Jing smiled. "I think my friend is falling in love with my sister and she with him."

"Jing!" I exclaimed, not pleased that he would speak so freely about my feelings in front of the family.

My mother laughed. "You can't be serious."

"Why not?" asked Jing.

"He is at least twenty years older than Shu, with children and no money to speak of and no position. How would he expect that we would permit . . . besides, I hear that he has a love for the aristocracy. Is he only interested in our status?"

"What status?" asked Jing wryly.

I stood up. "Enough. You speak about me as if my feelings don't matter at all." Turning to my mother, I calmly but firmly said, "I won't have you say a word against Li Bai. He is the most talented, admired, and respected poet in all of the Tang Empire."

"To respect him as a poet is one thing," replied my mother just as firmly. "To consider him as a suitor is quite another."

I retreated to the sanctuary of my room, but as I was leaving, I heard my brother say, "He has no money to speak of because he is a most generous man. How many times he has bailed out friends in need, including me."

"That is not generosity, it is foolishness," declared my mother.

Jing's words made me step back into the doorway of my room. "Is that true, Jing?" He nodded. "I didn't know that, but I am not surprised."

Jing followed me into the room. "I know how much you admire him, but you should also recognize that while he is the best of friends, he may not be the best choice for a husband."

"What do you mean?"

"He was married to a woman who died after the birth of his second child, a son, but he had hardly spent time with her, being mostly on the road. I heard she was of an aristocratic background, a literary family, and very fond of poetry. That is all I know about her, but it must have been lonely to spend most of your married life apart from your husband. After she died, he found a woman to care for his two young children. He had a child with her, but they never married. She took their son and left him because she saw no future with him. Now there is another woman caring for his two children by his first wife, but he hardly goes there. It seems the women in his life have been there . . . well, just in a way of support, to care for his children. You have such an independent spirit, Shu, and I don't think you would be satisfied with that. Li Bai is a solitary man, living the life of a traveling poet. You should know these things about him, and he . . . well, you know how much he loves his wine. He can outdrink all of his companions."

Although Jing's words disturbed me, they did not stop me from meeting Li Bai, but instead of him coming to the house, I would often meet him outside. We went for long walks through a nearby park, to the river, or through the town, so engrossed in our conversation that we would lose all sense of time. Often, I wouldn't return home until sunset, only to meet the disapproving eyes of my parents.

One day we had gone to the forest, and as I leaned back on the ground to gaze up at the sky, I said, "Bai, recite to me some of your poetry. I love to hear the way you almost sing the verses."

"Which poems do you want to hear?"

"Any. I love them all."

He was quiet for a few minutes. Then he began with a poem I loved.

Drinking in Moonlight

I sit with my wine jar
among flowers
blossoming trees

no one to drink with

well, there's the moon

I raise my cup
and ask him to join me
bringing my shadow
making us three

but the moon doesn't seem to be drinking
and my shadow just creeps around behind me

still, we're companions tonight
me, the moon, and the shadow
we're observing
the rites of spring

I sing
and the moon rocks back and forth

I dance
and my shadow
weaves and tumbles with me

we celebrate for a while
then go our own ways, drunk

may we meet again someday
in the white river of stars
overhead!

"You recite so beautifully. Keep going," I whispered with closed eyes when he had finished. He started another poem.

Conversation Among Mountains
You ask why I live
in these green mountains

I smile
can't answer

I am completely at peace

a peach blossom
sails past
on the current

there are worlds
beyond this one

Waking Up Drunk on a Spring day
Life is a huge dream
why work so hard?

all day long I drink
lying outside the front door

awakening
looking up through the trees
in the garden

and one bird singing in the flowers

bird, what season is this?
"Spring! I'm a mango bird
and the spring wind makes me sing"

now I grow sad
very sad

so I have some more wine
and I sing
out loud
until the bright moon
rises

what was I upset about?
I can't remember

The last words I heard were "until the bright moon rises," and then I must have drifted off to sleep. In my dream I saw Bai standing with me by a river, a great body of water, and his voice was drifting over the sound of gentle waves, filling me with such a sense of well-being. Suddenly I awoke and as my eyes opened, I found myself lying on Bai's lap, my head resting there. I looked up at him and he leaned over as if to kiss me, but I was startled and jolted forward into a seated position. Embarrassed, Bai drew himself up. Then I rose and brushed myself off, also embarrassed by this first intimate moment between us. He looked at me for a few minutes as if unsure of what to say, but then I began to speak to break the awkwardness.

"I had such a strange dream, Bai, in those few minutes that I fell asleep . . ."

He interrupted me, "Come, Shu, sit down again." He took my hand and seated me next to him. "I know your hesitation about marriage, but surely you must know my sentiments. I want to marry you."

This was not what I expected to hear, and I was unprepared. I was quiet as a mix of emotions rose within me. He must had sensed my inner turmoil. At last, I replied, "It is a great honor that you think of me this way, but I fear it is an honor I don't deserve."

Over the few weeks that I had come to know him, Bai had recounted to me many stories of his travels, meetings with eminent personalities, and his time at the court. His stories intimidated me. I listened admiringly to his loquacious speeches, impressed by his knowledge and wit, but where did I fit in among all of that? I didn't want a husband who I thought was so superior to myself. I didn't want to be his shadow, like the other women in his life who were there simply to care for his children. Yet I knew I was much attracted to this man, who had such a dynamic personality and striking appearance. The attraction was such that sometimes I had to move myself away physically so as not to touch him or fulfil the urge to embrace and wrap myself around him. I was well aware of those feelings, which I had never before experienced, and for some reason they frightened me.

"Why do you say that?"

I fumbled for words. "You are a man of great literary accomplishment, with extensive knowledge of the world. You have recited your poetry before the emperor, mesmerized the court with your talent, are considered a creative genius by so many. What educated person in the Tang Empire doesn't know the name Li Bai? When I first met you, I was overwhelmed at the thought of being in your presence. Now that I have come to know you, I see you as Li Bai the man, not the poet. There is nobody on this earth I can speak with as freely as I can speak with you. You seem to know my mind, my innermost feelings. But in my understanding of the union between a man and woman, there should be balance and equality, each one contributing as much as the other to who they are as a couple. What can I contribute to this union? Tell me, Bai? I have no knowledge of the world, no experience. I am not a creative genius like you, and yet, as much as I care for you, I am unwilling to be nothing more than a support, as the other women in your life have been. That is not the purpose of my life. I cannot live in your shadow, Bai." I hoped that my eyes would express what my lips did not—my extreme affection for him.

"You undercstimate yourself, Shu." He spoke quietly. "Outer circumstances mean nothing to either one of us. You have wisdom well beyond your years, and what draws me to you is your inner knowing of the Dao, a knowing that years of study cannot grant. One has to be born with it or gain it through much cultivation. You are right, I have seen the world. And what I have learned is that the accolades, the position one gains, how the world regards one are not what matter; rather, it is this inner knowing. It has taken me many years and many missteps to learn this. That is what you can contribute to this union, and this is more precious than anything I can give. I know that I am asking a lot. I have no possessions, no home to offer. I live the life of a wandering intoxicated poet, at the mercy of the gods who inspire me. But sometimes, Shu, the river that wanders aimlessly needs the mountain to keep it flowing."

"Bai, let me reflect on this. It is a big decision." He nodded and we rode back to my home in silence. The next day Bai was gone, leaving no note or explanation. I feared he had taken my reply as a rejection and I berated myself for not having explained my feelings better. In the short time that I had gotten to know Bai, I had come to care deeply about him. My brother saw my depressed state but expressed no sympathy.

"You have turned away a creative genius, the very kind of man you are seeking?" he said in disbelief when I told him what had happened.

"I didn't turn him away. I told him I needed to reflect."

"Shu, what is truly the problem? Is it what I told you about his life?" I shook my head and replied quietly. "It's not that. It is just, honestly Jing, who am I to marry such a man? I am a nobody. There are many well-known women writers who would jump at the opportunity to marry him. How am I fit to be the wife of such a man? I can't help but wonder why he wants to marry me." Sadness nearly swallowed my voice as it trailed off and I fought to hold back the tears.

"Stop right there!" he interjected. "Could it be because he loves you? I have met many prominent women, Shu, and I can't think of anyone more worthy to be his wife. Although it will be a difficult life for you, I know Bai well and he is a good and generous man, with the creative spirit that you so love. Although I cautioned you at first, I have come to believe that you two are made for each other."

"Really, Jing?" He nodded. "Then can you try to find where he has gone?"

"I will try to find him, but I know him well enough to understand that he wants to have something to offer you, so he has probably gone to find employment. But why didn't you tell him your feelings, how much you care for him?"

"I was so startled!"

"You have kept yourself locked up for so long that you don't know how to open your heart. I know you well. You are so used to keeping everything inside. This will never work with a man like Li Bai, who is so expressive of his feelings."

Later that evening, when I sat to reflect, I realized that there was some inner resistance in me that I couldn't understand. Did I truly feel unworthy, or was there something else that I couldn't discern? I didn't mind at all his age or financial situation, or even his family matters. His reputation was definitely that of a man who defied all convention, but this appealed to me. Yet while I was incredibly attracted to him—physically, emotionally and spiritually—I also was aware of an inner resistance. Perhaps I needed a sign, one that only I would recognize, to know that this marriage would bring me closer to the Dao and not further away.

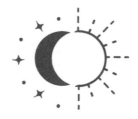

Chapter Nine

FINDING THE MASTER

J ing was not able to uncover the whereabouts of Bai as he was once again on the road, and the months passed without his return. I had begun to think that Bai had forgotten me, and with each passing day my longing for his presence increased. I felt lonely and abject without him, but still I couldn't bring myself to try to contact him, and I didn't even know how to find him. My parents did everything they could to make me forget Bai, but it was no use. I was very much in love and my feelings were impossible to hide.

Finally, one day, without any advance notice, Bai showed up and asked me to walk with him in the park. I had imagined so many times the moment when I would see him again, thinking I would rush into his arms and tell him how much I wanted to marry him, but that was not the way it turned out. A serious reserve inserted itself between us when he appeared unexpectedly at my home, and we hardly spoke a word on the walk to the park. *What is the matter with me?* I berated myself internally as we strode in silence. *Why can't I share with him what is in my heart?*

Once we sat down, he placed his hand under my chin and, lifting my face to his, looked deeply into my eyes. As was the case with his previous visits, I was again struck by his steady, penetrating gaze, the likes of which I had never seen in another person. After a few minutes, he quietly spoke. "I had a vision of you and that is why I returned."

"A vision?" I asked quietly.

"Hmm." He nodded ever so slightly. "Shall I share it with you?" I nodded. "I was seated on a mountain top, on a cliff overlooking a wide expanse, engaged in cultivation, when something caused me to open my eyes. As I gazed at the valley below, out of nowhere a beautiful bird emerged, a blueish phoenix, and it was flying directly toward me. I watched in amazement as it drew closer, and then I saw a woman seated on that phoenix. The phoenix came up close to the edge of the mountain, and I could see clearly who the woman was. She smiled as the phoenix hovered in mid-air for a few minutes, and then it turned around and began to fly away, but as it did, a thread of light emerged from my center and attached itself to the woman, as if my qi (life force) was joining hers. Soon she and the phoenix were out of sight, but that thread of light still extended from my center, linking us together."

As he spoke, he continued to look deeply into my eyes, and I stared back at him. "Do you know who that woman was?" I shook my head slightly. "It was you, Little Phoenix."

For a moment I wavered. Was he being serious? "Are you being poetic, Bai?" I asked, continuing to look directly at him.

He smiled. "Of course I am being poetic, but that is exactly what I saw." He was quiet for a few moments and then said, "But I don't know what is in your heart."

I lowered my head as he released his hand from my chin. I turned away and was silent. Clearly, his dream was the sign I had been waiting for. Then facing him, I replied, "I have missed you a great deal, and I have been trying to understand my feelings. Why this resistance? Am I afraid of losing what I have worked so hard to gain—my independence? You are the only man I would ever marry, but . . ." I smiled. "Bai, how did you know about the phoenix?"

"Know what?"

"Throughout my growing up years I used to dream of flying on a phoenix, seated as you describe. Nobody knows that, not even Jing, for I have never spoken of it. The phoenix would take me high into the sky on an exhilarating ride, and I would always awake from such dreams feeling as if I had visited the celestial worlds and the phoenix had been my spiritual guide, my vehicle to those worlds."

He bent over and gently pressed his lips against mine, resting them there for several seconds. It was the first time I had ever experienced such an intimate moment, and it felt so right, so natural with him. When he had withdrawn his lips he said, "I think my heart can read yours, can know your experiences without you needing to speak them."

"I suppose we should marry now," I replied quietly.

He laughed. "I have finally found a woman who is as much of a wanderer as I am, only you travel the inner worlds as I wander the outer one. We are a good match, Little Phoenix, a very good match. The only problem is, I don't know where we will live. I was not able to find employment."

"I would rather live here under this tree with you than in a grand house with any other man. We can live with my family until we are able to afford a place of our own."

"Oh, I nearly forgot. I have brought you a present." From the bag he had been carrying, he lifted out a silk pouch and handed it to me.

"What is it, Bai?" I asked in surprise. In the past he had brought me gifts of small items, flowers or sweets, nothing of great value.

"Open it," he replied.

Undoing the pouch, I lifted out a beautifully carved jade phoenix. After running my hands over the smooth stone, I looked at him. My face must have shown my amazement because a broad smile shone across his face.

"You like it?"

"Like it, Bai?" I said pressing it to my chest. "I can think of no greater gift. I can hardly believe you bought this. It must have been expensive."

"It is antique. I happened to see it after I saw you flying on the phoenix in my vision and couldn't resist buying it."

Still holding it close to my chest I said, "Bai, this is the most precious thing you could have gotten me. Now I will have my phoenix with me always."

Bai and I got married and he moved into my family home. Those were difficult months for him, and for me as well. We tried our best to avoid time with the family, to escape Yue's snide remarks and the disapproving looks of my parents, but we were not immune. We sought the refuge of our private room as much as we could, but there was a limit to how much we could stay apart from the others. I could see the situation was making Bai restless. After a few months, Bai decided to go to Nanjing where he hoped to get some commissions. I was reluctant to let him leave, but I knew that he was languishing at home. "How long will you be gone?" I asked, clinging to him.

"Not long, Little Phoenix, only a few weeks."

Those few weeks stretched out to months; it was to be the first of many such partings. After being home a little while, Bai would become restless and seek to get on the road again, claiming that it was the only way for him to earn money, which was true. He would always return with money from a benefactor or commissioned essays and poems, and so it was hard for me to object, but this didn't make our separations any easier.

Soon we had our own cottage, and our times together were loving and served to deepen our relationship. When Bai was absent, I sought to engage in Daoist inner cultivation, but I was not successful. I couldn't tame my wandering mind. I tried to write poetry, but the verse that I wrote showed the dearth of my life experience. I had little to write about and my frustration grew. I saw that increasingly I was leaning on Bai emotionally and I was not happy with myself. He was flourishing while I was withering. Each time he prepared to leave, he sensed my dissatisfaction, but when he inquired, I closed up, not wanting him to stay home out of guilt.

As I struggled with Bai's comings and goings, the condition of the country was deteriorating. While earlier in his life, Emperor Xuanzong had led many reforms and overseen a stable and prosperous empire, the present situation had become more uncertain. A number of years earlier, our emperor had become infatuated with a concubine of one of his sons. He convinced this son to give her up and took her as his own consort. Much, much younger than the emperor and a famed beauty, she soon came to control him. Consort Yang Guifei brought her relatives into powerful positions and became known for leading a lavish and frivolous lifestyle, organizing parties and plays and outings to the mountains while the country began to fester. Government affairs were neglected, poverty increased, and corruption was endemic, as many officials now sought to curry favor at court. I had heard much about this, as had Bai, but neither of us believed the country was in any serious danger.

On one of his excursions, Bai went to visit an old friend; upon his return I saw how worried he was for the fate of the country. The situation had taken a more dangerous turn when Consort Yang convinced the emperor to empower a man who claimed to be a relative of hers. He was a foreigner who had been adopted and consequently many questioned this claim, but Consort Yang went along with it and brought him into the central power structure of the court. Over time, General An Lushan came to be close to the emperor and favored by his consort. Eventually, he was given command over much of the Tang army, notably the regiments in the northeast.

When I married Bai, I didn't know of his skill in swordsmanship, although this realization did not surprise me as he excelled in so many areas, and I also didn't know about his inclination toward military matters. When he returned from visiting his friend, he told me that this man had received a letter from a mutual friend of theirs encouraging him to join the army in the northeast to fight tribal groups at the border. Bai then told me of his inclination to go. I didn't know whether this was Bai's poetic imagination or his wanderlust speaking, but I grew concerned.

"The northeast region is under the command of General An Lushan, Bai. He has a horrible reputation and is considered a fraud by many. It is too dangerous for you to go."

"He's effective and clearly very smart. He has worked his way up from being a nobody to one of the most powerful positions in the country. One has to admire that."

"Or bemoan it. It seems that our emperor, bewitched by that woman, has lost all discrimination." Our disagreement continued through many such discussions. It was about this time that I received a letter from a highly respected Daoist master, with whom I had been communicating. Shifu Li Tengkong had a small hermitage on Lushan Mountain (Mt. Lu) near Yongzhen Cavern. She spent much of her time caring for villagers and was said to be able to cure diseases and perform other such miracles. Bai had known her father, Li Linfu, the grand councilor to Emperor Xuanzong, but had little respect for him, and I had heard that the dislike was mutual. Fortunately, Bai didn't hold this against her; he greatly admired Li Tengkong because she had publicly rejected court life and left her aristocratic family to become a Daoist nun.

In her letter, Li Tengkong invited me to come for a visit. When Bai announced that, despite my objections, he would leave shortly to meet his friend in the northeast to see how he could be helpful, I could not help but allow my feelings to surface. "How long will you be gone this time, Bai?"

"It may be a longer trip, Little Phoenix, six months, maybe nine, or more."

"That long?" I asked tearfully.

"I am hoping to find employment there." He drew me close to him and I wiped my tears.

"Fine. Then I will go to visit Li Tengkong." At this point I was not thinking that she would become my teacher, but at the very least she could instruct me in cultivation practices. Bai had spoken to me about the beauty of Mt. Lushan, a famed place for Daoists, and I had long been wanting to visit. This was the perfect time.

"I will bring you there."

"It's in the opposite direction, Bai. I will ask Jing to bring me. He and his wife can enjoy the landscape." A few days before I was to leave, Bai handed me two poems he had written for me.

Seeking Mistress Tengkong
You should go to her on the azure mountain.
Water pounds the mica reef.
Wind scatters the Photinia flowers.
If you long for the secluded life of an immortal,
Let's frolic together in the purple clouds.

I admire the daughter of a councilor
Who studies the Way and aspires to be an immortal.
Her white hands scoop up the blue clouds,
Her silk robe dragging in the purple mist.
When she departs from the Folds Screening Heaven
She rides a phoenix and carries a jade whip.

I read the poems, then looked up at Bai. "What is the Folds Screening Heaven?"

"That is the name of the peak where she lives."

"So, she also rides a phoenix," I murmured.

"And carries a jade whip," he replied with a slight smile. "She is known to be quite austere and strict with her students, so be cautious, Little Phoenix. She may carry you to the heavens, but the ride might be a rough one. Are you prepared for that, for whatever may come? One never knows what will emerge during cultivation practice. All the demons of one's inner life can break forth."

"Demons?" I asked nervously. "Are there demons inside?"

"We don't know what lies hidden within. Be prepared, but you will be in good hands. Her jade whip will guide you."

"I will take your poems with me and read them if I have any difficulty. They will remind me that you are waiting to frolic with me in the purple clouds."

My sadness over parting from Bai was now replaced by a nervousness at the thought of meeting the famed master. I was apprehensive as to what might lie ahead for me, but I also knew that I was fulfilling a long-held desire. Everything in my life had led up to this point when I could finally learn cultivation practices. Bai had been vague about how long he would be gone, and I knew that if I stayed home, I would grow increasingly dissatisfied. Here was an opportunity for me to progress in my spiritual life.

As we discussed this, Bai said, "Stay at the hermitage as long as need be. When you are ready to leave, I will know and will come for you."

But as the day of departure drew near, I sighed and asked him, "I have been waiting my whole life for this. Why am I so anxious?"

"It is natural to be anxious, Little Phoenix. You have never traveled far, and you are going to an unknown environment. Do not expect the comforts to which you are accustomed."

"You know me well enough to know that comforts don't matter, but what if those inner demons arise?"

"Don't take my words too seriously. You have no inner demons. The first lesson with a teacher is to trust. You cannot advance if you don't have faith in your teacher, that he or she will do what is in your best interest. You must have that faith."

"I am going to meet her for the first time. I don't know that she is my teacher. How will I know if she is the right one?"

"You are worrying too much. Would you feel better if Jing stayed with you a few days, until you became comfortable?" I nodded.

The day we were to part, I clung to Bai. Suddenly the thought arose that I might lose him, and I couldn't bear to think this. At that moment, how I yearned to undo both of our plans so that we could remain together in our home.

"Why this anxiety, Little Phoenix? It is only a temporary separation."

"I am so afraid I will lose you, that you won't come back," I said tearfully.

"Do you think you can get rid of me so easily?" he replied with a slight chuckle. "Even in our separation, I will be with you, Little Phoenix." Unwrapping himself from my arms, he looked at me tenderly, and I spontaneously took off the jade bead necklace I was wearing and placed it around Bai's neck. It had been given to me by my grandmother and was very precious to me. I always felt it protected me and in giving it to Bai I felt it would protect him as well.

"What is this for?" he asked.

"So that you will remember your wife. It is valuable and you can always sell it in case you need money." He began to take it off to return it to me, but I placed my hand on the beads and said, "Please keep this in case you need it. We don't know how long you will be gone or what awaits you. I will feel better knowing that you have this."

When we arrived at the mountain home of Li Tengkong, she was not there. A nun who seemed just a little bit older than me received us at the doorway of the master's cottage.

"Our teacher is away at the moment, but she is expecting you, Lady Zong, and I will help you get settled," she said, taking the few belongings I had brought with me. Then turning to Jing, she added, "I know you have had a long journey and so I have prepared some food for you to take on your return home."

"I was hoping that my wife and I could stay with my sister for a few days until she gets accustomed . . ."

"I am afraid that is not permitted," she replied in a kind voice. I looked at Jing anxiously. "Don't worry," the nun smiled at him. "Your sister will be fine. Shifu has gone to one of the villages to provide some assistance there. She will be back by evening. I will look after your sister until then." Jing took me aside. "Shu," he whispered, "if you are uncomfortable you can come with us to an inn nearby and we can have a nice time traveling through the mountains. Don't feel you need to stay here. The accommodations seem quite inadequate."

For a moment I vacillated. But I realized that if I left, all my aspirations would dissipate like mist in the air. I feigned a smile. "Jing, I have come all this way for training, and I will not consider leaving. This nun seems very kind and caring. I am comfortable with her. Please go and enjoy your time in these beautiful mountains."

"Are you sure?" he looked at me doubtfully.

I nodded and indicated to my brother that he and his wife should now leave. I saw him pause. With somewhat forced good cheer, I waved him off. "Send a message if you need me, Shu, and I will come for you," he said before retreating to the waiting horses.

As I watched him ride away, a veil of sadness fell over me, but I was determined not to reveal my feelings. With some apprehension, I followed the nun, who introduced herself as Ying, to the small cottage where I was to stay. The cottage consisted of a small room with three mats on the floor.

"You will be sharing this room with two other women," she explained. "They have already been here for several months and so are quite familiar with the routine. They will help you with anything you need, although our general rule is silence. You can, of course, come to me with any questions. My job is to help those newly arrived get adjusted. I will show you where we take our meals, two meals day, at 9 a.m. and then at 2 p.m. and then tea and some fruit at 5 p.m. We consume no meat here as diet is an important part of our practice. Once a month we fast."

I nodded. That didn't seem too difficult for me. The only hard part might be sharing the small room with two other women. I had never slept in a room with anyone else except Bai, but I would adjust.

"I will keep your things in Shifu's cottage, and you can get them when you leave. You will be given two white robes and a simple wood pin for your hair. Nothing else is required here." I discretely slipped the paper containing Bai's poems into my sleeve and handed her my small box of clothing. "Let us go for the afternoon meal and then you will be assigned your tasks. Each woman is given a task for the week and we all rotate through the different duties. We have women from aristocratic families here and commoners as well. Shifu does not distinguish. Everyone gets the same training. Some women find this difficult and don't stay long, but those who remain are very glad that they did. It is rare to find a teacher like our Shifu. I am sure you will soon come to know this."

There were about ten of us eating together. I soon realized that most of the women only stayed for a few weeks, but a few stayed for months, even years. That evening, after I had retired to my cottage, Ying came to tell me that Shifu had returned and inquired after me. She would meet with me tomorrow. After placing Bai's poems beneath my pillow, I lay down and felt at ease, thinking that I was exactly where I belonged.

I was somewhat surprised by Shifu's appearance when I saw her the next morning. Although dressed simply in a white robe like all the other women, there was an elegance and nobility about her that couldn't be disguised. Her hair was tied neatly atop her head, held by a simple wooden pin. She was about Bai's age or a bit older, but the years did not show themselves on her face or her hair, which was as midnight black as any of the younger women. Her eyes were large, and her gaze was firm, yet a gentleness peered through; her presence strong yet peaceful. One was aware when she entered the room.

As I stood in the doorway of her cottage, I remembered Bai's words about the necessity of trusting one's teacher. Could I trust her? Could I place myself in her hands? But that was exactly what I was being asked to do, and I knew this to be a gift. How rare to find a teacher!

After she invited me to be seated, she looked at me for quite some time. "I am glad to receive you, Lady Zong, but I must ask, have you come to visit me and the region, or to receive training?"

"For training."

"Then let me ask you, my dear, why do you seek training?" I didn't know how to answer, and so she rephrased the question, "What are you seeking?"

"Immortality," I replied quietly.

A half-smile crossed her face. "What do you treasure most?"

I thought for a moment and then replied, "My husband."

"And what do you fear most?"

"Losing my husband."

"I appreciate your honesty," she said with a smile. "There are no right answers to those questions. The purpose is to know what is in your heart. Many women who come here try to guess what answers I want to hear. That is not the purpose of those questions. The whole goal in coming here is to know yourself, what your potential is, and how to reach that potential. You will find that your answers change as you go deeper into the Dao.

"Since you are new to our ways, we will teach you some basic cultivation practices—how to work with the breath and the qi, the flow of life force. There will be three hours each day of cultivation practices, one at 5 a.m., another at noon and then a third at 7 p.m., before retiring for the night. You will do the morning and evening cultivation in your room with the other women you stay with. We will all gather for the noon practice under some trees outside my cottage and then take our afternoon meal. When you perform your duties in the kitchen or in cleaning or anywhere else, keep your mind here"—she pointed to my heart—"or there," pointing at the middle of my forehead. "These are key centers for the qi. The more you concentrate there, the stronger will be your qi. Do you have any questions?"

I shook my head.

"Ying will be your guide and will meet with you every day to see how your practice is developing." I nodded. "One more thing. Every day you must spend at least an hour outside among the trees, deeply breathing in and out and releasing yourself into the flow of nature. That is as important as anything you do here. Some of the women choose to sleep out among the trees in the warmer weather, but that will come later. These mountains are extremely beautiful, and you should wander in them whenever you have some free time. That is part of our practice. Connect to the trees, feel the strength of the mountains and the lightness of the mist and clouds. Notice the flowers—there are so many varieties—and take time to be with the animals." Her counsel pleased me greatly and I eagerly nodded. Then she called to Ying. "Please take Lady Zong to the kitchen. She will help prepare the meals this week."

"Please call me Shu," I said to Shifu as I bowed low before her. I repeated the same to Ying as she led me to the kitchen. I was not very familiar with meal preparation, since we had always had a servant who worked in the kitchen, but I eagerly took to this new task.

Life gained a certain rhythm, and slowly I came to understand the true meaning of simplicity. The days flowed one into another in silence, like a stream that passes quietly without any disturbance when there are no rocks to break its pace. Gradually my mind settled down. Our daily life consisted of early rising for cultivation practice, morning tasks and more cultivation, then the afternoon meal, more duties, free time to merge with nature, tea, and then evening cultivation practice and early to bed. A subtle joy entered my heart. I came to see that I was beginning to trust Shifu and would not question any request or order of hers.

I climbed the hills and watched the silken clouds linger below the distant peaks, circling the mountains like the hem of a robe. Tall rock outcroppings stood like guardian figures watching over the lands. Walking further, I found slopes of yellow and purple wildflowers, gracefully swaying in the breezes. I watched until I felt my body gently move with them, my rhythm becoming one with theirs. Birds fluttered all around, peering at me from branches, unsure of whether I was friend or foe and keeping their distance. The pine trees filled the air with perfumes I had not known before; I could not help but inhale so deeply that I became intoxicated with their fragrance. Families of wild macaque scrambled here and there, and I watched with amusement how their young clung to them. The most magical of the creatures, the white deer, would occasionally peer out discretely from behind clusters of trees, one moment there and gone the next, as quickly as a fleeting illusion.

My many silent walks were teaching me the way of the Dao, and after a few weeks I felt as if I had lived lifetimes in that quiet state of unity with the natural world. After I had been at the nunnery for about a month, one of the women with whom I shared the room disappeared for a few days. No explanation was given and, as we rarely spoke to one another, I hesitated to ask. Passing Ying on the way to the vegetable garden, where I was assigned that week, I asked if the woman had left.

She shook her head. "Shifu has sent her to the cave for a few days. After that she will return."

"The cave?" This was the first I was hearing of a cave.

"When someone's cultivation is deep enough, Shifu allows that person to spend some time in the cave. It could be a few days or longer, depending on the situation and the need."

"Oh," I replied simply.

She must have guessed the thoughts passing through my mind because she hurried to say, "Time in the cave is not something to ask for, Shu, as it can be very intense if one is not ready. Shifu knows what is needed and when." I nodded, but after three days, when the woman returned to our cottage and I saw the glow on her face, I could not help but wonder if I would ever be ready.

The weeks passed and I was retrieving Bai's poems from under my pillow with less and less frequency. Whereas at first I would read them every day, now I hardly looked at them. Initially, I had longed for him, especially at night, but now after evening cultivation practice, I would simply slip into sleep without thinking of anything. Bai's presence was drifting further and further away as I began to release the subtle clinging that bound me to him.

Chapter Ten

IN THE CAVE

"I will explain to you about Wu Wei," said Shifu one morning.
"Wu Wei?"

She nodded. "Non-action or effortless action. In the second chapter of the *Dao De Jing*, Laozi describes it like this:

> *. . . the sage acts by doing nothing,*
> *And teaches without saying a word.*
> *The ten thousand things arise but he is silent.*
> *Things grow but he takes nothing for himself.*

"This state of acting without acting comes about when one is in natural alignment with the flow of life. During your first few weeks here, I wanted you to develop a life of simplicity and connectedness to nature. These are two essential principles of the Dao and they were easy for you because you were already practicing them in your life. A third principle is Wu Wei, which means being in balance, without effort, flowing with the Dao so that you spontaneously know what to do and when to do it. It comes when we put the thinking mind aside and rest in an inner knowing, when we can act externally but internally be disengaged.

"The concept has political implications and has been used in that sphere, but I am referring to a personal state of composure, an inner awareness, an inner compass, so to speak, which guides one. The absence of Wu Wei often looks like grasping, holding, desire, ambition, seeking to control, and thirsting after that which is not innate to oneself. I want you to watch your mind carefully and see when you are in this state of Wu Wei and when you are not. For this purpose, you will spend some time in the cave so you can devote more hours to cultivation."

"The cave?" I didn't know whether to be glad or fearful. Going to the cave meant that Shifu felt I was ready for testing. I might encounter difficulties, but also, I might reach a deeper state of peace. All the women I had seen return from the cave emerged with a radiance, an inner glow, and that was reassuring. "When am I to go?"

"Now. Ying will take you and explain everything."

Without any time to prepare, I followed Ying to the cave. It was a bit of a climb from our cottages. My chest tightened as we approached the large opening and then walked down a dark, narrow passageway until we came to another larger room, lit only by a small oil lamp. As my eyes got used to the dark, I saw the cultivation area: a thin wool blanket on the ground next to the lamp, with an extra wool blanket for covering. Beside the sitting area was a pitcher of water and a cup.

"Are there any snakes here?" I asked nervously. Since childhood I had had a fear of snakes and this seemed the perfect place to encounter one.

Ying smiled. "The only snakes here are the ones in your mind. I don't know how long Shifu will keep you here, but every day a meal will be set at the entrance to the passageway, one meal a day, with a new pitcher of water. And every other day a new robe will be set there with a basin for washing. There is also a place to relieve yourself, which will be cleaned every day. It is best that you don't leave this area except to go to the passageway for food and water. You know cultivation practices now, so engage in them as much as you can."

I nodded. "Ying, what if there is an emergency?"

"What kind of emergency, Shu? If you absolutely cannot stay here any longer, Shifu will know and will send one of us for you." With those words she turned and left.

It was only when I went to sit down that I noticed the jeweled dagger resting by the wool blanket on the ground. I picked it up and ran my fingers over the many jewels that lined the handle. *If there are no snakes here, why the dagger?* I mused. *Perhaps there are other wild animals. Could I kill them with this little dagger? But no, we are meant to live in harmony with nature; surely this dagger is not for killing.* Nobody had died in here, at least not since I arrived.

The presence of the dagger set my mind off in many directions, and it was a long time before I could get it to calm down and remember Shifu's words about Wu Wei. Finally, I scolded myself. I was creating situations out of nothing. "Stop!" I yelled as loudly as I could, speaking to my own mind. I was alone, far from another human presence, and felt no inhibition about crying out. *Whatever is to come, let it come. If it is death, let it be.*

I began to practice the breathing techniques I had learned, and gradually my fears subsided. Then I began to work with the qi, moving it up and down between the center of my torso, my heart and forehead. Within a short time, a gentle peace came over me and gradually I slipped into a sweet state of sleep. I awoke after what seemed like many hours later, but I had no accurate notion of time, and again began practicing cultivation. That day and night were spent in quiet inner reflection, sleeping, and walking around the cave.

As the second day began, I found myself getting restless and so had to struggle more with my mind, which was beginning to imagine all sorts of things. I was again on guard, lest a snake or other creature should quietly arrive, and so my sleep was somewhat shallow as I tried to be alert for sounds. Many hours into the second day, I found myself drifting off to sleep again when I was suddenly awakened by the hissing of a snake, which sounded as if it was right in front of me. Snapping into a fully awake position, I clutched the dagger.

"Where are you?" I asked fearfully, as I stood up and looked about. Slowly I moved around the enclosed room and checked every crevice, but the creature was nowhere in sight. Perhaps it had slithered down the passageway. That was where my food would be, but there was no light there. I returned to my seat and closed my eyes and began to practice my breathing again. After some time, I heard the hissing sound again. My eyes flew open and there it was, a large cobra-like animal, its head raised in what seemed like a threatening pose. Again I grabbed the dagger and then froze in my seated position, afraid to move a muscle. As I stared at the snake, what struck me most were its eyes, which were not like what I imagined snake's eyes to be. They were large and green and shone with a translucent light. I couldn't tell if it was dangerous or not, but in my mind, it was a creature on the verge of striking.

Looking into those eyes, a feeling of confidence arose in me and I spoke to the snake. "You are going to curse me, I know, but I don't intend to harm you. I have no anger toward you and will not kill you. I would rather you curse or kill me than I harm you." My voice began to quiver as I let the dagger drop to the ground. "I will not fight you," I mumbled again. Closing my eyes, I prepared for death. "I will not."

Later as I thought about that moment, I wondered if my inaction was due to a lack of courage on my part. Did I not have the strength and mental focus to strike the snake? I didn't know. I heard the snake slither closer until I felt it right before me and my body began to tremble. I could feel its energy, its qi, and I spontaneously began to send qi out from my heart, without thinking about it, without directing it. The qi began to move. *I know there is a hidden cause behind every act, I silently pleaded, so if I have harmed you in the past, please forgive me.*

As I felt the qi moving between us, I remembered what Bai had told me when he returned after several months absence, about the thread of light stretching from him to me; I imagined those very same threads of light emerging from my heart and dispersing into the air, again with no thought, no direction. It was a spontaneous arising and with it came a feeling of warmth, fully engulfing me. I sat there for a while, afraid to open my eyes. When I finally did, I saw that there was no snake and heard no hissing sound. Had I imagined the whole experience? But no, I had seen the snake with open eyes. I had been fully awake, and I had heard its loud hissing.

I was determined not to allow my mind to dwell on this. Immediately I began practicing the breathing techniques. I felt the qi flowing up and down between my heart and forehead, as if the qi was replenishing itself, as if it had been strengthened by the experience. After some time, I felt the need to walk around. I picked up the oil lamp and slowly made my way down the dark passageway to fetch my food, watching every inch of the ground to see whether the snake might be lurking there, but found nothing.

After eating and drinking and walking back and forth for a while, I sat down again to practice cultivation. As my body relaxed, I fell into a semi-sleep state. In that state, I saw a young woman in a forest, walking down a narrow, overgrown path and looking as if she were searching for food. I saw her bend down to pull up one plant after another, and then she began to dig up some roots, examining each one and shaking off the dirt before placing it in a basket. Just as she finished putting a root plant into her basket, suddenly from behind the brush she encountered a very large snake. Seeing her, the snake lifted its head and its large piercing eyes caught hers. I could feel her fear as the snake began to hiss vehemently. Picking up a large stick that lay on the ground by her feet, she smacked the snake on the head again and again and again as if she were battling a mighty enemy, until it lay at her feet in pieces.

I awoke with a start and uttered a small cry. It took a few minutes for me to recapture the dream, but when I realized I had seen a woman kill a snake in a most dreadful manner, I was greatly disturbed. The dream was so vivid, so very real. Was there a connection between the dream and what I had experienced earlier? I didn't know what to make of it.

It was useless to try to cultivate in this state of mind. I got up and paced the small enclosed area, trying to make sense of what I had seen. I dreamed of a woman killing a snake, and yet I experienced the horror of the scene as if it were real. How was her experience related to the one I had had? Surely the snake that had come before me and then mysteriously disappeared was a magical creature, not an ordinary snake. How I wished I could ask Shifu to explain! After walking back and forth, I slowly made my way back to the wool blanket on the floor. As I dwelt on both experiences, I realized that the hissing had been entirely different. In the dream, the snake had clearly been angry and cursing the woman, but in my awakened state the magical snake that appeared was not angry, was not cursing, rather it was communicating, and I had misunderstood the exchange. "Was my dream imagination or a memory?" I exclaimed out loud. "A memory of something that happened long ago?"

I fell asleep again, sitting up in cultivation position, and Bai came to me in another dream. We were sitting in the park near my home, surrounded by snakes. "You are not afraid of them anymore, are you, Little Phoenix?" I shook my head. "No Bai, I am not afraid."

"Good," he replied. "There are different kinds of snakes. Some are of the ordinary kind: they defend themselves and mean no harm. But there is another kind and they can bring a message. You should try to understand that message." As he spoke these words, I saw the snakes slither away one by one until there were no more left around us.

When I awoke, the dream was only a faint recollection. "Why is my cultivation time preoccupied with snakes?" I asked out loud. Getting up, I slowly walked around the enclosed area. I had no notion of what time it was since I was steeped in darkness all the time, except for the faint glow given off by the oil lamp. Day and night had no meaning in the cave, which was dark and still and silent always. I sat down once more and began my cultivation practice. After some time, I drifted again into a semi-sleep state and saw before me a large river. There was a woman standing by the edge of the river, about to step in, when a man's voice called out, "Don't enter. Her current is very strong here. She will carry you away and you will drown."

In my sitting/sleeping position, my body had begun to lean over and it suddenly jerked forward, bringing me back to normal consciousness, but then I drifted away again. I recalled a time I had spent with Bai when we had walked through a forest and come to a small lake. It was a very hot day and he began to take off his robes. I watched as he started to lower himself into the lake and I suddenly called out, "Bai, don't go into the water. It is too deep. You don't know how to swim, and you will drown." He glanced back at me surprised and asked, "How did you know that I don't swim?"

My eyes flew open and I had to steady myself. That was a true memory of something that had happened one day when I was out with Bai, but why was I remembering that now, and what relationship did it have to that other woman stepping into the river? My mind was clearly playing tricks on me. I decided to stay awake for the rest of my time in the cave, so I played little games to keep from falling asleep, to keep from drifting into a state of cultivation. Finally, I peered down the passageway and saw a glimmer of light in the distance. Day had come. I had passed two days and nights in the cave.

I hoped that Shifu would send for me that morning, but she didn't. Throughout the day I kept hearing her words about Wu Wei. She had told me to pay attention. The girl who was about to step into the rushing river was not in harmony with the Dao, but when I stopped Bai from stepping into the lake, I was in harmony. There was an inner knowing that made me call out to him. The woman who beat the snake to death was not in harmony, but when I refrained from thrusting my dagger at the snake in the cave, I was functioning in harmony with the Dao, or so I thought. Throughout the day I reflected on the meaning of Shifu's words and wondered if the purpose of these experiences was to help me understand how to be in tune with the Dao.

The next night, night three of my stay in the cave, I again drifted into an altered state. I saw that young woman again, the same one I had seen by the river, the one who had killed the snake, but this time she was in a forest collecting plants. I saw her searching carefully, placing her hands over many plants before choosing the one she desired. A man suddenly appeared and called to her. "What are you doing here so late? It will soon be dark."

Looking up at him she smiled and replied, "I am gathering food. I have everything that I need, and I am almost done."

"There is plenty of food in the market. Why do you need to come to the forest to gather food?"

"They don't have these plants in the market, and this is what we are used to eating. I have come to gather them for my mother."

"Here, let me help you." He looked around and then reached toward a plant.

"Not that one. It is poisonous. Don't touch it or you might get a rash." She pulled his hand away but kept her hand over his for a few moments, looking up at him with admiration. Then noting his embarrassment, she withdrew her hand. He took the basket from her, and together they walked down the narrow path that led out of the forest.

The scene changed and I saw her bringing some cooked food to a hut. The man emerged and she said, "I have brought some food that I cooked with the plants I gathered. You will see how tasty the forest foods are." There was an awkward moment and he hesitated, and I saw a strange look come over his face.

I came back to my normal consciousness with a start. *What am I seeing? Who are these people and why am I seeing them? Are those scenes a real-life memory or something imagined.* Then the memory came to me of a walk through the forest with Bai when he suddenly stopped to gather wildflowers. "We have so many flowers in the garden," I had said. "Why are you picking these? Let them stay here for the forest creatures to enjoy."

"These wildflowers are beautiful. Look at the variety of colors. Let's pick some for the house."

"You are right. They will make a lovely bouquet."

I had bent down to pick a flower with small yellow buds, when he reached over to stop me, placing his hand on mine. "Not that one, Little Phoenix. It is poisonous. You will get a rash if you touch it. See all the prickles on the stem?"

"Oh," I had replied, withdrawing my hand. Then he took my hand and held it as I looked up at him with a faint smile, thinking how knowledgeable he was about plant life.

After he had filled our basket with flowers, he found a place for us to sit. I lay back against a tree and looked up at the canopied sky, as I often did on our outings. After a while I noticed he had made a necklace of flowers for me. Placing it around my neck, he said, "Wildflowers make a beautiful garland."

As I started to see eerie connections between the scenes that were appearing in my mind, I became uneasy. Was this about learning to understand Wu Wei or was it something else? I tried to ease my confusion by saying that Shifu was trying to teach me about being in the flow of the Dao, and I began to dissect the scenes I had remembered and dreamed. If I allowed fear or anxiety to enter, surely I was departing from the Dao. I had to let all these thoughts and memories flow, without attachment, without placing too much importance on them.

Throughout the night, I tried to keep at bay discomforting feelings that were creeping up in me about what I was seeing, and I realized that by pushing those feelings away, I also was not in the Dao. Shifu had said not to cling, not to pull at anything or to push it away, not to exert effort. I was to be in a state of inaction, not to strive for it but to be in it. The night passed slowly with hardly any sleep.

Day four was the same. I tried not to yearn for Shifu to send for me, but I failed miserably. On the fourth night I again drifted back into dreams of the life of that woman. I saw her on a boat going down a vast river. The man was standing on the bank, partially hidden, watching as the river was taking her further and further away. She must have felt his presence. Suddenly she turned around as he was turning his back to walk away, and she exploded in tears. My heart grew heavy as I saw her tears. Then I remembered the day Bai left me after he had mentioned marriage. We had ridden back to my home in silence, and when we reached the door, without inviting him in, I said goodbye and watched him as he walked away. He didn't look back. But as I turned to go inside, I felt him pause and I knew he had turned around for one last gaze. I also paused at the door, but by the time I turned around he was gone.

Rousing myself, I straightened up and exclaimed, "Why am I reliving the past? I am married to Bai and we are happy. Why am I returning to incidents that have passed? Why must I feel the sorrow of this other woman who I don't know, who may even be an imagined person?" I paced the room and stayed awake for the rest of the time.

Thankfully, Ying came for me in the morning. When I heard her cheerful voice and saw her smiling face, I nearly fell at her feet in gratitude. She looked at me in surprise. "You are exhausted, Shu. Did you not get any rest?"

"Hardly any," I murmured.

"How was your time in the cave?" I feigned a smile and didn't answer. She hurried to say, "It is better not to speak of it, except with Shifu, of course."

"When will I see Shifu?"

"I don't know. She will call for you. Meanwhile, take my hand and I will guide you to your room. You are unsteady. That is often the case after spending a few nights here." As we walked through the dark passageway and into the daylight, I stopped and squinted as I looked around me at the bright landscape. The colors seemed more vibrant than ever before. Never had the trees seemed so green, the sky so blue. Never had the bird songs sounded so sweet.

"I have never appreciated the sunlight so much," I murmured, as I looked up at the cloudless sky. Tree branches were dancing in the wind, which swept through me as well. It was a beautiful spring day. I stood for a few minutes breathing in deeply the air and the sunshine.

"Come, you need to take some rest. Shifu has changed your room. You now have a small cottage to yourself."

"Why is that?" I asked.

"She said a poet needs solitude, so she shifted you to a room with a writing table. No need to come for the afternoon meal. I will bring you food. When one comes out of the cave, it is best to spend some time alone."

She led me to a little cottage and left me there in the small room, furnished with only a mat on the floor, a few cushions, and a low desk equipped with paper, brush, and ink for writing. A window was open to let in the fresh mountain air. I stood before the writing table for many minutes and then sat down and wrote. The words flowed without much effort and without me truly understanding their meaning. After I had written the poem about the Naga, I looked at it in amazement and could not help but wonder whose words they were. That could not have been me, who killed that serpent, I said to myself firmly. I would never have done such a brutal act, so who is this about?

The Naga
I met an ancient naga
Who had been killed long ago,
So long that the memory of the deed
Lay buried in the sand 'til now.

In the cave he befriended me.
I bow before that magical creature
Who came from a distant star
To forgive the one who killed him.

In the Cave

Ancient memories seep
From every crevice of this cave.
I came not to play on purple clouds
But to be cast into the depths of sky
Where unknown faces people my mind.
Do they come to disturb the flow of time,
Or did I create all of this?

I slept from mid-afternoon until the next day, when Shifu called for me in the morning. After a good sleep, I was steadier on my feet and my mind was less disturbed. Sitting before Shifu, my questions fled.

"Is there anything you want to share with me, Shu?"

My eyes were cast down and I didn't respond.

"Anything you want to ask me?"

I shook my head.

"Were you able to go deep in your cultivation practice?"

"I don't think so, Shifu," I replied with a still bent head. I was afraid that if I looked into her eyes, she might see something of my confusion. "My mind was very restless."

"That is natural, especially the first time in the cave. Next time might be easier."

"Next time?" I raised my eyes briefly and then lowered them again.

"You should return to the cave in a few weeks. You are beginning to understand Wu Wei."

"Wu Wei," I mumbled. "Inaction. Effortless being. I don't have a good grasp of that, Shifu. I don't know how not to be affected by what I experience." *So, all of this was to teach me about Wu Wei, I thought. Nothing more than that.*

"You know what it is to be at one with the flow of nature. You have experienced that. Keep that experience in your mind. When you stopped Li Bai from stepping into the lake, you were in the state of spontaneous knowing. Remember that, but do not strive for it. Don't strive for anything. Let it all go, observe. Watch." I raised my eyes to look at her and wondered how she knew of that incident with Bai. Was she able to read my mind, to peer into the restless waves of thought? She smiled. As if in response to my question, she said quietly, "It is the teacher's responsibility to know the mind of the student. Are you sure that you have no questions for me?"

Without thinking, I shook my head, as if embarrassed to share my confusion.

"You may return to your duties now and to our regular routine."

I nodded and, bowing to her, got up to leave. As I reached for the door, I heard her say, "Not everyone experiences the awakening of old memories. Don't let it confuse or frighten you. Don't seek to awaken what lies asleep, but don't resist what awakens on its own. That is the path of inaction. In time you will understand what you need to know."

"Thank you, Shifu," I replied quietly, as I turned and bowed deeply.

"One more thing, Shu. As you go about your duties, reflect on these words of Laozi in the *Dao De Jing*:

Dao is the bottomless cup that need not be filled.
Profound and deep, it is the root of ten thousand things."

I looked up at her and nodded and then took my leave. Those words were to reverberate through my mind in the days and weeks that followed, yet I could not say that I truly understood them. I was glad to return to the normal routine. The weather was getting warmer, and I was assigned to work in the vegetable garden. An older nun named Changying, who had been with Shifu for many years, oversaw the care of all the gardens. I had admired her from a distance because she seemed quite close to Shifu. She had a cheerful and peaceful presence, rarely speaking but often casting a loving expression. That was her way of communicating. One day as I was walking through the rows of newly planted vegetables, I came to a patch of what looked like herbs and bent down to smell them. Changying was there picking the herbs and I watched as she looked at each plant, closed her eyes, and reflected before deciding which ones to pluck.

"Are these medicinal plants?" I asked her, curious about the great care she was displaying toward them.

She nodded. "Shifu tends to these herself as she knows how to strengthen the qi in these plants so they will be more effective."

"I have heard that Shifu is able to cure deadly diseases. Is it because of that?"

She smiled and leaning close to me replied quietly. "As you will discover, Shifu has many magical powers, but she displays them discretely."

"I think I have already discovered that. But have you seen any of these healings?"

"I often accompany Shifu when she goes to the villages, as do some of the others who live here. We have seen many wonderous things but Shifu does not like us to speak of them."

I nodded.

"Come, help me gather the plants she needs, since we are going to a village later. Watch me and I will show you which plants to pick and how to gather the leaves very gently. We speak to the plants before taking what they have to offer. This is how we show our gratitude and respect."

Working in the garden was healing for me. Slowly the discomfort remaining from my time in the cave began to dissipate, and I began to return to a feeling of ease, but this was not to last. As I was starting to rest in the peace of the monastic routine, Shifu sent me again into the dark depths of my mind.

My return to the cave was not a welcome one, but I tried not to resist. Don't seek and don't not seek, those were the words I took with me as I reentered the place where I had experienced the emergence of images I still didn't understand. On my second night of this second stay in the cave, my mind was again thrown into an altered state, and I became the witness of another life, although this time I knew with certainty that the life I was revisiting belonged to me.

Chapter Eleven

LIFE AS A CONCUBINE

Early Tang Empire, 7th Century CE

I was only sixteen when I became aware of my father's ambition to advance his position in society. A minor government official, my father eagerly eyed the intrigues of the court of Emperor Gaozong, who had many sons and an overbearing wife, Empress Wu. Marriage into the royal family was clearly out of the question, so it became my father's greatest desire to have one of his daughters be taken as a concubine for one of the princes, even a junior one. It didn't really matter which one. This would give him access to the inner working of the court. I was the youngest daughter in the family, and for some reason I was the chosen one, selected to be put forth and bartered away. My father tried every trick in the book and finally hooked one of the younger princes. He was an overweight and unattractive man, far older than I, and one indulgent in sensory pleasures. He took a liking to me and I was given to him, the youngest concubine in his harem.

Too young to resist and too timid to object, I allowed myself to be a pawn for my father's desires, not realizing what was in store for me. My life became one of total frivolity, hours spent on shaping myself to be the image of beauty, as others flocked around me to paint my face, decorate my coiffed hair with jeweled ornaments, and adorn me in embroidered robes so abundant that they prevented me from moving freely. The first night my lord called me to him, I struggled to hide my distaste. I was young and had no voice of my own and so I submitted. The next morning when I returned to my room, I vomited profusely, sickened by the smell of the man who was now lord over my being. Then I scrubbed myself, weeping as I tried to erase the memory of that night from my body. But neither washing nor tears could do away with what was now inscribed in my mind, a memory that could not be eradicated.

My lord took delight in me, or secretly sought to torture me; I could not tell the difference. He called me often to him, and each time I would return sickened and desperate to wash off his touch. I scrubbed and scrubbed the places where he had handled me and tried to disavow that they were part of my body. I would look at myself and think, *You are no longer mine. I have no more rights to this body.* I began to hate all signs of beauty, all decorations and accoutrements that would make me more attractive.

The attention paid to me slowly began to arouse the resentment of the chief consort, who was much older and so much more adept at handling her lord. Her desire was for power over her little petty kingdom, the world of his concubines, and she began to plant stories, turning one against another. My only hope was that I would someday be evicted from the circle of the select and our lord would no longer visit me. Perhaps then I could erase forever the taste of his lips from my mind, a taste that haunted me day and night. Over time my distaste turned to indifference, and this lack of care infuriated him. No matter what he did, I displayed no emotion, as my heart had grown as cold as the frozen ground in winter.

It was to be ten years before the day of eviction came, and those ten years stretched out like a vast sea without shores. For the duration of that time, I drifted on the monotony of waveless water, numbed by what I could not change. I turned a blind eye to the intrigues in front of me, and mentally secluded myself as best I could. It was a lonely life. As I grew older, the coldness I exhibited toward him spread like a disease and he became bitter toward me. Every encounter entailed a mental and spiritual battle, but he seemed to relish the fight and, instead of staying away, sought me out more often. Our physical relationship became abusive, which only made me drift further away. I became like a faint shadow that one cannot catch and can barely see.

The only joy I had was in the occasional musical performance. The main consort, Consort Niu, did her best to exclude me, but on occasion one of the other concubines named Biyu, whose heart was soft and who saw my hidden pain, would steal an invitation for me. One day she came to me with such a proposal. "Meihua, a poet is coming to recite his newest works. I don't remember his name, but I hear he is quite well regarded. You love music, and you will enjoy his performance. I can get you an invitation, but I must be discrete because Consort Niu has already told us who will be invited. She has mentioned me, but I have no desire to be there. You can take my place, saying that I fell ill at the last moment and offered you the invitation. You deserve some entertainment."

"A poet?" I inquired.

She nodded.

"You don't know which one?"

She shook her head.

"I am willing to take a risk for this. As a young child, my mother used to recite poetry to me. She often told me that poetry was one of the emperor's gifts to his people, that he arranged for the printing of poetry and organized poetry readings at the court to elevate society, but I have never heard poetry read by the poet himself. I am sure that is another experience entirely." Then

I became thoughtful, remembering the venom of Consort Niu. "I don't want to put you in danger. She can be vengeful and may take it out on you."

"I am protected by my family. She cannot really touch me." Unlike me, Biyu came from a prominent family, who had used her relationship with the royal household to gain more power in the court. My father had risen slightly in his position but never achieved what he had hoped, often blaming me for failing to please our lord.

"If you think this will work, I will gladly go in your place. I will be indebted to you."

She placed her hand on mine. "There is no question of indebtedness. Consort Niu is insanely jealous of you, but I know the torture you endure. You don't have to speak what is in your heart for me to know it. This life is not one you have chosen. Our lord's affection for you is not something you welcome."

"Quite the contrary," I managed a small laugh. "I don't think he has much affection for me at all, but I have learned to tolerate the intolerable."

"Nobody should have to do that," she replied quietly. "I find our lord amusing and so don't mind my time with him, rare though it is. I don't envy you at all. To be with a man you find repulsive is beyond what one should have to endure," she said very quietly.

"Never mind, Biyu. I have stopped trying to change what can't be changed. If this poet manages to lift my spirits for a little while, I will be most grateful to him. Perhaps this will be my way of escape."

"Be careful, though, you know how quickly rumors spread here. There are eyes watching everywhere. Don't look at the poet at all, not even a glance. Keep your eyes down or Consort Niu will start some story about you."

The night of the poetry reading came and Consort Niu was indeed incensed by my presence, but I pretended not to notice. I kept my mind on the poetry and with closed eyes listened to the musical recitation, which carried me far away from the world in which I lived. When it was over, I opened my eyes and could not help but catch a brief glance of the poet, who was a young man, slightly older than I was, a man of great talent although still relatively unknown. There was nothing striking about his appearance and I didn't take much note of it as all my attention was on his words and the musical cadence of his voice. When I returned to my room that night, I felt a joy I had not known since I left home, and for the first time I realized the power of poetry to lift one out of one's troubles. *It is truly a gift, not from the emperor, but from the gods*, I thought.

I had a desire to thank the poet but had no idea how to reach him. I knew that it would not be wise to send even a brief message through a third party. The next day as I was passing through the main hall, to my great surprise I saw the poet walking toward me, alone. The heavens had answered my desire! As I reached him, I paused, and he stopped as well to greet me. After a moment I told him how much his reading had meant to me. He smiled and handed me a few sheets of paper.

"Here are the poems I read last night. They have not yet been printed, but I am happy to give you a handwritten copy since you have expressed appreciation. I noticed you last night. As I read the poems, you were in deep concentration. It means a lot to a poet when . . . when someone like you understands his work." For a moment as I took the papers, our hands met. It was at this moment that I saw Consort Niu with a few of the concubines cross the hall. I quickly received the papers, and then bowing low I took my leave.

It didn't take long for the embers of misunderstanding, a calculated one, to enflame my world. I returned to my room and waited, hiding the poems as best I could. A few days later Biyu came to me disturbed, telling me that Consort Niu was spreading the story that I had had a secret tryst with the poet. "She has told our lord that you have been unfaithful, that she caught you in a secret meeting with the poet. He is furious and they are debating your punishment," she conveyed in a voice full of sorrow.

"Biyu, this is ridiculous. I met the poet quite by accident the day after his reading as I walked through the main hall, and when I expressed my admiration for his poems, he handed me copies of his poems. That is all. There is nothing more to it. I cannot even say what the poet looks like. She cannot make up a story out of nothing."

"She is an expert at that. You do not truly know her. She has ruined many women here."

"Let her ruin me with our lord then. I won't be sorry if he doesn't call for me ever again."

"I hope she doesn't kill you."

"Over such a silly thing?" I asked incredulously.

"Meihua, after so many years here, you are still so innocent. How have you managed to keep that? When you came here, you were young, so very young. And now after these many years, you still haven't learned the ways of the world."

The thought suddenly dawned on me that the wretched woman might seek to harm the poet. "Can she do anything to him?" I asked hesitantly.

"That will depend on the story they concoct, but I have been told that the only way out is for you is to claim that the poet seduced you."

"I would never do that, say such a complete lie!" I exclaimed. "I would rather be punished myself. But really, Biyu, could they do this over a two-minute exchange? There was nothing more."

The next few days were ones of anxious waiting. I had begun trying to prepare myself for punishment, not knowing what to expect, but even so I was not prepared for what awaited me. Early one morning an official came to my room to fetch me and brought me to the public courtyard outside the palace where a large fire pit had been created. Then reading my crime of infidelity, he tried to get me to sign a paper admitting that I had been seduced. After refusing several times, the official stripped me of my richly embroidered robes and threw at me a simple grey item of clothing. He ripped the ornaments from my head, causing my hair to tumble loose around my chest and back. Then the printed poems of the poet were cast into the fire and he was declared a banished person. I watched the scene as a nightmare unfolding, unable to believe this was truly taking place.

I was taken to a small room behind the palace, isolated from the rest, with only a small courtyard for relief from indoor life. Biyu came to see me soon after. Whispering to me, she said, "If you have any poems of the poet on you, give them to me for safekeeping. They will soon search your belongings. I will return them in time, but it will be difficult for me to visit you as we have all been forbidden any communication with you.

"Biyu, why has this happened?"

"You have underestimated the hostility of Consort Niu and of our lord, who now claims your disrespect for him stems from this secret affair, which he believes you have been carrying on for a long time. Since you won't confess to being seduced, he believes it was a willing alliance. Something you did, I don't know what, has incensed him. I went to see him and told him of your innocence, and he said that even now if you admit to the seduction, he will allow you to return."

"Return to him? I am finally free," I replied bitterly. "Why would I confess to something untrue. The poet has already suffered on my account. I have had to endure humiliation, but what he has had to endure is far greater.

That is the crime I will have to live with—to have caused this innocent man to suffer, and to have deprived society of the beauty of his poetry." I began to cry, but quickly suppressed my tears as a fierce defiance took over me. "I will make it up to the poet, sometime in the future," I said quietly.

"I knew you would feel this way. But Meihua, the crime you speak of falls squarely at the feet of Consort Nui, not to any doing of yours."

She left me there to begin my life of isolation and humiliation and to mourn deeply for the fate of the poet.

I came back to waking consciousness, unaware of my surroundings. It took me a few minutes to recall that I was in the cave, and that I was Shu, not Meihua. I had no notion of time, as the days had slipped into nights, which had slipped again into the dark of days. But I was weak and faint from lack of food. Slowly I rose from the wool blanket on which I was seated and took small steps down the dark passageway to retrieve the food at the entrance. I didn't know how long the food had been there. I carried the tray back to the cultivation room and began to eat, although I had no appetite and had to force the food into my mouth. As I did, the memory of being intimate with my lord of that former time overcame me and I began to vomit profusely. I lifted myself to get some water, but then dizziness overcame me, and I felt myself fall onto the hard ground.

When I regained consciousness, I was lying on the mat of my cottage, with Ying sitting beside me. Opening my eyes, I couldn't remember how I had gotten there. "What happened, Ying?" I asked in not more than a whisper.

"When the attendant told me the food she left hadn't been eaten for a few days, I became worried. She was supposed to be leaving fresh food every day, but she hadn't changed the food and it must have gone bad. Shifu sent me to check on you. I found you lying unconscious on the floor. You must have hit your head hard when you fell.

Remembering that I had vomited all over myself, I turned my face to the wall in embarrassment. "I made a mess there, I am sorry."

"Don't worry. I have cleaned everything up."

"How many days was I in the cave?" I asked, turning to face her again.

"Five days."

"Five days," I repeated quietly. "Time stops inside those rock walls."

"You should rest now. It is best if you don't eat today, but drink. I will keep bringing you tea and water."

"Ying, I have to wash."

"I have cleaned you, Shu, and changed your garment."

"I have to wash again. Please bring me a basin." I looked at her with pleading eyes.

Realizing the urgency of my need, she replied, "You lie here. I will get what you need." She returned a short time later with a large basin of water, a towel and some soap.

I slowly undressed and began to scrub myself, but I couldn't erase the memory, the memory of that man who had invaded my body and of the humiliation. I scrubbed and scrubbed until my skin was raw. Ying stood by helplessly, a look of concern on her face.

"What are you doing, Shu?" she finally asked. "You will tear off your skin if you don't stop digging into it."

"I have to clean the stain, Ying, clean the stain of those memories, but they won't come off." I sank down onto the floor and dissolved into tears.

She wrapped the towel around me and hugged me, waiting for the stream of tears to cease their flow.

"I will go get Shifu," she finally said.

I put out my hand to restrain her. "I can't let her see me like this. Give me a few days to gain control of myself." She nodded. After helping me dress she led me back to my mat on the floor and began to clean up the basin and water from the washing. I don't know how long she stayed because I drifted off to sleep.

Sadness sat with me day after day. I couldn't shake off this unwelcome companion. I didn't leave my room. Ying brought me food and attended personally to all my needs. Again and again I relived the scenes I had witnessed. Finally, one day there was a knock on my door and Shifu entered. I was seated on my mat attempting to engage in cultivation, but the atmosphere in the room was anything but peaceful or joyful. I tried to rise to greet her but couldn't. She sat down on the floor in front of me without saying a word. Many minutes passed before she spoke.

"For how long will you wallow in self-pity?" she asked in a stern voice. I cast my eyes down, afraid to look at her. "My dear, in one life or another we all have been concubines of some nature. That woman is not who you are today."

I raised my eyes to look at her. "Why do I feel such shame? Shifu, I have to understand why I took that birth and who that man was to me. Why did he torture me so?"

She replied in a gentler tone. "You did not see the rest of that life. You only saw the sorrow, not what came after. Every life is a mixture of sad and joyful events. To live in the Dao is not to be swayed by either. Close your eyes, breathe in deeply, and I will take you back." Placing her hand on my heart, I felt a warm flow of energy pass from her to me. It began to circulate through me, moving up down between my heart and forehead, and within a short while I was back in time, in the life of Meihua.

My isolation from the rest of the household was a relief, a hidden blessing, and oddly enough, it gave me a tremendous sense of freedom, despite being locked in a small room with no freedom of movement. No longer did I have to hide behind the mask of a painted face. No longer did I have to follow protocols and wait to be called by a man who repelled me. I was released from all of that, but in addition to this mental freedom, I also gained loneliness and boredom. Confined to my small room and tiny courtyard, with no visitors, except a servant who brought me food twice a day, there was little for me to do. I requested books and was refused. I requested some flowers for the courtyard and was again turned down. I requested writing implements and none came. A deaf ear was turned on me and nothing that I could say or do elicited any response. It was like speaking to the wind that carries the words away, and so the weeks and months passed.

Then one day Biyu showed up. I hadn't seen her since her visit at the beginning of my imprisonment and was so glad for her company. "I have brought you some scrolls and copied some poems out for you, and I also brought the papers that the poet had handed you," she said quietly, taking several scrolls of poetry from inside her robe. "I saw how much poetry uplifted you and thought you would do well to educate yourself on the subject."

"Where did you get these, Biyu?" I asked, flipping through the pile she had place on the floor beside me.

"Never mind. I took a great risk in coming here and had to bribe the guard, but I could no longer bear to think of you here alone with nothing to keep you occupied. I will come again and bring you as much poetry as I can find. Keep the scrolls hidden under your quilt, as we know well that the walls here have eyes and ears. You must at least use your time here well. I hope our lord will reconsider and one day let you come back."

I shook my head. "I don't want that, Biyu. As difficult as this is, I much prefer it." Biyu did not stay long, but a few months later she returned with many more scrolls and a few newly printed books.

"Biyu, there is a poet I have come to like very much. His name is Cao Cao. When you were here last you gave me one of his poems that you had copied. Can you find me more of his writings?"

"The warlord Cao Cao of many centuries ago?"

"I don't know about that, but his poem is very thoughtful and moving. There are others I like from the Han Empire as well, perhaps you can find more writings from that time. I never realized it was such a culturally-rich period." And so, every few months she would bring me more scrolls and printed copies of poetry and I would spend my days studying them, memorizing the poems I liked the best. Sometimes I would go out into the courtyard at night and recite them to my lone friend, the moon, and tell myself how much the gods there enjoy listening to our human poetry.

Many years into my imprisonment, one day I looked out into the courtyard and found a Daoist priest standing there. I couldn't imagine how he had entered as the only door was the one leading into my room and the small open area was surrounded by a tall wall, too high for anyone to climb over. Eager for a visitor, I gratefully greeted him, and was surprised that he seemed to know of my plight.

"You have the right conditions here to engage in cultivation, and I will share with you some practices," he said as he seated himself on the ground and indicated that I should sit in front of him. "Engage yourself diligently for several hours each day and you will see wondrous results." He handed me some writings on Daoism and began to teach me exercises for breathing and for balancing the inner energy, the qi.

Before leaving, he said, "Take this small abode as your hermitage, as your mountain cave, and cultivate your inner life. In your mind, practice simplicity, holding no desires, yearnings, likes or dislikes, or any harmful thoughts. In this way you will become one with the Dao."

"The Dao," I whispered quietly. "What is the Dao and where will I find it?"

He replied:

> *"Dao is the bottomless cup that need not be filled.*
> *Profound and deep, it is the root of ten thousand things."*

"A bottomless cup?" I asked, perplexed.

He nodded and added:

> *"The doorway to wonder."*

"How will I find it?"

He smiled and said, "There is nothing to seek, nothing to find.

> *The sage travels all day,*
> *And never leaves his supply wagon."*

I was even more perplexed. "He travels yet never leaves?" I inquired, wondering how that could be.

He replied, "Be like the sage. Remember:

> *Dao does nothing,*
> *Yet nothing is left undone."*

Bowing, he made a motion to depart and I asked, "Will you come again to teach me?"

"There won't be a need. She will be your companion." He looked up at the moon, visible in the day sky. "She is there, waiting for you to call her."

I followed his upward gaze and wondered what he meant. Before I could say another word, I saw him rise and then walk through the wall that enclosed the courtyard and disappear from sight. He left me wondering if I had imagined the whole encounter, but I had the writings as proof of his visit.

From that day onward, in addition to my reading of poetry, I tried to engage in cultivation, but I was more successful at studying Daoism than practicing it. I found my mind impossible to control, and every time I sought to enter inner cultivation, I would reach for some poetry to read. As much as I tried, I was unable to find that inner life or understand the mysterious words of the sage who had visited me. Three times I sent a request to my lord asking that I be allowed to enter a Daoist nunnery and three times I was refused. Remembering the priest's words, I accepted this with no anger or hatred in my heart. My small abode was my nunnery. What need was there for anything else?

One evening, I stepped out into the courtyard and recalled how the priest had pointed to the moon. *What had he meant?* I wondered. *Surely, he was not referring to the physical moon.* Although I had been reciting poetry to the moon, I didn't imagine that there would be a response. It had been a way to relieve my loneliness. That night I sat for many hours gazing into the dark sky. Night after night drew me there, until one night I found myself talking to some being, a female being who was somehow linked to the moon, as I would talk to a friend. She became my companion. It was a one-way conversation, but I didn't mind; I imagined her listening and responding to my every word.

The years passed and I continued this exercise. Then one night when I was seated outside, looking up into the expanse of sky, I saw her emerge from that round rock body we know as the moon. She descended, and for the first time I heard her voice, a musical tone that carried me into a peaceful and loving state of being. The love that she embodied filled me, and I felt it expand beyond the confines of my body. I rested in this elevated state throughout the night and, when daybreak came, I knew that she was with me and I would ever be with her.

I lived in that small abode for twenty years. One day a distraught Biyu arrived to convey that our lord had been brutally murdered while in the middle of a sexual act. Nobody knew who had done it, but there were many accusations and there was much chaos in the palace.

"What will happen to you, Biyu?"

"I am not worried. I will be given to one of the other princes, but this is your chance to escape. Take advantage of this opportunity while nobody is noticing."

That night I found my door unlocked with no guard there and I simply walked away.

"Now you have a complete picture." Shifu's gentle voice brought me back to the present. Where shame and humiliation had engulfed me, a deep sense of peace now took its place. If I had to undergo years of torment at the hands of that man in order to find the goddess, it was a sacrifice I was more than willing to make. "Now you understand. It was your efforts in that life that led you here, that led you to the life you now have. Every one of us must make sacrifices to attain spiritual treasures, and if we are crushed by the hardships that we endure, then we are not ready to progress. That is why the Dao teaches us to flow with whatever comes: whether the currents of life carry us this way or that way should be of no concern."

She leaned forward and spoke quietly. "You learned, in that life, one of the essential teachings of the Dao: to attune oneself with the Dao is to attune oneself with the currents of love that sustain the universe. There is no difference between that love and the Dao. They are one and the same, but not many know this." I was speechless, as I was not yet able to comprehend all that she was saying. My mind was still lingering on the past that I had seen. "Although you had the vision of the moon goddess, it was not the depth of your cultivation that brought this, but your devotion to her. You were not able to advance much in cultivation in that life, and that is why you are with me now, to learn to go deeper. But she became your friend and she responded to your years of devotion."

I was still unable to speak, and we sat for some time in silence. "You have a question. Ask it."

"Shifu, what happened after I left my confinement? Did I find that Daoist sage again?"

She shook her head. "You wandered here and there for a while and finally ended up in a Daoist nunnery. You died shortly after that. This is why in your younger years the thought of entering a nunnery keep coming to you. It was where you last died."

"What happened to the poet, Shifu? It was my fault that his poems were burned and he was banished." A shadow of pain flickered across my face.

She took my hands in hers and looked directly into my eyes. She said firmly, "That was not your doing. That was his own karma. I can go back into his past and find out why, but is that necessary? I don't like to pry unless there is a reason. Your paths crossed briefly, and you served each other's needs at that moment. Perhaps he also needed banishment for his spiritual growth.

197

You must trust the Dao, Shu. There is perfection in all that happens. The universe is continually balancing itself through the law of cause and effect, and that is called justice.

"To understand this universal law is not easy, as there are many hidden facets. If you believe that you caused harm to a poet in one life, you can bring benefit to another in a later life and that will compensate. If you feel you caused harm, you must rectify this in your mind. It doesn't have to be the same soul. Think now about your life. Are you not bringing joy to one of the great poets of our time? Are you not serving the cause of poetry? It is not you but those other two from that time who will bear responsibility for his banishment. You and the poet were both victims."

I nodded. "I understand this, but why did I have to be a concubine, Shifu, a position I so detest?"

"We all have to pass through many different stations in life to have the full human experience and to truly have compassion for others who are now in that position. You will never look at a concubine in the same way again, am I right?"

"That is for sure, Shifu. He was so fat and ugly," I smiled. "I think that was his curse. Everyone used him, thinking he could give them access to political power, but he was powerless, a useless man in a useless court. He was not intelligent, literate, or kind, but was also not the most terrible. He wasn't shrewd enough to cause much harm."

"Sadly, as we speak, the same things are going on today."

"I wonder why I took the life of a concubine?"

"To understand the causes that led you to become a concubine, you will have to go back further, but do you really want to engage in that?"

I vehemently shook my head. "I think I have seen enough."

"For now," she said. "You identify strongly with Meihua because that was your life just previous to this one; you took birth very quickly, so there was little time to submerge those memories. I hope you will be able to release whatever sorrow you have been holding. That is part of living in the Dao, not holding on to anything that comes. That is what is meant by inaction, showing a neutral face to all outer events. As Laozi says:

Do without doing, and all will be peaceful."

After sitting a few more minutes she said, "I think you are now ready to take up your normal duties." I nodded and bowed before her as she took her leave. With her hand on the door, she turned to me and said enigmatically, "Shu, don't seek a gift, but also don't refuse one. Memory of a past birth, although at times painful, is a gift." After she was gone, I realized I had forgotten to ask her not to send me to the cave anymore.

Sitting at my writing table one morning soon after, I tried to capture my memories in verse.

The Abandoned Concubine

Finally I free my hair of its ornaments.
Like withered feathers they fall away.

I put aside my folds of silk
And dress in the leaves of spring.
No longer hiding behind a painted face
Or the smile of sunset.

Unvarnished and naked,
Who will desire the concubine now
Stripped of all that is not me?

The Old Daoist

A poet stirred the life in me.
For this he was banished and I
Cast aside like a wounded doe.

An old Daoist took pity on me
And stepped into my heart.
He saw the songbird in my eyes
And taught me the path of patience.
"Be still," he said,

"And listen to the laughter of the wind.
Be attentive

For the footsteps of joy are approaching."
"How do I find the Dao?" I asked.
He smiled and replied,
"There is nothing to do, nowhere to go
For the Dao has found you."

Many years later, sitting in the courtyard
A small pigeon flew onto my shoulder
And whispered in my ear,
"A mountain has moved.
In your next birth
The songbird will be free."

Waiting

I wait for eternity to pass
For the moon to erase the sun
So I no longer have to stare
Into the cold heart of day.
I yearn to no longer be
But that time does not come.

I watch as gullies line my face,
And my midnight hair turns to snow.
I watch myself grow old
Alone and uncared for.
As slow as an idle stream
That is how time passes.
Oh, when will you come,
Goddess of the Moon?
I have no other friend.

The Moon Goddess

Years passed without the sight of you.
Then in the abandonment of night
I saw you slip from a half moon.
Surrounded by silver light.

You came before me,
From a world the eye can't see.
All my torment, the deceit
In which I lived,

Fled like the quick-footed deer
Disappearing into a forest mist.

It was not your beauty that struck me
But the love you awakened
In this deadened heart,
The love that strings the stars together,
That animates the sun
And floods the skies
Holding the earth in its arms.

I came to know your secret,
Oh Goddess of the Moon.

Chapter Twelve

THE CELESTIAL MASTERS

Eastern Han Dynasty, 2nd Century CE

If I thought that was the end of my time travels, I was sorely mistaken, but I did get a reprieve of a few months. Every so often while performing my tasks, and especially during times of inner cultivation, I would drift back into the past, adding additional memories to my life as Meihua. She was becoming more of a distant figure and I no longer cried over her experiences. Increasingly, I reflected on the latter part of her life, her love for poetry and interest in Daoism, and these memories explained much to me about my current birth. Her desire to live in a Daoist monastery had followed me into my current life, which was why I kept making this threat to my parents. Meihua's father had forced her into a painful relationship and I wasn't about to let that happen again, and thus my resistance to an arranged marriage.

I saw that one life flows into another; interests taken up toward the end of a life are naturally pursued and advanced at the beginning of the next one. This is the flow of the Dao. I was beginning to understand it, and I realized that the revival of my memories was helping me to gain deeper understanding of Daoism. I continued to spend as little time as possible thinking about my first stay in the cave as I still didn't understand what I had experienced. I attributed those visions to Shifu's teaching of Wu Wei, not to the emergence of old memories.

A sense of peace and contentment came over me, and I was beginning to think that the rest of my stay with Shifu would be like this. Two months passed before Ying came to get me one morning saying that Shifu wanted me to return to the cave.

"Today?" I asked hesitantly. She nodded. I was quiet for a few minutes and then asked, "Ying, I know that one must always follow Shifu's directives, but is it possible to . . . to ask that I not be sent there?"

Her eyes softened in understanding. "I know you have had difficult times in the past, but this retreat might be different. It is a rare opportunity. Everyone waits for the moment when Shifu will allow this time of seclusion."

"Everyone but me, I suppose."

"Trust her. She would not send you there if not for a special purpose." I nodded and reluctantly followed her back to the scene of my last visitation from the past.

As we stood before the entrance, Ying counseled me. "You are now settled more deeply in the Dao. The most important thing to remember is to engage in cultivation as much as possible. If you do that, you may have tremendous realizations." I nodded. Then she added, "Shifu wants you to reflect on these words from the Dao De Jing:

Act without acting,
Work without getting involved,
Taste without tasting.

No matter how great or how often,
Repay injury with De."

"I don't understand the concept of De, Ying, but perhaps I will when I emerge from the cave," I replied as I left her, thinking how many times I had read those lines but that I still had not been able to internalize them and act accordingly.

For the first two days, I managed to keep my practice steady, reflecting on the lines as Shifu had instructed, but on the third day I was drawn back again into the river of time long past. Like a vortex sweeping me inside, I could not resist the voices pulling me, the images seeking to burst forth.

I was born during the late *Eastern Han Dynasty* (25 CE-220 CE) into a family of ardent Daoists who were very much inspired by the teachings of the great sage Zhang Daoling, who had been instructed by the blessed Laozi himself, in a vision, to help free the world of falsehood and corruption, which had become endemic. Without a return to virtue, he warned, political and social instability would increase and cause much suffering.

It was true that the countryside around us was filled with poverty and misery, and Zhang Daoling inspired a vision of what we could create together to transform the world into a paradisal one. It was with much hope and passion that a small band of followers left their homes and came to the western province of Sichuan to create a community that would be ruled by Daoist principles, a community of people bonded by their commitment to a common ideal of equality and peace. I was fortunate to grow up in such an environment, where the ideals of the virtuous state were taught.

I was born after Zhang Daoling had already left the world, having mysteriously disappeared at the age of 123 years, leaving his son Zhang Heng and then his grandson Zhang Lu to fulfil his vision. Some say he died, but others say he ascended to heaven on a celestial creature. I chose to believe the latter and was fascinated by him from an early age, eager for any story.

From a small band of followers, a movement grew called the Way of the Celestial Masters, or the Five Pecks of Rice Movement, because to join our community one had to offer five pecks of rice. Our movement continued to expand, and late in my childhood Zhang Lu, who had become the head of our religious community, formed an independent state called *Hanning* (Peace of Han) in the valley of Hanzhong in northern Sichuan.

My parents were active in the formation of Hanning and I, being the youngest of three children, was often left in the care of my maternal grandfather while they busied themselves with the small group of people charged with setting up the structure and laws of the state. After his wife died, my grandfather had become a hermit, living alone in one of the forests of the valley. He was a tall, thin man with grey hair that reached well below his waist, partly knotted up in a rather messy way atop his head. His face was weathered by age, but animating the lines and creases were two bright eyes that sparkled with joy, as if he was always on the brink of laughter. To me, he was a beautiful sight. I never saw a worried or sorrowful expression on his face, and when he spoke there was always significance to his words. The community respected him greatly because as a young man he had known Zhang Daoling and had become his disciple. He was eager to share stories about the old sage with anyone willing to listen.

Often, when I would stay with my grandfather, he would relate magical tales while I rested my head on his lap, and these were among my fondest memories. One time, when I was about eight years old, I was lazily listening to him as I rested my head against his leg, when he suddenly stood up, jolting me. Taking me tightly by the hand, he led me through the skies to a mountaintop, where several bearded men and two elderly women sat in a circle. Stooping down, he placed his finger on his lips to indicate that I should not ask any questions or speak, and then sat me down beside him. The group remained in silence while I rested my head upon his lap and fell asleep. When I awoke, I was in my bed in his small cottage tucked away in the woods.

Quickly I got up to find him. "*Yeye* (grandfather)," I called. He appeared in the doorway.

"What is it, child?'

"I dreamed I flew through the skies with you."

"Where did we go?"

"To a mountaintop."

He smiled enigmatically.

"It seemed so real, Yeye."

"Did it?"

I nodded.

"If it seemed real, then perhaps it was. What is so strange about flying? Sometimes it is the only way to travel."

"Yeye, you are teasing me!"

"Am I?" Again, that enigmatic smile. "Come, I have fixed some food for you." That was the end of our conversation and I assumed that I had dreamed the whole event.

A year or so later, I came down with an illness while staying with him. The medicinal plants that Yeye applied did not bring down the fever. "Some magic is needed," he said mysteriously with a glimmer in his eyes. "Come, I have to take you to a hermit I know. He has the magical medicinal plants we need, but his place is not so close."

"Magical plants?" He nodded. "Will we fly, Yeye?" This was the first time I had mentioned flying since that time of the dream.

He leaned close to me and whispered with a grin, "No, this time I will call my tigress friend and we will ride her, as this hermit lives deeper into the forest, not on a mountaintop."

"Yeye," I protested in a hoarse voice. "You are teasing me."

"Am I? Get ready and we will leave." Stepping outside, he issued a high call. As I followed him, a large tigress approached. I drew back in fear, but he pulled me forward by the hand. "Come, don't be afraid. I know this tigress well and have ridden her many times. She is as swift as time that stops for no one." Lifting me into his arms, he climbed onto the back of the animal and away we sped. Within a short time, we reached the entrance of a cave. The hermit was there to greet us with a handful of plants and a liquid mixture.

"I knew you were coming, so I made this medicine," he said. "Here are extra plants. Feed them to her for three days and she will recover." As we rode back on the tigress, I fell asleep, and sometime later I woke up in my bed.

In my feverish state I stared at Yeye, who was waiting for me to drink a liquid medicine. "Take this and you will soon feel better."

"Yeye," I whispered. "Did we really ride a tigress?"

"If that is what you saw, then that is what we did," he responded with a small smile. "But a fever can cause one to see many things."

I was too sick to ask any more questions. After I recovered, I asked Yeye why I had taken ill. In our way of thinking, it was wrong thoughts or behavior that brought illness. He replied that fever is a form of purification. "Your body was burning impurities. If you were older, I would tell you to fast for three days, but you are still too young for that and you have hardly eaten these last days." Then in his teasing manner he added, "But perhaps it was your doubts that brought this illness."

"Doubts?"

"Hmm," he responded. "Do you have any doubts?" I shook my head. "Good, then that is why the illness fled so quickly."

My grandfather's cottage was a magical place, and many of the stories he told me were of fantastical creatures, dragons and phoenixes and the like. One day I asked him if he had ever ridden a phoenix.

"Of course, many times. Would you like to ride one?" I shook my head. I could never tell whether Yeye was serious or teasing.

"But one day, Yeye, when I get older, perhaps then I will ride a phoenix. Of all the creatures, that is the one I like the most. They are strong and beautiful and can take me up high in the sky, higher than a mountain."

Leaning close to me, he replied, "I will make sure that you ride one."

"Yeye, you are teasing me again!"

"Why do you say that, Chunhua?"

"There are no such things as phoenixes. I know they are imaginary beasts."

"Really?"

I nodded.

"If you would like to see one now, I can beckon it."

"Yeye, why are you never serious?"

"Hmm," was his reply.

One day when I was a little older and beginning to take an interest in mystical matters, I asked him to tell me a story about his teacher Zhang Daoling.

"Zhang Daoling," he began, "was a rare man. One day when he was sitting in cultivation on a remote mountain, a goddess appeared to him and said she would show him the celestial world." I drew closer so that I would not miss a word he spoke. "He had already had glimpses in dreams and visions, but he wanted to see that world up close. He thanked her and, before he knew it, he was in a place of such beauty, such harmony, in the presence of such loving beings full of virtuous qualities, that he didn't want to return to earth. His visit was meant to be brief because one cannot stay in the celestial world for long while in a human body, but he didn't want to leave. The goddess saw his reluctance. She showed him the misery on earth—people without food, with disease, losing loved ones, corruption, greed—all the causes of suffering. His heart was moved, and she gave him a choice: 'You can leave your body, die right now and remain here, or you can return and try to bring this vision to earth, but you must know that you won't succeed, because humanity is not ready.'" My grandfather paused and looked at me. "Do you know what he chose?"

"Is that when he died and was taken to the celestial world?"

"He didn't hesitate for a moment. He told the goddess to bring him back to the human world so that he could implant the seed of a more virtuous world, a higher reality. Even if he didn't see that seed come to flower, he would know that he had done his part. He opened his eyes and found himself sitting alone on the mountaintop."

"He came back here for us?"

"For all of humanity. He lived another fifty years, trying to show people how to live in harmony with the Dao. He thought that if he could create a society where virtue ruled, this would be a model for the rest of the world. He knew his vision would not be fulfilled, but he also knew that he was planting a seed. Earth is not the celestial world and will not become like one, but we can cultivate a little more virtue, a little more goodness so that we come somewhat closer to the heavenly worlds."

"But Yeye, his vision did come to fruition. Isn't Hanning the fulfillment of that?"

An almost scornful laugh escaped his lips. Without answering my question, he rose and started to prepare some food. As I had grown older, my grandfather had left enough hints for me to understand his dissatisfaction with the way our state was governed, but he never openly criticized. During my youth I hardly paid attention to the forming of our independent state of Hanning, although I knew it was a religious state and that our religious leader was Zhang Lu, the grandson of Zhang Daoling. I came to realize that my grandfather felt Zhang Lu had not understood, or for some other reason had departed from, the teachings of his grandfather.

Once I questioned him about Zhang Lu and he replied, "Zhang Lu is a warlord and formed this state based on military victory. While he has done many good things, his ideas are far from the ideals I learned under his grandfather." When I asked him what he meant, he added, "To achieve victory, he allied with and later killed a powerful shaman named Zhang Xiu, then integrated his followers into Hanning. I am afraid they have brought some of their practices with them, which to my mind deviate from the way of the Dao." His words had great impact on me, as there was no one I trusted more than him, so I began to look more critically at the society we were forming.

My parents knew of my grandfather's attitude and were afraid it would spill over to me, and when I reached a certain age, they stopped sending me to spend days and weeks with him. This was a crushing disappointment, as I greatly missed the world he lived in, one filled with joy and supernatural events, lots of laughter, and stories. My parents were strong supporters of Zhang Lu, as was the husband they chose for me. I spent much time in my early adult years internally debating what I had learned from my grandfather and what I had been taught by my parents. Having been immersed in the movement my whole life, I knew no other reality and could not compare our enclosed community with the outside world.

My parents had taught me that poverty, corruption, power struggles and violence pervaded society and that we, who were able to escape that lot, were a chosen elite. Our mission was to spread our ideals throughout the whole empire and thus transform society. They had also taught me that the imperial authority, the Eastern Han Dynasty, was challenging the Daoist communities and that for our very survival we had to isolate ourselves and live by Daoist principles alone, guided by the one chosen for us, Zhang Lu.

When Zhang Lu established our independent state, he sought to set new laws for our community, leniency for those who transgressed the laws, free places to stay and free food for travelers, the end of animal sacrifices, no alcohol, new religious rituals, and healing by faith.

When I brought up these points to my grandfather, he quietly acknowledged these good laws, but then asked if the name of our state was Hanning (Peace of Han), why did we use military force and amass large armies? And why was our leader also a warlord? He would shake his head and say, "This is not what I learned from Zhang Daoling."

From the beginning Yeye opposed my marriage. I knew it was because of my prospective husband's family's association with the shaman leader Zhang Xiu, but my parents overruled his objections and the marriage took place. My feelings for my husband Wang Wei were not ones of affection and love but rather of respect, due to what I believed was his commitment to the ideals of Hanning.

Wang Wei was an average-looking man, with nothing special about his appearance. He was slender, dressed meticulously, and believed that demeanor mattered a great deal, so he was careful about his words and courteous, but there was a certain coldness in his manner, a disconnection. His face ordinarily wore a solemn expression and rarely did I see him smile. When Wei looked at me, I felt he was seeing through me, a feeling that often made me uncomfortable, and so I would turn my eyes away. His was an imposing presence and I was somewhat intimidated by his knowing airs and his pride over what he saw as his achievements. I had married a man who spent much time in cultivation, often throughout the night, and soon I also be came proud of his endeavors, as I had not nearly the abilities that he had, but this did not ease the strain in our relationship.

The values that I had imbibed from my grandfather were very much about living a life of simplicity as an integral part of the natural world and the cycles of nature, and practicing inner cultivation to help safeguard against the negative influences that disturbed the flow of life and created diseases and other forms of suffering. My parents were more concerned with the nature of governance and would often point out to me that we were not under any imperial authority and lived with far greater equality than people elsewhere in the vast Han Empire. I soon noticed, however, that those who showed greater interest in military matters were gaining more prominence in the state. My husband Wei was such a one.

My grandfather judged Hanning according to the ideals set forth by his teacher, but for others the important thing was the military strength that would enable us to maintain our independence. For this purpose, the state gave each of us a number of what it called "divine generals" to fight off what they called "wandering demons," the kind that brought misfortune and illness. When one of us turned six years old, we received our first general, and with the advance of age we gained more generals and a higher ranking. Marriage would unite two sets of generals, giving a couple a rather large army. After marriage, religious practice and merit would yield further increases in ranking. Several years into my marriage I realized that my husband's intent and ambition was to build his own formidable army.

I came to realize that Wei's inner cultivation was not for the purpose of bringing him into harmony with the Dao or to increase his virtue, but rather to bring him greater ranking, more divine generals, an increase in stature and power. This brought me great distress as it was opposed to the ideals I had learned from my grandfather, who always taught me to be wary of the stealthy rise of ambition. By the time I realized this, I already had two children and felt trapped between loyalty to my husband and loyalty to the ideals of my grandfather. I dealt with this contradiction by trying to suppress my uneasiness and even suspicions, and for a while this worked.

A number of years after the birth of my second child, I was awakened in the middle of the night by my crying son. After putting him back to sleep, I heard murmurings, quiet conversation, and so I went to check on Wei, who was practicing inner cultivation in another room. The door was bolted shut, but I stood there and tried to hear what was being said, wondering who he could be speaking with so late at night. Between pleading words and stern replies, I heard bits of a conversation, mention of a border village and the creation of an incursion. I was baffled because there was nobody else in the house. Our two servants lived in a building adjacent to ours. I quietly crept back to bed and waited for Wei, but he didn't return to our room that night.

A few days later, Wei told me he was going to take our generals to a border village as he had a hunch there would soon be an incursion there. I nodded and waited anxiously for his return. They were successful and repelled the invasion, and Zhang Lu awarded my husband a higher ranking and more generals. When I asked who had incited the incursion, he didn't answer.

Uneasy inside, I began to keep closer watch on Wei. A few weeks later, I heard a similar conversation in the quiet of the night, and then there was another incursion and another rescue. Taking aside one of the generals who had come with me at the time of marriage, I asked who was causing the conflict. "Did you see anyone? What did they look like?"

"They appeared in the dark of night, with covered faces, and we couldn't tell to which tribe or army they belonged."

"Please keep careful watch and let me know in the future, and don't tell Wei of my concern. I wouldn't want him to know of my worries." Soon after that, things returned to normal and I began to forget the strange night-time happenings. But then another incident occurred that made me suspect my husband was working with spirits, something only advanced cultivators were able to do. I overheard another conversation in which Wei asked what-ever spirit he was speaking with if he could spread a disease in one of the villages. I heard the affirmation, sending waves of anxiety through me. Sure enough, a disease began to spread through one of the villages and Wei was able to find the medicinal plants to cure the disease, although not before several people died. Again, his status and prestige grew.

This is getting serious, I said to myself. *People are dying.* The only per-son I could seek counsel from was my grandfather, who I had not visited in over a year. I hesitated to involve him, as I had no proof, no witness, only whisperings overheard in the shadows of the night.

It was after I was awakened by a foul smell one night that I decided to act. In the morning I went outside to trace the origin of the smell; it led to a fire pit behind our cottage where I clearly found the remains of an animal. I hurried back into the house when I found Wei looking for me.

"Where were you?" he asked harshly.

"Getting a horse ready," I replied in an unsteady voice. "I fear some-thing is wrong with Yeye and I must go bring him some food today."

"Why all of a sudden? You haven't visited your grandfather in a long time."

"I have a feeling. He is old and out there in the forest . . ." I hurried from the room and went to the kitchen area to pack some food. Then I took off alone on horseback for the hour's ride into the valley's forest. When I reached my grandfather's small cottage, he was outside and appeared to be expecting me. I quickly alighted from the horse.

"My favorite granddaughter has finally come for a visit," he called with a broad smile.

"Yeye, I am your only granddaughter," I reminded him, giving him a warm hug.

"I should reprimand you, Chunhua, for staying away for so long, but I know you have your children to look after. Now tell me, this is not a casual visit, is it?" I shook my head. "Come, let me make you some tea."

"I brought you some food I have cooked myself," I said as we entered his cottage and I lay a package of cooked goods on the table.

"You should not spend your time cooking for me. Yu Yan takes care of all of that." Yu Yan was a disciple of my grandfather's, about my mother's age, who lived alone in a nearby cottage. She had served him faithfully for many years and so my mother looked at her more as a servant than a student, but since childhood I had come to respect her greatly for her advanced cultivation practices.

"Yu Yan works hard for you and deserves a little time off," I replied playfully.

"Now tell me what is wrong. Although you have hardly come to visit these last few years, I can still read the expressions on your face as clearly as when you were a small child."

I turned serious. "It is my husband. For many, many months now I have heard him speaking to some entity at night when he is supposedly engaged in inner cultivation. He bolts the door to the room so I can't enter, but I hear him talking as if another person is there, and then shortly afterwards terrible things happen, border incursions, disease, and then miraculously he solves the problem and advances in his ranking. I don't know who to go to about this, Yeye."

"You suspect him of sorcery?"

I had not allowed myself to even think that word, but as Yeye spoke it, I spontaneously nodded my head. "And there is another thing. A few nights ago, I smelled something foul. The next morning behind our cottage I found a fire pit and the remains of an animal." I lowered my trembling voice although there was nobody else in the room. "Yeye, I think he is performing animal sacrifices. When I think back over the last few weeks, I realize I had smelled that awful thing before, numerous times. Only last night, it was much stronger."

My grandfather drew back in surprise. "That is forbidden here, against the law, one of the few good things Zhang Lu has done." His voice had become serious. "You must report this, or it could have adverse effects on the whole community." I didn't respond, and he began to ruminate. "From the moment I met him, I saw that something was amiss, that his spirit was susceptible to negative influences, that his cultivation was not genuine, but your parents would not listen. They were impressed by his outer achievements and paid no heed to his inner weaknesses. Without that inner purity, what can we achieve in Hanning? How are we different from the rest of the world? We pride ourselves on adhering to the principles of the Dao, but then we allow our young ones to go astray." He shook his head. "I am afraid you will have to report this."

"But I have no proof." I was quiet for a few minutes and then asked in disbelief, "Yeye, are there really such things as demons?"

He smiled. "That is not something you have to worry about. There are many worlds and many types of beings. Most likely your husband believes his powers to be greater than they are and is summoning up lower spirits. He should be worrying about the demons in his own heart—his arrogance and desire for power— instead of fooling around with entities about which he knows nothing."

I then related to Yeye what I had overheard in the late-night conversations. He grew thoughtful and didn't respond right away. Finally he said, "I wish I could take you away from him, but you now have two children and it won't be so easy."

"I'm afraid of him, Yeye. It feels like some entity has entered him. One minute he is fine, his old self, but at other times, I see something in his eyes that scares me. He becomes totally detached in an eerie way, as if he doesn't see or hear me. He looks at me with a blank expression, without any emotion, any kindness, any . . ." my voice began to crack and Yeye drew me to him. "I can't control my fear," I said in a quivering voice.

"That is your challenge, to overcome your fear. You are not doing enough inner cultivation."

"I feel that if I say the wrong thing, he could harm me. If he finds out I have been listening, spying on him . . ."

He replied hesitantly. "I don't believe he would harm the children."

"I also don't think he would, but if he feels that I am a threat, I don't know what he is capable of doing. He watches my every move. I had to make an excuse to come here, and I know he will make me pay for this visit. He has become vindictive, angry, capable of I don't know what."

"Let us walk among the trees and listen. It will calm you. We can learn so much from nature, which has a way of balancing herself, something we all need to learn. The forest air is good for nurturing the qi." He led me outside and, picking up a walking stick that rested by the front door, he moved in a slow gait down a narrow path until he found a slight opening and a downed log where we could rest. Setting aside his walking stick, he sat on the log and motioned me to sit beside him.

We were both quiet for a while and then he asked, "Do you remember what I used to say to you when we would come here?"

I smiled. "You would quote Sage Laozi: *Nature's words are few*, and then you would add 'yet Nature has so much wisdom.'"

"I am glad you remember. Let's listen to Nature."

We again fell into silence. After a few minutes, I heard the flutter of bird wings and, looking up, saw a small family of birds flying overhead.

"What do we learn from the birds?" he asked very quietly, as if not to disturb the stillness of the forest any more than necessary. He was questioning me as he had when I was child.

I was silent for a few moments and then replied, "Freedom. From the birds we can learn how to be free."

He nodded. "And from which animal do we learn to be fearless?"

"From the tigers," I replied automatically, as I had so many times when I was a child.

"They are fierce and fearless. We must at times be like them. What do we learn from the deer?"

"To be circumspect."

"And from the trees?"

"Inner strength and patience."

He smiled. "You have learned well. Is anyone more patient than a tree?" I shook my head. "What do we learn from the snakes?"

"Fear," I replied immediately.

He chuckled. "You have always responded like that, and what is the answer I have always told you?"

"Intelligence," I said quickly. "But I have never understood that, Yeye."

"There was an ancient species called the nagas. They were a very intelligent kind of being, living in a different world. They could cross into our world and disguise themselves in a serpent form, but we could not cross into theirs. Most of them were benevolent, but there were some who were greedy and ambitious, like some people in the human world. Eventually these greedy ones gained power and the door into our world had to be closed so they wouldn't disrupt human life. The higher ones of the nagas closed that door and then fled to another place, where they now live. We are left with these poor relatives who don't have their level of intelligence, but when I see them, I think of their ancestors. Now tell me, what do we learn from the small forest creatures?"

I was thoughtful. "I don't know, Yeye. What do they teach us?"

"To be carefree. They are the food for the larger creatures, and yet they scamper around the forest floor as if they have no worry in the world. That is how we are meant to be. All these creatures live in harmony with the Dao; it is only we humans who try to impose our own will on the natural way of things. You must learn to be free, fearless, strong, patient, intelligent, and carefree, and fierce when necessary. That is what the animals teach us and that is the way of the Dao. Which animal teaches us kindness, compassion?"

"I don't know."

"The wounded ones. They serve a purpose, too. Who can see a wounded animal and not feel care for that being?"

"I feel like a child again, Yeye. How often did you bring me here when I was young and try to teach me how to become one with the natural world!"

"All of our problems can be solved by simply observing and listening. Listening is the key."

"What are you trying to tell me, Yeye? That I should not interfere with Wei, that I should simply observe him?"

"What does the Dao teach? To act without acting. Your husband will do what he will do, and you must act according to your inner guidance, without being moved internally. He has transgressed at least one of the laws of our state, animal sacrifice, and that cannot continue, but you must not be fearful of the consequences of reporting it. This is the time for you to be fierce in your adherence to the Dao, to the ideals of virtue."

"What consequences could there be?" I asked hesitantly.

"It might incite his anger. But you don't have to accuse him. Report that you suspect an animal sacrifice was committed behind your cottage and request an investigation." I wondered if I had the courage to do this and didn't respond. "Let us sit here in cultivation for a while. Breathe in the pure forest air and hold it in your chest, then slowly breathe it out as you feel the qi rise to your forehead. This will give you inner strength and help ease your fear."

We sat for some time in silence. Every now and then I would open my eyes and find Yeye settled deep within his own being. Then, closing my eyes, I would try again to follow his instructions, but without much success. Finally, he opened his eyes and indicated it was time for us to return. I stayed with my grandfather for the rest of the day and before I left, he gave me a piece of paper with a name written on it.

"If you decide to report the sacrifice, this is the man to approach. If you are unable to come forth openly, you can always send an anonymous message to him. I am sure he will send somebody to check on the matter." Before leaving, Yeye asked that I find some excuse to bring my husband to him so that he could see for himself what was amiss. "Remember, my dear, if you are strong inside and of pure intent, no human or demon can harm you. The Dao is the ultimate protection."

It took me a few days to gather the nerve to send an anonymous message to the official my grandfather had indicated. A few days later, two men came to inspect the land behind our cottage, but they found nothing. All evidence of an outdoor fire and sacrifice had been removed, but I was sure that Wei now suspected me of betraying him. His attitude toward me seemed to grow more hostile after that.

It was not an easy task to convince Wei to visit my grandfather. He tried every excuse but finally when I mentioned that it would be an insult to refuse, he consented. After a few pleasantries Yeye congratulated him on his success in fending off the incursions and curing the disease that had plagued a village. Then he went on to say that perhaps we should stop the practice of growing our military and granting more generals as it was causing a sense of competition among the younger men.

"It is one of the reasons for our success," insisted Wei. "The dangers are growing. I don't mean to be disrespectful, but perhaps you don't realize the external dangers facing our state. The warlord Cao Cao is growing in power, now nearly controlling the Han central government."

"The dangers I see are internal ones," replied my grandfather curtly. "As the great Laozi said:

Use the Dao to assist the lords of people,
But don't use military force

For there will be retribution.
When armies camp thorns grow.
After armies leave, the harvest is poor."

"That was a different time, long ago. The Dao must adapt," replied my husband.

"The Dao that must adapt is not the Dao," said my grandfather sternly. My husband ignored this remark and went on to brag about his victory in pushing back the recent incursions. "I wonder who or what is causing these incursions," responded Yeye wryly. "A state only falls when it is weak internally. It is not an army that offers the true protection, but the virtue of the people."

"You are a respected elder in our community, but you have been hidden away for so long in this forest that you may not be aware of our current situation. Virtue is fine in an ideal world, but we live in a world where might rules."

"What was the purpose of Zhang Daoling's efforts then? If we are no different than the other states and kingdoms, why go through the effort of creating a new society based on the principles of the Dao? Might lies in the ability to be in balance with universal laws, not laws manufactured by humans. I thought that was the whole purpose of forming an independent state, and if that vision no longer applies, we might as well assimilate into the other kingdoms." My grandfather's message was clear and firm, and yet when I saw my husband's reaction, I became agitated. He sat there coldly glaring at Yeye as if his words had no import.

"You are upsetting Chunhua by such talk," he replied. "Let's not discuss matters of state."

My grandfather changed the subject. "There's a man I used to know by the name of Li Quiang. Have you heard of him?"

Wei shifted uncomfortably in his seat. "Why do you ask?" I looked over at my husband and saw the strange look that came over him. Without waiting for an answer, he hurriedly replied, "I don't know anything about him," as he rose and indicated to me that it was time to leave.

Unsettled by this visit, I went alone a few days later to visit my grandfather and asked who this Li Quiang was. He refused to answer at first but when I continued to press him, he finally responded. "I knew him years ago during the time of Zhang Daoling. He had a dispute with my teacher, and it was not clear whether he was asked to leave or left on his accord, but I had the feeling that in his anger he would try to destroy Zhang Daoling's vision. I heard that he then went to study with a shaman who was also a sorcerer. That was many years ago. Recently I learned that some of the younger people here had contact with one of his most advanced students who claimed Li Quiang had been unfairly treated when he left the community. I believe your husband is one of those people, and if that is the case, he would have learned methods of summoning up unwanted forces."

I looked sullenly at my grandfather. "Then I have to make a choice, to take my children and run away, or . . . or . . . I don't know what. How can I leave my children with him?"

"I would go to Zhang Lu, but frankly I don't trust him. He has also developed a military mind. The best of the disciples of Zhang Daoling are now hermits, hidden away or wandering from here to there. They want no part in governance because they see the failing of Zhang Lu's efforts. Perhaps it is not his fault alone, perhaps it is the times in which we live. I am sure the intentions of Zhang Lu are good, but humanity may not yet be ready for the creation of an ideal state founded on the principles of the Dao, not at this time, not in this place. I will go visit some of my hermit friends and see what they advise."

"Yeye, I don't want you to travel far," I protested.

"I will not go by foot," he laughed and then with a twinkle in his eyes added, "but I can traverse the skies or call upon my tigress friend." I smiled. It had been a long time since he had teased me in this manner. "Come see me in a week and I will know whether I have been successful. In the meantime, try not to be so fearful. You are protected, my dear. I have placed the celestial masters around you."

The days passed slowly as my husband now kept a close eye on me, questioning my every move, and his distrust was turning into a meanness that truly hurt. After putting the children to sleep at night, I would also feign sleep, while he would go into another room for solitude and cultivation. I would lie awake, listening for any sounds. For the first few days after my return from visiting Yeye, I heard nothing and began to feel relief. Then one night I heard sounds again, and quietly approaching the room where he was,

I found the door unbolted. Gently pushing it open, I peered in and I saw my husband speaking as if somebody were there, as if engaged in a full conversation, although nobody else was present. A voice was answering him, coming through his mouth but speaking in another tone. I stood in the doorway wondering what to do, when suddenly he turned around and saw me. It was my husband's body standing there, but there was another entity as well. I saw it in his eyes, which were not the eyes of my husband. They were cold and distant and frightening, sparking a fury that I had never seen before.

"Get out!" he screamed. "Get out!"

I ran from the room, slamming the door behind me and took refuge in the bed of my son, hugging him as tightly as I could. The next morning, I was afraid to meet Wei and so busied myself with the children. I made sure to keep one of the servants with me at all times. When he finally came to me mid-morning, he appeared as if nothing was wrong.

In the early afternoon, he went out. I was determined to get into his cultivation room to see if I could find any evidence of sorcery. As usual, the door was locked. Going around to the back of the cottage I pried open the lone window to the room and climbed in. I looked around but could find nothing suspicious. As I was about to leave, my eyes caught a rather odd-looking stone resting on a table; it seemed to glow with minerals or gems. As I drew closer, I felt a strong energy coming from it. I thought I should bring it to Yeye, so I grabbed the stone and quickly climbed back out of the window and, slipping it in a pouch, hid it in the basket of food I was preparing. I decided to leave for my grandfather's cottage right away before my husband returned. After leaving a message with one of the servants that I was taking the children to visit my mother, we quickly left.

I could only manage to secure one horse, and the children and I piled on it together to make our way to Yeye's cottage. They were eager to meet him after a long absence, as they loved his stories as much as I did. When we arrived, Yeye had just returned from visiting one of his hermit friends. When he saw that the children were with me, he didn't say a word about my husband. Greeting the children, he engaged in some play with them, and only when he had seen them off to bed did he speak with me about the situation.

"He will come looking for me soon. I left a message that I was going to my mother, but he will find out that I am not there and will come here. I don't know what I will do."

"After you left here, I decided to go see Zhang Lu to listen to him. It is a difficult situation because your husband is very well regarded. After all, he has countered numerous border incursions, seemingly cured an epidemic, and now controls a sizable army."

"Some force inhabits him. I am now certain of that. Surely there must be a way to rid him of that entity."

"Yes, there are rituals we can perform, but he must be willing. In our system the first step is confession, acknowledgement of what has taken place, and then time spent in true inner cultivation. Zhang Lu was very hesitant to take any action. He offered to speak with your husband, but then he will know that I have issued a complaint against him and I fear he will take this out on you. So, I told him to be cautious but to investigate if he can. You and the children can stay here with me for the time being."

"Yeye, I am too tired to think clearly."

"Go rest, Chunhua. I also visited a distant hermit friend, and tomorrow we will go see the one in the cave deeper in the forest. He may have some wise counsel."

"The hermit who once cured me when I was young?"

"You remember him?"

I nodded and smiled. "We rode on a tigress to his cave. How will we go this time?" I never actually believed that I rode on a tigress or flew in the

226

skies, but always thought these were sweet dreams that came to me in the home of my beloved Yeye.

My grandfather's eyes sparkled with delight. "It is time for your children also to learn to ride the tigress." That is what I loved about Yeye. The real and imagined worlds were ever one in his mind.

We didn't ride the tigress, but somehow Yeye managed to manifest two horses for us, in addition to the horse that had carried me and my children from our home. That was as much of a miracle. My grandfather never possessed any animals as he was opposed to the very idea, but they seemed to respond to his call or his need, and when I awoke the next morning, the horses were waiting patiently by the back door.

Turning to my children, he advised them, "Now observe the horses carefully. Listen as they carry us on our journey so you can tell me what you learn from them."

"I already know the answer," replied my daughter, the older of my two children. "From the horses, we learn to be swift, to have a sharp mind, and to make the right decisions in keeping with the Dao." My grandfather turned to me and I could see that he was impressed by this answer. From him, I had learned to help my children feel close to animal life, as if we and the animals were all one family, because in truth we were. The children were pleased to go on an adventure, and when we arrived at the hermit's cave, there were many nooks and crannies for them to explore, as well as many small animals, and a variety of birds for them to observe and enjoy. While they were engaged, my grandfather explained the situation to his friend.

"I can put a protection around you," the hermit told me, "so whatever entity is using your husband will not be able to approach you."

"I have done that," responded Yeye. "That will protect my granddaughter but not Hanning, not the state."

"Ah, Hanning," replied the hermit solemnly to my grandfather. "It is already gone. What is there to protect?"

As they were speaking, I suddenly remembered the stone I had brought. I had not wanted to show it to my grandfather in front of the children, but they were now busy. Taking it out of the pouch I had with me, I showed it to them. "Before leaving my home, I entered the room my husband uses for cultivation and found this. It seemed to emit a strange energy and so I brought it for you to see." I handed the stone to my grandfather.

The two of them looked at each other in a strange way and then went off into the forest. They were gone a few hours before they returned. I told Yeye that the children were restless and asked if we might return to his cottage. Taking me aside, he said, "I will perform a stronger protection ritual for you, Chunhua, before you leave tomorrow. You will need to go home for some time, while we think this through, but you have nothing to fear now, the stone has been broken and buried. It was a portal your husband used to engage with the lower spirit entities.

By the time we reached the cottage, my father and husband were already there, impatiently waiting for us. At the sight of my husband, fear once again possessed me. I watched as my son ran eagerly to greet the father he thought he knew, but my daughter clung to me as if she felt something was amiss. My own father took me aside and, unwrapping my child's arms from my waist and sending her to her father, he chided me in private. "You have always had a wild imagination, dreaming up all kinds of fanciful tales about your time with your grandfather, but whatever has possessed you to make up damaging stories about your husband? You know it is a serious offense, Chunhua, to accuse anyone falsely, let alone one's husband. But our laws are lenient. If you confess your error, you will only need to spend time in the Chamber of Silence, perform some community service, and then all will be fine. I promised your mother and brothers that I would bring you back."

I looked at my father blankly in disbelief. He had turned the tables on me and now I was being accused, not Wei. I wondered what and how much he knew, and to what extent my husband was aware of my feelings. I glanced at my grandfather pleadingly, who, sensing the course of our conversation, came over to us and spoke quietly to my father. "You take the children home and let them stay with you and my daughter. I will keep Chunhua here for a little while longer, until this whole thing can be straightened out, but ask my daughter to come visit me alone. I want to speak with her." There was much back and forth, but my grandfather held firm, and because of the respect he commanded they could not counter him.

Before departing, my husband came to me. Casting my face downward so I wouldn't have to see the fire in his eyes, I heard his whispered words biting the air between us as he tightly gripped my arm. "Give me back that stone." It was then I realized that I had forgotten to close the window that I had climbed through.

"I don't know what you are talking about," I whispered, as fear overcame me.

"You have imagined all of this, creating a scene and disturbing the peace of our home. Admit your mistake and return with that stone if you want to see your children again." I tried to free myself from his grasp but couldn't. Raising my eyes to his, I said fearfully, "Let go of me. You are possessed by dark spirits. You have become a sorcerer!"

Instead of releasing me, he tightened and twisted his grip so much that I thought my arm might break. It was not until my grandfather came over that he let go, and as he did, a feeling of terror crept over me like an ominous cloud. As they mounted the horses, my daughter cried out to me, but I stood aside helplessly as they rode away. Once they were gone, I gripped in pain the arm that had been badly bruised, and tears flooded my face.

Chapter Thirteen

THE END OF AN IDEAL

My heart felt as if it would burst, such was the pressure building in my chest and I could not help but cry out.

"Shu . . . Shu." Faintly I heard a voice calling as if from a distant place, but I didn't respond. Again, this time slightly louder and more commanding, I heard, "Shu, open your eyes." Slowly my eyes unlocked, and I looked around in confusion. Where was I?

"Shifu?" I whispered. "Have you come to Hanning?" My teacher was seated before me in the cave. I looked around. "Where is Yeye?" At that moment, there was no distinction between the past and the present. Time flowed in a confusing fusion.

"We are not in Hanning," she replied firmly. "We are in the cave on Lushan Mountain. You are Shu, here with me. What you saw happened long ago. You have again visited the past."

The image of my sorcerer husband was as real as if he were standing before me, and the feeling of his presence still lingered, refusing to depart. "Shifu, he will come for me," I said in a frightened voice. "Where can I hide?"

Placing her hands on my shoulders she gently shook me. "Come back to the present moment. Your actions have long ago been decided. Whatever was to be done, has already been done. You can change nothing now. Try to understand what you are seeing and why. Shu . . ." I felt her grip relax, but I could no longer follow what she was saying as her voice began to drift into the distance. I could not keep my eyes from shutting as I surrendered to the memories that beckoned me back.

As soon as my father and husband left, I ran into the other room of the cottage, sank down onto the floor, and hid my face in my hands in the attempt to hide the emotions that had overwhelmed me. My grandfather hobbled over and sat beside me, then pressed my head against his shoulder as he had done so many times during my childhood. "It's okay to cry, child, but I don't want you to be consumed by fear. Fear is not the way of the Dao. We must face all trials with an inner strength, an even mind."

Slowly my sobs subsided, and I looked up at him inquiringly. "Yeye, my father said I imagined it all. He said I have a vivid imagination. Perhaps it is true. Perhaps as I once imagined that we flew through the skies and that we rode a tigress . . . perhaps this too is all my imagination."

He smiled. "That was not your imagination, child. We really did fly through the sky and you really did ride a tigress when you were young and ill. Why do you think those things did not happen?"

For a moment I thought he was teasing again in an effort to bring a smile to my face. "You are not being serious, Yeye."

"I am being most serious. You have assumed that those things did not happen, and I allowed you to believe that, but I do not want you to doubt yourself. When you were a child, Zhang Daoling beckoned me for an important matter. I had no other means of traveling there and brought you with me the only way I knew how. This is not such an amazing feat for a follower of the Dao. And it was the same with the tigress. You thought those travels were dreams and I didn't dispute you because I didn't want your parents, who have little understanding of these matters, to grow concerned and keep you from me. Eventually they did that anyhow."

"Yeye, they believe I imagined the whole thing about Wei, but I didn't imagine what I saw in his eyes, and I didn't make up about the animal sacrifices." I paused and then added, "It was the stone he wanted. That is why he came after me. What was so special about this stone that made him so desperate to retrieve it?"

He chuckled. "I am not surprised that he is so eager to get that stone back, but it is gone and won't be found again. Without it, I doubt your husband will have the power he craves. I suspect he will do anything to get it back and so it won't be safe for you to return there."

"I can't even go to my parents as they don't believe me."

"I'm not surprised that your father is siding with Wei. He is impressed with the outer garb more than with what lies within." He shook his head. "Let me reflect on the situation and see what the best course of action is. This is no longer about you and your husband, my dear. There are implications for all of Hanning."

"What do you mean?" I asked, momentarily forgetting my own grief. He got up and started to walk away but I grabbed onto his hand. "Yeye, please explain what you just said."

"It's not important, my child. Haven't I always told you to stay steady in the flow of the Dao no matter what comes?"

"Yes, but what is coming? You were talking to that hermit for a long time. It couldn't have been just about me."

On tired and aged legs, he returned to his seat and said, "I learned that Zhang Lu had gone to see my friend the hermit to seek his advice. Zhang Lu knows that sooner or later the warlord Cao Cao, the ruler of the kingdom of Wei, will attack and he will have to make a deal. My hermit friend advised him not to abandon the ideals of his grandfather, but the inner core of our state has already grown weak. Without that inner knowing, we cannot last."

"What will happen then?"

"We will be absorbed into the larger kingdom, and Zhang Lu will make sure that his family and the other leaders will be protected, and even perhaps given prominent positions. That is why your husband is so disturbed with you. He is seeking to be one of those rewarded. Zhang Lu is not a bad man. He will fight for Hanning as long he can."

"Yeye, how can you accept this calamity so calmly?" I asked in an agitated voice, my own worries now compounded by concern over the fate of our state.

He smiled. "Calmness is what the Dao teaches.
Without desire, all is peaceful,
And the world settles itself.

"Remember those words, Chunhua." He was quiet for a few minutes and then continued. "Long ago, a very long time ago, people lived in harmony with one another and with the natural world. There was an inner knowing of the right way to be and to behave, a natural oneness with the Dao. Virtue was the natural state. The great sage Laozi knew this and tried to give us the guidelines for recapturing that way of living, but this must be done on an individual basis. Zhang Daoling had the vision of how each of us could live a virtuous life, with no thought of power or greed or control, a simple life close to nature, but humanity is not ready. As soon as a religious state develops and the state dictates how to be, it overrides the inner knowing of the individual.

Until people change from inside, such an ideal kingdom cannot last. But does it matter? We still have the Dao to guide us on how to live a fruitful life.

"I am ready to depart this world, having lived for nearly 100 years, but I am most concerned about you. Hanning will be dispersed and our people will be moved to other parts of the empire. Some, and I count your husband among those, will be given land and titles and find themselves in positions of power. Now I ask you, are there any conditions you can imagine that would enable you to return to him?" I vehemently shook my head. "If you don't overcome your fear of him, you will have to face him at another time."

"Then let me face him in the future. After what has come to pass, I don't want to see him again in this life. I will never be able to forget the look in his eyes, the cruelty. But my children, especially my daughter, what will become of her?"

"No doubt he will take another wife and tell them terrible lies about you."

I didn't answer. He waited and finally I replied in a barely audible voice, "That will be the pain I have to live with, at least for now. If I can have a few months away perhaps I can get control of this fear. I can't think beyond that."

He rose abruptly. "There is a vacant hut not far from here. Nobody has lived there for years. We will stay there for a few days. No doubt your husband will return and search this place for the stone. Come, let us leave from here. My disciple Yu Yan will come with us. I will have her pack enough food and some essentials."

For three days we stayed in the hut. During that time Yeye filled my head with stories of my childhood. During the nights, as I drifted to sleep listening to the forest sounds, he would enter cultivation and only emerge in the morning hours. Despite my sorrow at the separation from my children, it was comforting to be with the grandfather I so cherished.

On the last night of our stay in the hut, a full moon lit up the sky, casting a mystical mellow light on the forest floor, drenching the trees in a soft glow. It was the kind of night when the magic of the forest comes alive, and the prowling creatures could be heard amid the symphony of sounds that penetrated the thin walls of the hut. Yeye called me to come outside to "bathe myself" in the moon's love.

"Does the moon have love?" I asked as I went over and sat by his side, resting my head against his shoulder.

"The deities there do." He put his arm around me and drew me close to him. "Did I ever tell you the story of the marriage between the moon and the sun?"

I smiled. "Many times, when I was young."

He chuckled. "You didn't believe me then."

"Yeye, do the deities really marry?"

"We may call it marriage; they call it something else. Whatever we name it, there is a deep exchange of love and that love extends to the entire universe. That is what sustains us."

"Is that real or our imagination?"

"Why do you think the imagination is not real?" I shrugged my shoulders. "The imagination is the doorway to the inner worlds, to the worlds of the celestials. Never shut that door. Those who do only see what is right in front of them, nothing beyond."

I looked up at the moon. "We can't stare into the sun, but we can stare at the moon for as long as we want. It is more accessible."

"That is why the moon was given to us, to reflect the light of the sun. Someday I hope you will see the deities who reside there."

"Where do they reside, Yeye?" I asked looking up at him, no longer dismissing his talk as a way of joking or teasing me.

"It is a world our human eyes can't see unless we are granted celestial vision. But they can come in dreams, and dreams are real as well. It is easier for them to speak to us through dreams."

He was quiet. Suddenly, I asked, "Yeye, what was it like to be with Sage Zhang Daoling?'

He smiled. "You have never asked me that before. Why are you asking now?"

"I don't know." I pulled away so I could see him better. I wanted to look into his eyes when he spoke of his master. Intuitively, I felt this might be my last opportunity to ask such questions.

Even in the dim light, I could see his eyes sparkling with delight as he began to speak. "By the time I met the great sage, he had already retreated into near silence. He spoke, but not much, and when he did, it was always about the need to cultivate virtue. I learned from him that in earlier times, much earlier, it was the sages who ruled our lands, and they were men and women of great virtue, speaking only truth, looking out for the welfare of all, not putting their own needs or desires first, caring for the creatures and the land just as they cared for the people. When it came time for a ruler to withdraw from worldly affairs, he or she would search for the wisest among them and that sage would become the next ruler. There were no dynasties then. It was not until Emperor Yu that dynasties come into being, and perhaps this was because the wise ones had all retreated.

"I often wondered if my teacher had not been one of those ancient sages who ruled our lands because he knew so much about governance and spoke so often about the qualities of a virtuous leader. I learned from him that the emperor is a reflection of the minds of the people. If virtue is strong, the leaders will reflect that, and if virtue is weak, that will also be reflected.

He said that among the creatures of the world, we humans are the only ones who seek to amass power and wealth, to take more than we need. Think about it, Chunhua, the animals do not live this way. It is this insatiable desire for more that has led to the decline in virtue—to the increase in deception, selfishness, greed, and anger. Sage Zhang Daoling often quoted Laozi:

> *No misfortune is greater than not knowing when enough is enough,*
> *No fault is greater than wanting more and more.*

"The way to counter this, he said, was inner cultivation. The more one receives from the inner worlds, the less one needs from the external one. At the end of his life, when I met him, my teacher taught less through words than by transmission."

I listened thoughtfully to all he was saying but couldn't understand this last part. "What do you mean by transmission?"

He replied with a broad smile, "I had heard of his travel to the celestial world and once asked what the world of the immortals was like. Instead of replying, he simply closed his eyes and remained like that for a whole day, while I and a few others sat before him in cultivation, waiting for the response. After many, many hours, he took me to the moon. That was his response."

"Yeye!" I exclaimed, pulling back and looking at him with wide eyes. "Do you expect me to believe that!" Flying to a mountaintop was one thing, but to the moon? I was no longer a child who would believe such things. "Nobody could go to the moon, Yeye, not even Zhang Daoling."

Yeye laughed that hearty laugh of his, which always brought so much joy to my heart. "Not the physical moon, Chunhua."

"Then what?"

"The inner world of the moon. It is there that some of the deities reside, and it is a most beautiful world. The problem is, it can't be described in words. None of the celestial worlds can; they must be experienced. He was leading me into deeper cultivation so that I could have that vision, that experience, which he was finally able to grant me."

"Really?" He nodded. "How does one reach that place?"

"By long and deep cultivation. One must have unending patience and determination."

I wrinkled my brow, wondering how I would ever get there. I had little patience, and my cultivation was not long or deep. "Is there no other way?"

He nodded and then replied gently. "There is one other way. That is through love, and that will be your way, my dear. If love for any of the deities is deep enough, and if one perseveres in this love, it is inevitable that this deity will appear. It is a law of nature."

I turned to look up at the moon, but I could not say that I had love for the moon or her deities. I thought her beautiful and I had gratitude, but love, that was another matter. "Will you help me cultivate that love, Yeye?" I asked in a quiet voice.

"When you are ready, I will be there."

"Do you promise?" My voice was serious as I knew that he was not joking or teasing me. I believed every word he spoke.

"I promise."

I sighed as a reassuring peace entered my heart. I rested my head again on his shoulder, realizing that this night might be the last time I would be able to do so.

The next day we returned to the cottage and I dared not ask what was to become of me, but my grandfather brought up the subject. "You must move away from Hanning. War is not far off, and Cao Cao is already making preparations to invade. Your children will be safe, don't worry, for I have already seen their future.

"There is a hermit that I once knew who had a daughter, about your mother's age. I lost track of the hermit, but I have his daughter's name and the village where she lives, further south, beyond Sichuan. Over the years she visited me a few times and even met you when you were young. She is quite advanced in cultivation and will help you with your spiritual practices. I will send you to her with a message and I am sure she will take care of you. But you must be certain you are ready to leave your family."

I nodded. "For now, that may be the best plan so that I can regain some peace of mind and not live in fear. At least I will have time to think about my future course."

"I will send Yu Yan with you. She is my trusted student and knows well how to maneuver through the forests and mountains. You will be safe with her."

"Yeye, who will care for you then?" He didn't respond, but I glimpsed a partial smile on his face. "You are not thinking of dying, are you?"

With a twinkle in his eye, he replied, "Dying? I am merely thinking of relocating."

"Relocating?"

"Returning to my celestial home."

"Yeye!"

"Child, I have tried to teach you that despite what some will say, immortality is not meant for the body, but for the spirit. I will simply move from one home to another." He allowed me to hug him tightly, but then slowly removed my grip. "I want you to remember one thing, my dear Chun-hua."

"What is that?" I asked tearfully.

"As Laozi has taught us:
No matter how great or how often,
Repay injury with De."

"Yeye, you have told me that before, but I have never understood what De is."

"Ah, De. It is hard to define, but essentially it the Dao in action: right action, harmonious action, acting out of virtue, out of love. That is De."

I was thoughtful for a few moments and then replied, "That can't be right. How is one to repay injury with virtue, with love?"

He smiled. "That is how one becomes immortal. That is how one overcomes human frailties. That is what I want you to remember."

Yeye began to pack the horses with goods I might need for the journey and soon it came time to say our last goodbye. "The greatest gift I can give you, my dear, is to help you overcome your fear. Remember, there is nothing in this world that can truly hurt you—no wild beast, not death, no demon even. It is only your insecurities, the fear created by the mind, that hold you back. That you must overcome." Looking steadily into my eyes, he added. "Your husband has taught you a great lesson, one we all must continually remember."

I looked at him, perplexed.

Gazing intently at me, he said, "Spiritual practice must never be used for personal outer gain. The greatest enemy is the desire for power." He repeated these words a few times, as if he wanted them to sink deeply into my mind and spirit. At that moment, his image was engraved on my heart, and I prayed to never forget my dear grandfather or his words.

On a lighter note, he added, "I could ride with you further south, but I want you to have this adventure on your own with Yu Yan, trusting in the Dao to bring you safely to where you need to be. Don't feel sad, Chunhua.

The survival of Hanning is not important, for there will always be hermits who live the life of the Dao and show others the Way. Seek them out."

I wiped my eyes. "I am not crying for Hanning, Yeye. I am crying because I will not see you again."

"Who says you will not see me again?" His eyes sparkled in that enigmatic way so characteristic of him. I took one last long glance at him before riding away.

The journey was a long one, entailing many, many days of travel, but it also brought many rewards. The landscape was beautiful, with towering mountains, deep valleys, and rushing rivers. Most importantly, I got to know Yu Yan, the reserved student of my grandfather. She had been a presence in his house since my childhood, but we had never spoken much. She cared for me through our travels, as she would have my grandfather, tending to my needs in a very motherly way.

When we arrived at our destination, we were warmly greeted by the daughter of my grandfather's friend. Over time, she tried to ease my sorrow over the separation from my children by engaging me in cultivation practices. Resting in her kindness, and the care of Yu Yan, I gradually began to settle my mind and release the fear, but it was the presence of the forest and the animal life that brought me peace rather than any deep inner cultivation.

Many months later, I learned that the vast army of Cao Cao had attacked our state, causing Zhang Lu to flee to eastern Sichuan. I wondered if my sorcerer husband had not been working with the spirits to this end. After all, he would now rise in power. When Zhang Lu surrendered, the state of Hanning was absorbed into the Wei kingdom. To win them over, the clever Cao Cao gave titles and lands to Zhang Lu and other family members and prominent people, including my husband, but he forced the rest of the citizens to resettle elsewhere, with some sent to the western capital Chang'an and others to the eastern city of Luoyang. Much later, I came to understand the grand bargain that had been struck. Daoism, which had long been seen as a way of life passed on by wandering hermits, became a more formalized religion, adopted by the authorities who now claimed the mandate of heaven. Some said this was a good thing, as it brought Daoism to a greater number of people, but others saw the danger in shaping the principles of the Dao to suit political needs. I knew in my heart that Yeye would have claimed the latter.

"He is an evil man, that Cao Cao," I exclaimed to Yu Yan one night as I was reflecting on the demise of Hanning.

"You should not think that way, Chunhua. Ambitious, yes, but I don't know about evil," she replied calmly. "Your grandfather taught me that the end of the state would come as a result of internal weakness, and that the external threat would be the last bit that broke the back of the beast."

"I know that is what Yeye would say, but I can't help thinking that warlord is an evil man."

"You have to let go of your anger," she replied with a smile.

"I know, Yu Yan. You are so much like my grandfather, and your words are like a balm on my wounds."

The ideals I had grown up with had died and so had a little part of me. I spent the rest of my years living a simple life in the village to which my grandfather had sent me, but I didn't live to an old age. The separation from my children was an ache that never left, and I think I died of that heartache. After a number of years, I had begun to yearn for them. One day Yu Yan announced that she would go to Chang'an in search of my children. I tried to stop her as she was getting on in age, but she refused to be deterred. "Let this be the last service I provide to my teacher," she had replied.

After traveling for over a year she finally came back and told me of my husband's position in the court. "He has taken another wife and has had additional children but has not given up his anger or pursuit of you. He is determined to find you one day and make you pay for having tried to expose him. Your son has taken a great liking to aristocratic life and is very loyal to his father. Your daughter is a different matter. She left home secretly not long ago in search of you. I tried to follow her trail but couldn't find her. However, I did hear news of her. I was told that she feels a strong affinity with her great-grandfather, whom she remembers well, and that she does not believe the lies her father has told her about you. She is determined to find you, Chunhua, and I am sure one day she will."

"She was only ten when I left her," I replied with tears in my eyes. "She must be around twenty now. I abandoned my daughter. How will I ever make it up to her?"

"Don't blame yourself, Chunhua. You did what you had to. I strongly believe she will find you one day. She is seeking the Way and surely she will come to know it."

Her words brought me some peace. I didn't have the strength or confidence to disturb the life I had made for myself, but I kept waiting for the day when my daughter would arrive. That day never came. With the death of my grandfather, I felt the dream of Zhang Daoling had also died, except among those who would carry those ideals with them into lives yet to be lived.

I sighed deeply as I opened my eyes, no longer tormented by fear of my husband, but still reflecting on the loss of Hanning and of my children. I looked around. I was still in the cave, but now I was alone. I thought that Shifu had been seated before me, but perhaps I had imagined it. The line between outer reality and inner vision was thinning day by day, and I was no longer sure of place and time. A plate of fruit and a glass of fruit juice sat in front of me, and I slowly sipped the juice. Why was it there, and who had brought it? The sound of footsteps quietly tapping the dirt floor of the passageway startled me and, as I glanced toward the doorway, I saw Ying enter.

"You have returned to waking awareness," she said in relief. "Shifu had us bring the food here to you because she saw you were not taking it from the passageway. Are you okay, Shu?"

I nodded as I sipped the juice. Moment by moment I was slowly sailing back to the present. "How long have I been in here, Ying?"

"Ten days."

"I was unaware of time," I murmured. "Ten years have passed."

She chuckled. "No, Shu, ten days, not years."

"Oh."

"Shifu has sent me to bring you back to your room, but first you must eat."

"I am not hungry, Ying."

"Take a piece of fruit at least. You must have strength to walk. I can't carry you." She waited as I took a few bites and then pushed the plate away. Then she bent down and helped me to my feet. "Take a few steps slowly." My body, which had become stiff from sitting so long, took some time to regain its movement, but little by little we made our way to my room. There was another glass of juice and some fruit waiting there. "Eat these when you are ready."

"Ying, help me wash." She nodded. After washing me and dressing me in a new robe, she helped me to bed, but I couldn't sleep. After resting for a while, I got up from my mat on the floor and went to my writing table.

Leaving Behind the State of Hanning

The sage Zhang Daoling traveled through the skies
Where he found flowering clouds
And dewdrops that burst into stars.
Gently placing them in his palm
He brought them to earth for us to enjoy.

Was it the sorcerer's mind or human frailties
That withered his dream
Like winter flowers falling in snow?
Before it could die
I hid that dream deep in my heart
And will care for it
Until humanity comes of age.

Shifu came to see me the next morning. I was seated on my mat in cultivation and she sat down in front of me. We stayed in silence for a while. "Shifu, did you come to me in the cave?" I asked.

She nodded. "I felt your fear and I came."

"I didn't imagine it then?" She slowly shook her head. "Was it real, or did I imagine what I saw, that state of Hanning? Did that really exist? And my grandfather, was he real?"

"It was as real or unreal as this life is."

"So, I was also Chunhua?"

She nodded.

"How long ago was that?"

"About 500 years."

"All night I have been reflecting on the connections. That man, that horrible sorcerer, I met him in my last birth. He was the prince who took me as a concubine and tormented me so, wasn't he?" She nodded. "That is why he repulsed me and that is why he tried to force me to make a false confession and that is why . . ." I couldn't finish my sentence as my voice broke off.

"It is over. It is all over. You are finished with that man and will not meet him again in any future life."

"But why did I have to meet him a second time and be bound to him?"

"Think back, Shu, why did he hate you so?"

"Yes, why?" I closed my eyes and sat in the stillness for a long time trying to recall. "It was the stone, that strange object I took from his room before I fled to my grandfather. That was his doorway to the world of dark entities, and I deprived him of that. That is what aroused his hatred."

"That is why he spread rumors about you that you were a sorcerer, because you had taken the stone, and that is why he tried to hunt you down to kill you. Shu, in that life you were not finished with him. You ran from him in fear, but he became obsessed with you. He didn't find you again in that life and he had to wait until you were strong enough in yourself so that you could stand up to him. And you did. Don't you remember your indifference, how you never truly submitted to him in your life as Meihua as all the others did? He may have subdued your body, but not your mind or spirit. You were the thorn in his side, and that is why finally he cast you away. He tried again to get you to submit to a false accusation, but you refused. That was your victory. Your freedom was the isolation, the release from court life. There in your solitude, you could devote yourself to the study of poetry and Daoism for the first time.

"To understand any one life, you have to see the whole scale of lives, where one has come from in the past, what the current conditions offer, and what the future presents." She paused and then said in a ruminating tone, "I suspect that through your life with that sorcerer you learned to stay far away from those who misuse their powers, which is a serious trap for many who pursue the way of knowledge. Powers come and it is easy to fall into deception. Those who take that road have a long and hard trek back."

"I pray that I have learned this lesson for all eternity. Never do I want to engage with such a person again."

"Do you remember the words of Laozi that I asked you to reflect on before you entered the cave?"

I had to think back. It seemed an eternity ago. Suddenly the words came to me:

No matter how great or how often
Repay injury with De.

"Shifu, those were the same words that my grandfather spoke to me as I was leaving him."

"I know that," she replied quietly. "Why do you think I asked you to reflect on those words?" I didn't respond. "One is not responsible for the actions or character of another, only for one's own character. No matter what anyone does to you, no matter how horrific, you must retain your inner balance and innate virtue and act accordingly. That is called De and that is living in the Dao. One can't learn this by words alone, but only through experience. You can see the difference in the way Chunhua and Meihua reacted to this person, and I think if you were to meet him again you would not lose your inner balance."

"You may be right, Shifu, but I hope I am not put to the test." She laughed. 'Shifu, when my grandfather spoke those words to me, I didn't understand De. Now, I feel I am beginning to understand it."

"I believe you are, Shu. One comes to know De through experience, and that is why we must go through all that we encounter in life. This is how we learn."

"Shifu, the Daoist who came to me in my life as Meihua, that was Chunhua's grandfather, wasn't it? He had promised and he kept his promise."

She nodded. "I am glad you understand that. Of all the people in Hanning at that time, he was one of the few who achieved immortality and didn't need to take rebirth, but his love for you was such that he came in your distress to give you a key, to teach you the true way of the Dao, which had survived and will in the future survive as a path to truth. You were not able to go deep in your spiritual practice as Chunhua or as Meihua, but it was your efforts then that brought you to me now."

"Shifu, both of the lives I have seen were lonely ones. I didn't have much love in those lives."

"Every life has its trials and gifts. It was a great, great blessing to have the grandfather that you did. That is a very rare gift indeed. Didn't that compensate for the lack of love in your marriage, to have had someone in your life of that spiritual stature?"

"You are right, Shifu, but I have not had much luck with husbands, have I?"

Opening her eyes as wide as could be, she brought her face close to mine and I saw her disbelief. "What did you say?"

"I have not had . . ." I began to repeat myself, but she cut me off.

"Have you forgotten Li Bai already? You have been gifted a rare man. One does not easily find such a man as he."

"Bai," I uttered a small cry. "I have flown so far from him, I don't know how to return. My Bai, I only hope he has not forgotten me."

"Shu, he has written to me asking when he can come for you, but I have held him off as you are not ready yet to return."

"How long have I been here, Shifu?"

"Seven months."

"Seven months," I repeated. "My Bai has had to wait that long for me?"

She uttered a small laugh. "He has waited much longer; he can bear a few more months."

At the mention of Bai's name, I was swiftly brought back to my present life. "Shifu, is Bai safe in the northeast? That is a troubled region. I should have been worried about him, but my mind has been elsewhere."

"No need to worry about Bai yet. He is fine and will soon be returning."

As she rose to take her leave, I reflected, "Isn't it strange, Shifu, that at one time I hated the warlord Cao Cao and thought he was such an evil man, and then, centuries later, I fell in love with his poetry, and his poems helped me get through a very difficult time. Isn't that strange?"

"Our lives take many unforeseen turns, and the unexpected often shows up. You had to let go of your anger over the defeat of Hanning and you did that through poetry. Cao Cao was actually a very thoughtful and cultured man, even though he was a warlord."

"I viewed that historical time period through the eyes of a simple woman who loved her grandfather and the ideals he represented."

"We all do that," she replied. "There is no one story of history. It is each man's or woman's story. We all see events through the people and places close to us, through our own experiences of that time. History is recorded in the memories of each one of us."

After Shifu left, my mind turned to Bai, and for the first time in many months I felt a longing for him. I missed his touch, the vibrant look in his eyes, his strong wit, his humor and sharp intelligence, and his loving embrace. From across the distance that separated us, I felt his love engulf me, and I began to yearn for him at night as I drifted to sleep. I began to wonder and imagine what he had been doing, what people he had met, what poems he had written. That night I wrote of the distance between us:

Separation

Your golden ship sails down the mighty Yangtze
Where people and poems and drink await you,
While I swim alone among the stars.
From earth they appear as candles lighting the sky.
But up close, they disappear in the mist of time.
Truly there are no stars, no sky, no me, no you.
Only the Dao can see me home.

I knew that I had to begin the climb back to the present, but there was so much about the past that continued to preoccupy me. For many weeks, my mind dwelt in Hanning, reliving those memories. The ideals that inspired the founding of the state had long ago been rooted in my heart by the grandfather I called Yeye. He was the living example of what Zhang Daoling had envisioned. I remembered how the accumulation of wealth by an individual was considered an afront to the community, not in keeping with the Dao, but how those who were later resettled were eager to gather lands and the wealth that came with them. I remembered how power was to be distributed, not held in the hands of one man or a few, but how this all changed as our people regrouped in other regions and sought access to court life. The ideals of Hanning were lost then, but I had held them tightly in my heart. As I remembered the qualities that Zhang Daoling tried to instill in the people, I thought of how many of those qualities Bai displayed. Later, when I was sitting with Shifu, I asked her if Bai had lived in Hanning.

She shook her head and replied, "His journey has been an entirely different one, but like many, he was on earth during a higher age, when humanity lived in harmony with the natural world, when there was an innate knowing of the Dao, that which is also called dhamma by the Buddhists and dharma by the Hindus. Subsequently, he lived as a wandering Buddhist monk, and that is why he is unattached to worldly things. That is also why he is, and in this life will always be, a wanderer, with no real home. You must fully accept that about him. His years as a traveling monk influenced his early life, and so in his youth he spent time in monasteries studying with Buddhist teachers. In another life, he was a great swordsman. He has retained this ability and also some chivalrous qualities. These are all remnants from his past. He has also been a ruler and that is why court life will always hold an allure for him, despite his disgust with court intrigue and corruption.

As she spoke, I thought of how eager Bai had been to travel to the northeast despite the dangers and my objections. A reflective expression must have crossed my face because Shifu added, "I know, Shu, that his inability to settle down, his wanderlust, is not easy for you."

"You are right," I replied softly, "but I know it is an essential part of his nature."

"You must give up any desire to hold on to him. Grasping is not in keeping with the Dao. That is not the purpose of your marriage. The love between you two is an ancient one that has finally found fulfillment after many years of searching and waiting. You must look to see what you are meant to learn from this situation, how you can grow."

"Acceptance, patience, and unattachment," I sighed. "That is what I am meant to learn. If he is fated to wander endlessly, I am fated to wait endlessly and can only cultivate my inner life."

"This is your opportunity. You have a perfect situation, a husband who loves you dearly but makes few demands, who allows you as much solitude as you need. Nothing can be achieved spiritually without solitude."

"I truly want to love him without clinging, for the sake of my marriage."

She laughed. "Don't worry. Your life with Bai will help you realize that. You two have been destined for each other, and nothing in the world can change that, but also, nothing you can say or do will keep him from journeying. This is what inspires his poetry."

Back in my cottage, I sat down and reflected on what I had seen about Hanning. As I wrote my thoughts, I hoped that I would remember the ideals and values that had been transmitted to me and that I could realize them in my life with Bai.

The Sage
Zhang Daoling reached into the heavens
And plucked a dream from a goddess.
She stirred and lifting herself
With the song of spring told him
that earth was not ready for her dream.

He replied, "I will plant it in her soil
So that earth can dream with you."
She nodded and with a smile
Lowered her flowering head.

Chapter Fourteen

VISION OF THE GODDESS

My forays into the past were depleting my qi. I could sense that my emotional identification with my previous lives, the waves of feeling being stirred, had weakened my energy. Shifu knew this and had me stay in the cottage to rest. She sent food to me and asked me to refrain from all activities except writing and cultivation practice. It was time for me to integrate and make peace with my experiences of the past, and slowly my identification with Chunhua and Meihua began to subside, as their struggles began to lose their impact on me.

Several weeks into my period of rest, I felt a need to touch the earth, to sink my hands into her dark soil. I asked Ying, who was visiting me regularly, if I could begin work in the garden again.

"This morning Shifu mentioned that she would like you to tend the flower garden."

"Flowers? Not the vegetable garden?" I asked.

She nodded. "She told me the scents of flowers have different healing powers, and that they would help restore your qi."

Eagerly, I accepted the new assignment and began to spend hours a day tending to the flowers: selecting some for Shifu's cottage, pruning, planting, picking off the stray insects. Soon the flowers became like my children, and I found myself speaking to them as I would to a beloved child. I was surprised to find that each variety had a different effect on me, and I thought of my grandfather's teaching about the animals, how each one taught a different quality. It was the same with the flowers. If I bent to smell a rose, it would lift my spirits and increase my overall sense of health. If I had any inflammation resulting from a cut or small wound, the peonies soothed it and decreased the swelling. Lavender released anxiety. Jasmine helped with digestive issues, which I had developed after finishing my first session in the cave. I began to realize that all of nature impacts us and teaches us, if only we know how to quiet our minds and listen. I was coming to understand that there was a purpose behind all that Shifu did. She was again helping me learn how to be in tune with nature.

Working with the flowers helped me recover, and I was beginning to feel like myself again, when one night I awoke out of deep sleep with a start. Thoughts of Bai filled my mind, and I had an intuitive sense that he was in need. Months ago, when we had parted, he had had enough money to see him through, but he was also hoping to find employment as an expert swordsman. If he wasn't successful in finding work, or if one of his friends needed money, he would give what he had away, and then what would he do? I knew my Bai. It was impossible for him to hold onto money. Then I remembered the jade necklace I had put around his neck when he left me. It had been a last-minute impulse before he left for the northeast region. I had suddenly taken the long string of small jade beads from my neck and placed it around his, saying, "This will remind you of your wife." When he had tried to return it, I had said, "Keep it in case you need money."

As I thought about this incident in the middle of the night, another image slid into my mind. I saw the man who had come before me in a dream during my first time in the cave; now he was handing the young woman, whom I had also seen at that time, a necklace strung of beads. "These are tulsi beads," he said. "Very sacred. We use them when we recite a mantra." That scene passed from my mind and another took its place. It was a scene of the woman throwing the string of beads into a river in a fit of anger. The images disturbed me, and I sat up to get my bearings.

I pulled myself back to the present. In the many months since I had first seen those two people in a dream during my first visit to the cave, I had not found out who they were and what my relationship to them was. "Why do I keep seeing scenes of their life?" I asked myself again and again. "And why do I only see them in connection with Bai?" Concern over Bai returned to me, and lying back down again, I whispered into my pillow, "It's okay, Bai, if you have to sell the necklace." Worry consumed me and it was not until near dawn that I fell back to sleep.

When I awoke it was already mid-morning. I had missed the 5 a.m. cultivation hour, but Shifu had not been strict with me these last few weeks. She had said that sleep was the most important thing for me now. Cheerful morning light flew through the small window of my room and fell upon me, bringing a smile to my face. Although I hadn't had much sleep, I awoke more refreshed than I had in many months. My time in the cave had made me feel as if I had traveled into the depths of darkness and back, but since my return, I felt cleansed of something, freed of whatever clouds had been secretly clinging to me, clouds I hadn't even known existed. I stretched and naturally entered a period of cultivation, sitting quietly for an hour before joining the others.

Two months had passed since my last visit to the cave and my qi was now strong. I felt ready to engage fully in the life of our small hermitage, but for some reason Shifu had slowed my return. Over the many months of my stay, I had come to completely trust her, and I dared not think of questioning any words or actions of hers. After I had finished my afternoon meal and was washing the cooking utensils, Ying approached me. "I was late this morning," I said apologetically. "I am still sleeping so much."

"That is good," she replied. "I can see how much stronger you are."

"I haven't seen Shifu in a few days. Is she here?"

"She left to attend to needs in one of the villages, but before leaving, she asked me to take you to the cave."

"Again to the cave?" I laughed. "I am ready right now."

"Come then, let us go." In silence we climbed up the hill that led to the cave. I refused to allow fear to enter my mind and was determined to keep the peaceful feeling that had awakened within me. At the entrance, Ying stood there for a moment and said, "Shifu mentioned that we should leave the daily food in the passageway, since you will be able to eat this time."

I nodded and replied in a teasing voice, "And if I don't eat?"

"I will personally check and bring you your food. This time, I am in charge of you, Shu." She took my hand and squeezed it before leaving.

As I entered the dark passageway and the room where I was to stay, I felt a sense of relief. During my recovery, I had been sleeping so much that I had not been able to enter deeply into cultivation. I knew that my stay with Shifu was coming to an end, and once I returned home, I would not have the same opportunities, so I was eager for this time to devote myself fully to my spiritual practices. The silence and solitude of the cave allowed this. There was not even the whisper of a bird or the kind caressing of a breeze to distract me. Closing my eyes, I steadied my breath until it rose and fell with even rhythm in and out. Finally, I was able to merge with the breath, flowing with the pace of a gentle stream, a stream that never ceases.

Peering into my internal organs, I saw the light of my qi gather from all parts of my body into a flaming ball in my stomach area and rise into my heart, settling there, becoming the life behind the beating heart. There it rested, and I concentrated on the light that fed my heart until I became that organ, drumming with the rhythm of pattering rain. I listened quietly until the distinction between it and myself disappeared. Hours passed. I felt myself sink into a half-sleep, not fully conscious of the external world but not unconscious either, rather, open to a different realm of being, as if I had fallen through a hole in the sky and found myself in a familiar yet foreign place.

In this dream state, my sight expanded, and the walls of the cave became transparent. There above was the beaming moon in all her bright glory. I looked up at the moon and felt the distance between us shorten until I could almost touch her. As her presence became stronger, I watched the moon turn into a body of light. A female form settled in front of me, a beautiful young woman, with dark hair that flowed to her waist, a pale face, and perfectly formed features with rounded eyes. I heard her words inside my mind: *I was the one who came to you in the courtyard when you were bereft of friends.*

I remember, I replied in thought. *It was the immortal who sent you.*

She made a slight nod of her head. *It was I who opened your ears to the song of the stars. It was I who expanded your sight so you could passage through the moon to find me.*

You were the friend who eased my sorrow, and you have come again, I replied internally.

She nodded and smiled, and as she did, a beam of light passed from her heart to mine, and then, bit by bit, her body began to withdraw and fade away, and with it, the image of the moon. Only the dark, cold walls of the cave remained, yet the memory lingered. I don't know for how many minutes or hours I remained in this state, quietly resting in that memory, but finally I emerged into the outer world and opened my eyes.

"It was a dream," I murmured, "a beautiful dream." Then I remembered the words of Yeye, telling me that dreams are real. "After so many centuries, he kept his promise," I whispered. "He brought me to the moon." I reached over to take a drink of water, and then after some time I stood up and walked down the passageway to see whether any food was there. I found a plate of fruit and slowly ate it, and then went back to enter again into cultivation, keeping before me the beautiful vision I had experienced. Thus passed the days.

When Ying came for me, she told me I had been in the cave for three days. I nodded, not wanting to speak. "There is a glow about you and your qi is stronger. You must have had an uplifting experience this time." I simply nodded and said nothing. That night I went to sit at my writing desk. Picking up the brush, I dipped it into the ink, closed my eyes to recall the image of the goddess I had seen in the cave, and then wrote:

The Moon
Last night I walked to the moon.
She led me on a beam of light.
There we sat on a ridge
And I awoke from the dream of Earth.

The Goddess
I looked into the eyes of a goddess
And saw myself there,
Beyond the edge of time,
Outside the boundaries of space.
Spring awoke that morning
And Earth called me back.

I needed no time for recovery and was able to return immediately to the rhythm of daily life. Shifu didn't come to see me as she had in the past. Perhaps she knew there was no confusion, no fear, no pain, only joy. A few weeks later, I had the opportunity to be alone with her. "Li Bai will be here in a few days to bring you home," she said casually.

"Already?"

She laughed. "It's been ten months. I have had to squeeze ten years of training into ten months for you. You cannot keep him waiting any longer."

"Shifu, I have changed. Will he know me? Will I know him? I am anxious . . ."

She smiled. "There is nothing to be concerned about. The love between you is very deep. You are old friends. Now you must enjoy your time with him. Treasure it, because it will pass like a dream, as all your other lives have." She paused and then continued in a thoughtful tone. "I think by now you understand that one must love without attachment, without conditions. That is what you will need to practice in this life. Make no mistake about your husband. He is a great soul, though he appears as a drunken poet. That is the disguise he has chosen for this life. Few people see through it as you do."

"Some of his friends call him the banished immortal," I said with a smile.

"He has not been banished but has come willingly into this exile we call life. He may be an immortal but is not a banished one. You have never asked me any details of his past births."

"Is there anything I should know?" I asked uncomfortably.

"I have told you about his Buddhist past and his time as a swordsman, but I have not told you much about his life as a ruler, which still has incompletions. That is why he has continually sought government positions but has eschewed the less important ones. He feels he should have the ear of the emperor but doesn't realize how fortunate he is to have been spared this. There are unfinished relationships, which may crop up again. One virtue of your husband is his loyalty, and this extends to past-life friends as well as current ones. This could present challenges for both of you, but I needn't tell you any more now and you should not worry about the future, which will take care of itself. Do your best to keep him away from politics, but if, in the end, deeds of the past propel him in a certain direction, you will have to accept this."

Her words did not provide me much comfort, but I could not press her for more information. I knew that Shifu would only say as much as she thought necessary about any matter. "Shifu, will I remember any more of my past?" I asked hesitantly. I was afraid that if such memories were to emerge and she was not near at hand, how would I cope? How would I understand?

"I cannot answer that. Time will tell. Most people don't recall their previous births, and in fact it is quite rare, with good reason. I don't encourage it. But you have been given this gift, which brings with it many difficulties. If you dwell too much on the past, it will distract you from your current life and cause confusion." Then she smiled, "It is good, though, for you to remember your grandfather."

I nodded. "That is the memory I treasure the most. But Shifu, I don't know if I am ready to leave you."

"Your training is far from over. In fact, it is only beginning. You now have to apply what you have learned here as you go back into the world. That is the only way to know whether you are truly living the Dao and the Dao is living in you. When you first arrived, I asked three questions. Do you remember them?" I nodded. "So, I will ask again. Shu, what are you seeking?"

"The Dao," I replied immediately.

"Not immortality?" she asked with a half-smile.

I shook my head. "I now know myself to be immortal as we all are, only we forget. There is, in truth, no death. We just change one body for another."

"What do you treasure the most?"

"The Dao," I replied again without hesitation.

"And what do you fear the most?"

"Losing the Dao," I said firmly. "My answers have changed, haven't they, Shifu?" She nodded.

"Your answers have changed because you have changed. It is easy to be in the Dao while you are here, but harder back in the world. That will be your challenge." She looked at me intently and then got up to leave.

A few days later, I climbed to the cave one last time, not to enter but to sit nearby and recall the many days and nights I had spent inside. Ying came to find me and, as she sat down beside me, I was glad for this time to express my gratitude to her. After a few minutes of silence, she asked, "Today you will go home to your husband. How do you feel about that?"

"Of course, I have missed him, Ying, and yet I am a bit nervous. I feel as if I have aged ten years in the months I have been here. Also, I have lived here in silence and Bai is a very social personality—how will I adapt?" I had been absorbed in the beautiful landscape before me but now I turned to look at her.

She smiled slightly and replied, "You will be surprised at how quickly you will adapt. You will need to find each other again in a new way. It won't be the same as before, because you are not the same, but perhaps, Shu, he has also changed. I don't know your husband, but from what you have told me I feel he is a deeply spiritual person and so will welcome the changes you have gone through."

"That is true. I don't need to worry about anything." I paused and then asked, "Ying, can I ask you about a spiritual matter?"

"Of course."

"Before I came here, I never thought much about death or rebirth. The question didn't arise for me, and I know Daoism does not speak much about rebirth. Yet, look at the experiences I had in the cave, where I not only recalled but relived lifetimes from long ago, in different bodies with different names. I knew those personalities to be me, and Shifu never doubted the authenticity of those experiences."

"Because she knew them to be real. Shifu is very discerning and can tell a person's past, although she doesn't reveal it unless for a spiritual purpose. The true Daoism is not an organized religion with a set of beliefs. It is a path to knowing one's place in the universe, to coming into harmony with all that is, to becoming one with that. Words can hardly describe the Dao."

Ying continued, "We know that a fundamental principle of the universe is the cyclical nature of all—the heavenly bodies and all of nature moves in cycles, and we do as well, because we are part of that. And so, we move through life cycles, not remembering from birth to birth. If we were to remember it all, how confusing it would be, and what a distraction! You have seen that. The law of cause and effect is a universal law and governs these cycles. In the past, before the formalization of all aspects of life, the hermit sages passed this knowledge from student to student. Now Daoist societies do this, but can an organization speak from personal experience as the sages did? It has changed and so much knowledge is now hidden. One must seek it out."

"I don't know what Bai feels about this, as we have never spoken about it. I fear if I tell him . . ."

"There is no need to share more than you are comfortable doing. What you have seen is for your own personal growth."

"Will you stay here, Ying?" I knew that she had never married and had come from a modest family.

She nodded. "I have been with Shifu for nearly ten years and made a decision long ago that I would spend my life in cultivation under her direction."

"Ying, I feel closer to you than a sister. You have helped me through some difficult times. You have seen me at my worst moments, and I don't know what I would have done without you. I will miss you."

"We are a spiritual family, Shu, and there is no saying goodbye. I am sure you will be back, and I am always here to provide whatever assistance you need. I will leave you now, so you have some time alone before your husband comes."

I stood up and bowed low before her.

After she left, my mind turned to the cave and I bowed in gratitude, then sat down to mentally review the experiences I had gone through inside that dark, womb-like retreat. So many memories, so many insights, so much growth in understanding. Despite the painful moments, I was grateful, enormously grateful, for what I had experienced. Breathing deeply, I took one last long glance at the scenery before me. How beautiful it all was: the tall rock outcroppings surrounded by trees and brush, silent except for the melodious bird calls and the subtle voice of the wind.

It was there that he found me. I was staring up at the cloud-strewn sky, wondering what it would be like to meet my husband again after so long. I had not recovered any memory of a past life with Bai, and yet our connection was so deep, surely this was not the first life in which we had met. Absorbed in thought, I did not hear him approach. It was only when I heard my name being quietly called, "Little Phoenix," that I turned to see him standing a few feet away. The sound of his voice calling me that endearing name chased away any concerns I had, as my husband's tender love once again filled my heart.

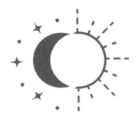

Chapter Fifteen

BURNING OF THE POEMS

"Little Phoenix." It had been so long since anyone had called me by that name, and they were welcome words. I stood up and for a few seconds we looked at one another, each becoming familiar once again with the sight of the other, and then I rushed forward and he gathered me in his arms. Embracing him tightly as if I were afraid he would fade away, I lifted my face to his as he bent over and kissed me on the forehead, and then on my cheek. I began to speak, but his lips firmly met mine, silencing the words. Arm in arm, we walked back to Shifu's cottage, where she was waiting.

Bai stood outside as I said my goodbyes to the women there. Then I stood before Shifu. "Shifu, will I see you again?" I asked, wiping the pearls of moisture that had crept into the corners of my eyes.

"How can you not? There is nowhere to go. The universe is infinitely large and yet infinitely small." She took hold of my hands.

"But in this life, Shifu, will I see you again?" I persisted.

"In this life, yes, we will meet again for sure," She smiled. "When the need arises, we will meet."

Her words gave me some comfort, and as I bowed low before her, I said quietly, "Then I don't need to say goodbye."

She nodded. "This is not goodbye."

I turned to Ying, who was standing near the door. We looked at each other without saying a word. She smiled; I tried to but could not muster any cheerful expression. Breathing in deeply, I bowed and walked out.

Quietly closing the door to Shifu's cottage, I took the hand waiting for me as Bai led me to the horses. After a brief ride down the steep, rocky road, we entered a carriage he had hired and I rested my head on his shoulder as we drove away, glad to be in his physical presence again. I didn't turn to say goodbye to Lushan Mountain, as instinctively I knew I would someday return.

As we made our way through the hilly roads, I turned to Bai and now noticed how the months had added age to his appearance, with more strands of grey hair, and new creases around his eyes and on his forehead. The months and perhaps the stress of military life had weighed on him, but I didn't want to ask any questions now. It saddened me to see him aging, and I realized how foolish I had been to be concerned about our reunion. I loved him every bit as much as I had before, perhaps even more. Not wanting to show my concern, I lifted the curtain of the carriage and began to take in the scenery.

"I have a surprise for you," Bai said mysteriously as we wound our way around a curve.

"Oh?" Lowering the curtain, I turned to face him.

"We are stopping by a lake for a few days. I've secured a room at an inn there. I thought it better than returning home right away."

I sighed in relief. Even though we had our own home, my family was close by and the thought of engaging again with them so soon was not a pleasant one for me.

"This will give you time to adjust to the world outside."

I looked at Bai with gratitude for this thoughtfulness. Hours later, we arrived at a pleasant inn, and after a modest meal we settled in for the evening. Our ride to the inn had included little conversation, as I was still very much in a silent mode, in keeping with my life over the past many months. Bai, who was naturally very loquacious, was also quiet and I assumed this was out of consideration for me rather than anything else. Now, alone in our room, we could not avoid a more serious conversation.

"You've changed. You are not my Little Phoenix anymore. Perhaps I should no longer call you that."

I smiled and shook my head. "Never stop. That is how we met, and that will always be my name with you. But it's true, I have changed."

"You have grown up."

"Perhaps." The age difference between us had always meant more to Bai than to me, since I never made any distinction in that way. The greater issue for me was what I considered to be his genius, his brilliant mind, which made me feel somewhat insufficient. "I have grown used to living in silence, and it has been a comfortable way for me. I think I have spoken more in the last few hours than in my ten months with Shifu."

Initially, I thought it might bring us closer if I shared something of my experiences, but it was difficult to find the words, and I didn't think they would be relevant to him. What would my struggles as a concubine or my life in Hanning mean to him? How could he understand what I had been through? And so, I kept quiet. I also wanted to show him the poems I had written, but I was terribly shy in sharing my writing with him, this man who in addition to being my beloved husband was also one of the great poetic minds of our time, so I refrained from saying anything about my verse. "I realize I can't stay in silence forever and don't want to. I am so glad to be back with you, Bai, but it will take some time for me to adjust."

"Take whatever time you need. I won't press you." We had been seated together on the bed, but now he got up and started to walk to the writing table. I grabbed his hand and pulled him back. I saw the anxiety on his face, and I wanted him to explain. "Tell me what happened in these many months. What is the situation in the northeast frontier? Were you engaged in any fighting?"

He shook his head. "I didn't do any fighting, but the situation is far more dire than I had imagined. You were right about that notorious man, General An Lushan. I had admired his effectiveness and strategic mind, which enabled him to rise to such a powerful position, but I didn't realize his treachery until I was there for a few months among his regiments. He's a complete fraud and has no loyalty to anyone, let alone the emperor. All along he has been planning to rebel and take over the government, putting his people in the top positions. Little Phoenix, the empire is in grave danger. The first place he will attack and take over is the eastern capital of Luoyang, which is so close to where we live. I have to think of where to move the family."

I was stunned. This was not the outcome I had expected. I had hoped that Bai would become disillusioned with military and political life and come home ready to give it up, but it had never occurred to me that a rebellion might be in the making. The threads of thought linking me to my past were abruptly cut, and his words brought me crashing back into the present.

"When I realized this, my first thought was to go to Chang'an (the capital) and warn the emperor, but he would not believe me, and they might accuse me of treason. He is still too infatuated with that Consort Yang, who fully supports General An Lushan."

"Bai!" I exclaimed. "It is far too dangerous for you to get involved."

"How can I not be involved when the empire and so many lives are at stake?"

"Bai, you are a poet, not a political man."

He looked at me sullenly and then replied. "I don't want this matter to ruin the few days we have alone together, so let's not speak of it until it is time to leave."

If anything would have thrust me back into my present life, this was it. Before leaving for Shifu's hermitage, I had been worried about Bai's presence on the northeastern frontier, knowing about the skirmishes there, but over the months all worries about that had fled as my preoccupations shifted. Now I was again deeply concerned for our future, and so it was hard to put aside the information he conveyed. I knew the only way to ease my concerns was to engage in cultivation, and so I went off into a corner of the room and sat in silence while Bai went to the writing table. He was deeply absorbed in reading when I quietly undressed and went to bed. We weren't intimate that night, but I awoke early in the morning to find myself in his arms, and his presence was a most welcoming and comforting one.

The next morning, Bai decided that we should head out while the day was still fresh to explore the landscape around the lake. As we walked, Bai began to speak about his experiences in the north, the people he had met, and I felt comfortable listening to him, responding every now and then. We found a deserted place to sit, and I lay back on the grassy bank and gazed up at the sky. A half-moon was faintly visible in the expanse of blue above, and I couldn't help but stare at it, remembering the goddess and also what Yeye had told me about the moon in the last conversation I had with him.

Noticing the faraway look in my eyes, Bai asked, "What are you thinking about?"

"My grandfather," I replied absentmindedly.

"Your grandfather? You have never spoken about him. Which grand-father is that?"

"My maternal grandfather."

"Tell me about him," said Bai as he lay down beside me and propped himself up on his elbow so that he could face me.

"He was a hermit, a very special Daoist who could fly through the skies." Bai's interest was piqued. "I spent much of my childhood with him, and he took me to meet some of the great Daoist hermits . . ." I stopped short and turned my eyes from the sky to face Bai.

"You never mentioned that your grandfather was a Daoist, and a flying one at that. You know how eager I always am to meet the hermits. Where does he live, and can you take me to him?"

"He . . . he is no longer alive," I replied in a muted voice.

"What was his name? Perhaps I have heard of him."

"His name," I murmured, realizing that I didn't remember his name. "I called him Yeye." I stopped short. Shifu had warned me not to dwell on the past but seeing the moon had reminded me of Yeye, and my mind had drifted back. "Someday I will tell you about him," I said, sitting up abruptly. "Come let us walk." As we strolled along the lake, I suddenly stopped and put my arms around him. "Bai, these few days we have alone together, I don't want to talk about my time with Shifu or about the country's troubles. I want to laugh with you, hear you recite poetry, listen to stories about your friends and the new people you have gotten to know."

He smiled. "We can do all of that." And so, we spent the next few days reviving our relationship, walking, talking, and enjoying the scenery. He recited poetry to me by a waterfall, as I sat with closed eyes listening to his musical voice, drinking deeply of his poetic talent. There was little I loved more than hearing the undulating tones of his voice as he sang his poems. We wandered in the wooded hills, breathing in the crisp air scented with pine, catching glimpses of forest creatures as they scampered away. I listened to his stories and could not help but laugh with him, so enticing was his wit. It was a time of renewal and return, and, day by day, memories of the past intruded less and less into my daily life.

At the hermitage, I had had little else to occupy my mind, and so for long stretches of time I would dwell on what I had heard and seen in the cave, trying to understand and make sense of the lives that had passed. Now I had Bai to occupy me, and he was a forceful presence, quite capable of drawing me back from my mental wanderings. It was on one of our walks that Bai confided to me that he had had to sell the jade necklace. He seemed repentant, and I hurried to reassure him. "It was for that reason that I gave it to you. I knew you might need money. It doesn't matter, Bai." My feelings were sincere, and, remembering Shifu's words, I was glad that I was able to let go of my attachment. Then I added, "The only possession I never want to sell is the jade phoenix you gave me when you proposed marriage. That is most dear to me."

"That, we will never sell, even if we have to go without food!"

It was on the last night of our stay at the inn, as we prepared to return home the next day, that I had an experience which again rattled my mind. Bai had gone to speak with the owner of the inn, and, I suspected, to share a drink with him, while I sat in cultivation. As I was beginning to feel the heat of my qi rising through my internal channels, I suddenly was transported to a river, a wide, rushing body of water. There I saw again that young woman I had seen during my first stay in the cave, kneeling by the edge of the river before the man who I had also previously seen. She was holding onto his legs, crying that she wanted to have his child. I had seen these two before, but this time I was not an observer. I was that woman, crying out to him as if my heart would break.

In the vision, I saw the woman lift her tearful face to his and cringe at the sternness, the coldness that had come over him as he pulled himself free and began to walk away, while she was left crying out that she wanted to have his child. This scene was frozen in my mind, and again and again I heard her—myself—cry out. I had become her. The heat of my rising qi turned into a searing pain, and before I could stop myself, I moaned, "I want to have your child," and then burst into tears to relieve the pressure building in my chest. I was so unaware of my surroundings that I hadn't heard Bai return to our room. When he saw my condition, he rushed over and put his arms around me.

"There is no need to cry, Little Phoenix. We can have a child. That is why I brought you here."

Opening my eyes, I turned to him. How could I explain that it wasn't his child I had cried for, but that of another man? I now had to question whether the glimpses I had been seeing were of a distant life, a life I could not avoid returning to and exploring, but how could I so without alarming my husband? I dried my eyes and replied in a broken voice, "Yes, Bai, let's keep trying to have a child."

"I know you feel badly that you haven't conceived, Little Phoenix, but we have been apart too much, and besides, we can't have a child if you continue to sit here in cultivation," he replied jokingly, taking me by the hand and leading me to the bed. Bai and I had been trying to have a child since our marriage, but with no success, and I was beginning to accept that this gift might not be destined for me. He was less concerned as he already had three children, but it was important to me. And so, I yielded to his urgings and was brought back into a most intimate and loving relationship with my husband.

"Did you write much poetry while you were on Mt. Lu?" Bai asked, when we were settled back at home.

I nodded. "I am still working on the poems, and as soon as they are ready, I will show them to you, Bai." Since the beginning of my relationship with Bai, I had been shy in sharing my poetry with him simply because I knew that his talent greatly outshone mine. On the spur of the moment, any moment, he could create exquisitely crafted verse in any of the classical styles. He was a poetic genius who took as his subjects the activities and lives of common people, merging them with subtle mystical images. My poems were more reflections on my inner life, of less interest, I thought, to others. This was especially true of the verses I had written on Lushan Mountain, and so I put off sharing them with him.

Our home had a guest room, which was also used as a writing room for me. Bai had his own place to work. One evening I entered my writing room to find him standing by my writing desk, holding in his hand and reading the pile of my recent poems, which I had inadvertently left out in the open on the table.

"Bai, they are not ready yet," I said, going over to him and trying to retrieve the papers, but he resisted. Folding them, he placed them in his robe.

"I'd like to reread these, Little Phoenix. I am very moved by what you have written. They show real emotion and experience. Besides you have not told me much about your time in the hermitage. These will help me understand what you have been through."

"Bai," I pleaded again, holding out my hand.

"Why are you so reluctant to share your poems with me? I am your husband."

At that moment, something came over me and I confronted a mix of emotions as the image returned of my concubine life and I again witnessed the burning of the poems of that poet who had been banished. Remembering the anguish I had felt then, I went over, and in an altered state of mind, lifted a torch that stood nearby and taking my old poems out of the box that lay on the writing table, lit them and watched them go up in flames. A look of shock crossed Bai's face.

"Shu!" he exclaimed. "What are you doing!"

"I am burning my old poems," I whispered in a distant and firm voice as I stared at the disintegrating papers. I stood there for a moment as if paralyzed and then guided the falling ashes into a metal bin by the side of my table.

"Why? Why must you do that?" His voice was sterner than I had ever heard. "A poet's work does not belong to the poet alone," he exclaimed as he left the room in a huff.

I sank down by my writing table. I was not sorry I had burned my older poems, the ones written before Lushan Mountain, as I felt them to be expressions of an immature mind. I had written them when young and was embarrassed that Bai might read them. I felt differently about the recent poems as they expressed my true experiences. As I sat reflecting on what I had done, I realized that I had just symbolically paid the debt I believed I owed to that unknown poet whose poems had been burnt when I was a concubine. "Now, I am finished with it." I said firmly to myself. "The debt is paid." And so, I addressed a poem to him:

To the Unknown Poet
Helplessly I watched the leaves of your poems

Burning in the fire of my lord's anger
Over a tryst that never happened,
An exchange of glances that never took place.
Unknowingly, I was the cause of your banishment.
Justice unravels as quickly
As a flight of birds,
Staining the whole land.

Spring comes, the trees bloom, mountains rise,
But who mourns the plight of the poet?
A century later, I burn my poems
As a tribute to you
Whose name I have long forgotten
And whose poetry drifts in the dust of time.

I put aside my brush and was about to get up, but then I sat down again and said silently to my grandfather, *Yeye, I have not written anything about you, and yet you are the most precious treasure I unearthed on Lushan Mountain, the memory that brought me the greatest happiness.* So I wrote another poem:

The Immortal Grandfather

Why do these memories still toss me
Like a river gone wild, a storm unabated
After five hundred years?
Fear of the sorcerer pursued me
Until you freed me of his shadow.
Then I remembered
A child's ride through the skies,

Passing the peaks of cloud
To where the hermits gather
On a mountaintop
Discussing the fate of the world
While I sleep in your arms.

"That was no dream,
And neither is she," you said
As you introduced me
To the goddess of the moon.
"She emerges
From the center of your heart
And waits for you
Where the Dao flows.
There you will also find me," you said.

When will that moment come, Yeye?
If not soon, my love will overflow the skies.
Let the moon goddess come
And lead me to where you abide.

After writing these poems, I put down my brush and rested my head on the low table, letting my thoughts drift back to the grandfather I so loved. I must have fallen asleep because some time later I was awakened by a presence. Lifting my head, I saw Bai seated beside me reading the poems I had written a few hours earlier. I didn't try to stop him from reading them. No words of reprimand emerged from my lips. No longer could I hide my inner life from my husband.

After putting the poems down, he looked at me lovingly and said apologetically, "I am sorry I was harsh with you. I didn't understand, but now I do. Come to bed. It is very late."

The next day he handed me back the poems he had taken, and I said, "I won't burn them, Bai. I don't need to anymore." I felt I owed him an explanation and was struggling with what to say, but he didn't ask any questions and acted like nothing had happened and so I didn't pursue it. He simply said to me casually, "You should have more confidence in yourself. You have become a very good poet and are a true Daoist."

"You are not saying that because you are my husband?" I asked meekly.

He shook his head. "I am not speaking as your husband now but as the poet Li Bai." Nothing anybody could have said would have meant more to me at that moment. To be complimented by the poet I respected most in the world was beyond what I had expected, even though he was my husband. Then he added, "But speaking as your husband, I hope that one day you will feel close enough to me to share your deepest spiritual experiences. That is the way husband and wife should be, and we are more than that."

I looked at him, curiously.

"We are both seekers of the Dao and what you experience will inspire me, for you have soared to heights I long to know as well."

Some days later as we were sitting alone together over tea, he asked me, "How do you know about Hanning and the sage Zhang Daoling? You write about them as if you had been there." I didn't answer right away but he pressed me.

Finally, I replied quietly as I looked down at the teacup in my hand,

"I was there, Bai."

"You remember?" He asked in surprise.

"Bai . . ." I fell silent and he waited for my response. "There is a cave near the hermitage and Shifu sent me there several times. For days I would remain in that dark, womb-like place, and it was there that many memories returned to me. Some of the memories were of Hanning—that is where I knew the grandfather of whom I spoke, the one who was so dear to me. I had never heard of Hanning or Zhang Daoling and so questioned whether there had ever been such a person. When I found out it was true, well, it was very difficult for me, having those memories return . . ." I looked up at him and added, "You don't know how I struggled during my time there, but also what gifts came, what insight and understanding. How much I have learned! I feel I have gained lifetimes of experience, and I guess I have."

"I don't think spiritual progress can be made without a struggle," he replied gently. "We all must make sacrifices for the higher knowledge."

"That is exactly what Shifu would say," I said with a slight laugh.

"I am glad you have shared this with me, Little Phoenix. I will now re-read those poems you wrote and understand them differently."

A few weeks later we had gone to walk in the forest and found a place to rest in a small clearing. As I sat there, my mind returned to the days after Bai and I had just met, when we had so often walked among the trees. Our times together had been relatively few, and yet so full. Despite his many absences, Bai had brought me much happiness. My mind drifted off and was only brought back when I heard his lulling voice chanting one of his poems.

Ancient Song
Chuang-tzu dreams he is a butterfly,
And a butterfly becomes Chuang-tzu.

All transformation this one body,
Boundless occurrence goes on and on:

It's no surprise eastern seas become
Western streams shallow and clear;

Or the melon-grower at Ch'ing Gate
Once reigned as Duke of Tung-ling.

Are hopes and dreams any different?
We bustle around, looking for what?

"The sound of your voice reciting, chanting, or singing always stirs something deep in me," I quietly said to him when he had finished.

"Now recite one of your poems, Little Phoenix." I resisted but he pressed me and reluctantly I recited "The Immortal Grandfather."

"You loved him a great deal, didn't you?" he asked gently.

I nodded. "And I still do. He hasn't left me. When love is deep, it remains forever."

In the years that followed, I would become more comfortable sharing with Bai poems I had written of my spiritual experiences, rather than speaking about those times of transcendence. Somehow verse felt like a more adequate expression than everyday conversation.

Now that I was back in my family milieu, I had to keep my relatives, with their intrusive meddling, at bay, and defend Bai against their unhelpful comments. My mother had assumed that my time alone in the mountains was due to unhappiness in my marriage. Before Bai had left for the northeast frontier, she had heard me arguing with him, trying to prevent his departure. One evening soon after our return, she called me to her and told me that if I wasn't happy with Bai, she could arrange a separation.

"I am perfectly happy, *Nanya* (mother)," I consoled her. "I have always wanted a Daoist teacher, and Bai found one for me, and so I stayed with her while he was looking for work at the frontier. I could not be happier."

She looked at me suspiciously and I wondered if perhaps that was not the answer she wanted to hear. Perhaps she secretly hoped I would be willing to part with him. To my sister, Bai was still a drunken poet who could not support a wife. "After all this time, he still can't provide adequately for you," she commented one day.

"What is adequate?" I asked. "I am perfectly happy with the modest way in which we live."

Meanwhile, I knew that Bai was preoccupied with finding a town further south that would be safer from the rebellion he foresaw, but I was also distracted, struggling to suppress memories that were seeking to burst forth, little suspecting that they would disturb the very foundation of my life with him.

Chapter Sixteen

ANOTHER LIFE RECALLED

"You are leaving already?" I walked into our room and saw that Bai was neatly folding some clothing for the trip. I couldn't hide the sadness in my voice. I knew that he wanted to start searching for a new place for us to live, but it hadn't dawned on me that he would leave so soon. We had only been home for a few months, and it had been a time of great tenderness between us and deepening appreciation for each other. Our months apart had served to make us both realize how precious was our life together, and now he was leaving again. He had been getting reports from friends about the growing militarization in the northeast, and his concern had greatly increased since we had returned.

Bai stopped what he was doing and looked up. "The sooner we leave this area the better. I have to find a safe place for us, and you and Jing must sell the family properties. Once fighting breaks out, it will be difficult to sell anything or to move about. I don't know how much time we have." I nodded. I understood all of that, but it didn't make it easier. Later that night, I wondered if there was not another reason I was clinging to Bai, so reluctant to let him leave. When he was with me, my excursions into the past were only momentary flashes, as his presence quickly brought me back, but I was afraid of what I might see when he was gone, without Shifu or Ying to guide me. I tried to hide my forebodings.

"When will you go?"

"In a few days." Seeing the sadness on my face, he came over to comfort me, saying, "Soon we will be settled somewhere else, and then we will have more time together."

"Please find a place for us far away in the countryside, an untamed place where we can live as true Daoists do, Bai, apart from the world." He nodded. "Where will you go?"

"To Xuan town. I have a cousin there who can help me. Once I find a suitable place, I will come back for the family. Hopefully you and Jing can sell all the properties by then." Xuan town was in the southern part of the province. I nodded but I couldn't make myself feel easy about his departure.

The night before he was to leave, I was filled with anxiety. "What am I afraid of?" I asked myself, trying unsuccessfully to ease my concern. Internally I heard Shifu's voice telling me not to cling to him, but I was unable to heed her advice, and the time of his departure found me holding onto him, refusing to let go as if I feared for my life.

"I won't be long, Shu," he said quietly, as he gently withdrew himself from my grip. Rarely did he call me by my given name and, as I watched him walk away, I wondered why he did so now.

A hollow emptiness engulfed me once he was gone, and I began to feel that all my cultivation, my many experiences at the hermitage, had not served to teach me how to live in the Dao. I felt as far away from harmony with the flow of life as I ever had. Despite Shifu's counsel, my attachment had grown. A few weeks after he was gone, I sent Bai a poem.

On Parting

Why must the sky separate us?
Why must summer suddenly end
And birds flee to winter havens?
Like the last leaf clinging to a branch
I cannot let go of the memory
Of the warmth that embraced us.

Am I fearful
Of what emptiness will reveal?
If this is the Dao
Why is there so much sorrow?

Months passed and I received only an occasional letter or poem from
Bai. I soon realized that he was not only looking for a place for us to live but
was also visiting friends, traveling, spending time in the taverns, and idling
along the wayside, despite the urgency he had expressed before departing.
None of this truly surprised me, but it awakened long-buried, aching feelings
of abandonment, feelings I didn't want to acknowledge. I knew he fully came
alive when he was traveling, meeting new people, engaging in the world of
ideas, and reciting his poems before powerful men, and so I had suspected all
along that this trip would not be a short one. What most concerned me from
his letters was his continued attraction to the cities. In one letter he remarked
how unsure he was of living in the countryside. "As much as I love to visit the
forests and mountain retreats, I cannot envision living there."

"I know that, Bai," I whispered. "I was only hoping that the Daoist
in you would come forth now."

I felt more apart from him now than I had during our separation
when I was in the hermitage. His absence haunted me day and night and

often I cried myself to sleep, but I was not able to understand my feelings. Had I progressed so little? Why wasn't my cultivation easing my pain? Why was I not able to heed Shifu's words?

Many months after his departure, during my cultivation practice, I began to feel the same vortex sucking me back in time that I had experienced in the cave on Lushan Mountain, but I didn't want to go back; each time I felt that pull, I struggled to stay in the present by thinking of Bai, the anchor to my current life. As more weeks and months passed and Bai's presence drifted further away, the anchor lifted and I was set adrift on the tides of time, once again finding myself in the distant past, with no notion of when or where. I was somewhere in a jungle, living among a forest clan, in a place unfamiliar, another culture entirely, and there she was: the one I had seen before, who I now knew to be me.

"Dada, tell me a story." I curled up next to my beloved elder as he sat cross-legged, leaning ever so slightly against a tree. The canopy of branches hid the sun from us, but soft light filtered through in flickering streams. It was late afternoon and there was much preparation underway for the evening meal. I had sneaked away to have some time alone with him.

"You want to hear again about the melting of the ice and the migration of our people? You always ask me about that."

I nodded.

"To some it may seem long ago, but to me, it does not seem so far back in time that the great rock was thrown from the heavens. It was so huge that it made a tremendous impact, cutting deep into the veins of the earth, sending forth fumes that warmed the air enough to gradually melt the ice, which at that time covered so much of earth. This was a good thing. If the human population was to flourish, more water was needed, and with the melting of the ice, the seas rose. Our people at that time stayed by a vast ocean in the east, living off the food of the sea.

"Our ancestors knew that the devas were sending a message that we should move inland, and so we began the long walk away from the sea. After many, many generations, we came to this wild forest, which had no human life. Muni Baba was seated alone here in meditation, under that tree where he still sits silently today. It is said that he created all of this—this forest rich in animal and plant life. He maintained balance among the animals and knew which plants to grow. He moderated the rains so there would not be too much or too little, because with the melting of the ice came a great increase in water from the sky. Everything we needed was here, and so we settled around him, recognizing him as one of the great *rishis* (seers) who was sent to guide humanity. Muni Baba never spoke out loud, but you could hear his voice internally. Even now he communicates by thought. I have often heard him speak to me inside my mind."

Lifting my head, I drew close to him and whispered, "We children can't go close. We look at him from a distance, from behind the trees so we won't disturb him."

"Who told you that, Sundari?" he asked, smiling down at me. "Nobody can bring Muni Baba out of his meditation unless he wills it, no matter how hard they try. His body is here, protecting this forest, but his spirit is roaming the celestial worlds, and perhaps other parts of earth as well."

"We children are afraid of him, Dada. We think he is a deva."

Again, Dada smiled. "He is communicating with the devas and the spirits of the forest, but it is better to think of him as a rishi."

"What is a rishi?"

"A rishi is a great soul that the devas have blessed with knowledge and sent to earth to guide the world. They can live for many thousands of years, either by renewing their bodies or migrating into new bodies. They are not compelled to take rebirth as we are, for they are free from all personal desires and come into our world voluntarily."

"I don't ever want to be a rishi, Dada," I said, sitting up straight. "It must be horribly boring to sit like that day after day."

He laughed. "You don't know how interesting and magical the celestial world is. It makes this world look very dull. There are so many beautiful beings in the heavens, and beautiful places, far more wondrous and colorful than this forest of ours."

"Are there animals too, like here?"

"Mystical animals that fly. They can take you anywhere in an instant." He snapped his fingers.

"So, while Muni Baba is sitting with closed eyes, he might be flying on a mystical animal?"

"Perhaps. Or he might be creating a new type of tree or fruit for us."

"Can he do that?"

"He has done that. He has helped create all of this. Not him alone, for there are others like him. They have the same creative powers as the devas."

"Then we shouldn't be afraid of him."

He leaned over and said quietly, "We should love him and thank him every day for what he has given the world. He could be enjoying the heavens, but he has chosen instead to come here and help us, to make sure there is enough food and that life here remains in balance."

I looked up at Dada lovingly. His long, grey hair was tied up in a knot atop his head, but many wild strands flew out, flowing down his back. His aged face was quite wrinkled and weathered by time, but his eyes sparkled with great delight, especially when he told such tales. His thin frame was tall but frail, as he hardly ate. He was a treasured storyteller, and nobody loved to hear his stories more than I. He was the elder of our clan, the great-great-grandfather of my mother, who now led us. He had watched several generations die, but he remained.

"Shu, your food is ready." Our servant Lui was calling me. I didn't know how many times she had beckoned me, but finally her words reached my ears. Opening my eyes, I slowly came out of cultivation. She was standing in the doorway.

"Has the rest of the family come?" I asked.

She nodded. "We have been calling you."

"Tell them to eat without me. I will take food alone in my room. I am not feeling up to coming out."

A few minutes later Jing's wife appeared at the door. "Are you unwell, Shu?"

I shook my head. "I want to spend more time in cultivation, so I will have a small meal here. Have Lui bring it. Don't worry, I am fine."

Slowly I ate the food that Lui set before me, reflecting all the while on what I had seen—a life truly in harmony with the Dao, I thought. There didn't seem to be any conflict. The scene I had experienced was one of peace and joyfulness. The image of Dada remained strong in my mind. Although his manner and dress were quite different, he reminded me of Yeye very much, and the love that I felt for him made me think of Yeye. Was I blessed to have two such grandfathers? The memory of Dada made me want to uncover more.

After finishing my meal, I tried to go back into cultivation, but nothing more emerged and so I went to bed.

Weeks passed before I was able to travel into the past again. This time, a different scene came before my mind. My head was resting on Dada's lap and I was drying my eyes. I wondered what had happened. It was a sad scene, but I heard Dada's comforting voice.

"Your sister has not died," he reassured me.

"Then she has been captured by those shadow people," I sobbed.

"No, no, Sundari," he said patting my head and stroking my hair. "She has left of her own free will."

"She would never do that. She wouldn't leave me."

Lifting my head and taking it between his hands, he looked into my eyes and said very gently, "Prema is happy. She is where she wants to be. You must let her go." Burying my head in his lap, I cried. "I will find her one day, Dada, and bring her back." He kept quiet and patted my head.

My mother came and taking my hands, lifted me to my feet. "Dada is old. Don't disturb him," she whispered into my ear. "We will continue to search for Prema."

Things were not the same after that. What had been a joyful life was suddenly darkened by the disappearance of my sister, the eldest of my mother's children, the future leader of our clan. The days of running carefree through the forest with Prema were over. I now made the evening rounds with my mother, checking on every family to make sure all the tasks were performed.

About a year after Prema's disappearance, I approached Dada. He was sitting apart from the others chipping away at a long wooden stick.

"What are you making, Dada?"

"A spear," he replied.

"Prema was so good at throwing spears, wasn't she?"

"She was the best. This one is for you, Sundari."

"For me? I don't know how to use a spear. Prema could send spears sailing through the forest further than anyone and always hit her mark, and she could do the same with arrows."

Putting aside his work, he looked at me and said, "You should not compare yourself with anyone. Each person has their own talents and skills. You make beautiful ornaments, but I want you to keep this spear by your side always. One day, when you don't need it anymore, it will disappear, but hold onto it until then."

I nodded. "Dada, you once told me that Muni Baba knows how to speak with the stars. Is that really true?"

"He knows how to read the stars. There is a great rishi named Bhrigu, who had a daughter, a high devi, who was born to him to help him understand the movement of the stars and how their movements measure the passage of time. She also taught him about the different qualities of the planets and how they affect us. Each planet has a personality and we need to know and understand its role. It is very difficult for ordinary people like us to know the meaning of what happens in the skies. It is very complex, but those who understand that meaning can predict events. Rishi Bhrigu passed this knowledge on to others, like our Muni Baba."

"But Muni Baba has not left here. How did he meet Rishi Bhrigu?"

Dada smiled. "I told you once when you were young that Muni Baba appears to be stationary, but actually he moves about quite a bit."

I looked at him perplexed. "You mean he leaves the forest at nighttime when we are asleep?"

With a glimmer in his eyes, he replied, "Not at all. While his body is sitting here, he can create a new body and be somewhere else. This is how he went to Rishi Bhrigu and learned to read the stars."

"Oh!" I exclaimed, truly amazed. "Are you sure he is not a deva?" I asked in a lowered voice.

"Sundari, someday you will understand. You might say he is like a deva, but he is still human, as we are."

"Dada, then surely Muni Baba can help us find Prema. He must know where she is. Perhaps the stars can tell him."

"You miss your sister." I nodded as a sad expression came over me. He sighed. "I wish I could bring her back for you. None of us can follow where she has gone. The stars will not help us because she has acted of her own will. Perhaps one of the planets has caused her to do so. I can't read their movements much at all, but if there was a way to bring her back, surely Muni Baba would have done so. He is aware of what happens to each and every one of us. He oversees not only our clan but many clans in this vast forest."

I sighed and said internally, because I didn't want to contradict Dada: *I know she will come back. She would never leave this way without even saying goodbye to me.* Changing the subject, I asked, "Dada, who and what are the devas and where do they live?"

He smiled. "You are asking difficult questions, Sundari. They don't have solid bodies as we do, but rather their bodies are made of light and change easily at their will. They don't grow old or suffer illness or die. They may move on to a higher realm, as there is not only one celestial world but many, some higher and some lower. It is difficult for me to explain where those worlds are. They are not above or below, not in space and not in time as we know it. It is a different world entirely."

"Why can't we see them?" I asked, now very curious about the subject.

"We can. I have often seen devas sitting around Muni Baba. They are very beautiful, but I have such respect for them that I don't approach unless they call me. Surely you have seen the nature spirits who reside in this forest?" I nodded, having seen spirits emerge from trees and plants. "There are so many deities all around, but most of us can see only the lower ones that hover on earth. The higher devas are of a different order entirely. They are cosmic forces that oversee not only earth, but the whole universe, all the seen and unseen worlds. We are a very miniscule part of their domain."

I was quiet, thinking over what Dada had said. He had so much wisdom and could answer questions that nobody else in our clan could. How I treasured these times alone with him! Taking my hand, he said, "If you want to learn about the devas, come with me." He led me along a narrow path to where the trees had thinned and the sun shone down. "I used to bring Prema here often because she loved to feel the sun on her body. All the clans in this forest have a special relationship with the sun deva. It is said that he is one of our ancestors."

"How can that be, Dada?"

His small laugh made me laugh, too. "Anything is possible, because the devas can assume a human appearance and mingle among us. But the way I understand it is that when the ice melted and we were forced to migrate, Surya Dev, the sun deva fed us and guided us. You know, we were used to eating from the sea and so there was little familiar food available to us at that time, but Surya Dev taught us how to live on light and on the prana that is all around."

"Prana?"

"Hmm. That is how Muni Baba lives. You know, he never eats, and the light of the sun rarely reaches him, and so he exists on prana, the life force. It is difficult to explain, Sundari. Someday perhaps you will understand."

"So, we should give thanks to Surya Dev for saving our clan," I murmured.

"For far more than that," laughed Dada. "Life would not exist without Surya Dev and so we should give thanks every day."

One day, about a year later, I went to seek him out and found him in quiet conversation with my mother. As soon as she saw me, she shooed me away. I could tell something was amiss, so I didn't immediately withdraw. It was then I learned that we were to leave our forest abode. The planning was left to my mother. I was disturbed that we would think of leaving before we found Prema, but my mother later explained that we had no choice. Some weeks after this decision, I learned that Dada would not be coming with us. He was too old for the weeks of walking that lay ahead. I hid myself when I heard this news, taking refuge in a boulder-strewn part of the forest not far from where we stayed. It was Dada who came to find me.

"I am not leaving without you, Dada," I said mournfully. After Prema, he was the one to whom I was closest. "As long as you are alive, I am not leaving," I insisted.

With a twinkle in his eyes he said, "Okay, Sundari. The clan will stay here as long as I am alive." I felt better and got up to help him walk back to his hut. Two days later, Dada died.

"Shu, are you ready?" There was a slight knock on the door. It was Jing calling me. I aroused myself from cultivation and went to open the door.

"Why are you here?" I asked.

"Did you forget? We are meeting a potential buyer for the winery today."

"For the winery? Yes, I did forget. Give me a moment and I will be ready."

"Are you alright, Shu? You look distracted."

"I am fine."

"Is it Bai? Are you worried about him?"

I shook my head.

"Is it because he has been away so long? I didn't respond. "Come, let's go."

Jing and I went on horseback to the one of the wineries that our family owned. The potential buyers, a family we knew, were already there waiting for us. Bai had told Jing a little about what he had discovered in the northeast concerning the treacherous nature of General An Lushan and the likely possibility of a rebellion, but he had asked him not to share this information with anyone, lest we be accused of treason, spreading false news about the general.

"Why are you selling your properties, Zong Jing?" asked the older of the two men who had come to meet us. "Your family has owned them for so long and they produce a decent income."

Jing began to speak but I interrupted him. "My husband would like us to move further south for the warmer climate. He is getting on in years you know, and he has relatives there."

"Yes, Li Bai is no longer young. Where is he thinking to move you?"

"He is in Xuan town now looking for property."

"A good place. Not much literary life, but the countryside is nice."

"My husband is a Daoist and is hoping for a more secluded life," I replied, speaking what I hoped to be true.

"Let me show you the winery," interrupted Jing, "and the account books."

"I will wait for you, Jing," I said quietly as I found a place to sit. The accounts were not of interest to me and I knew nothing about them. I preferred to sit in silence and try to understand what I had experienced with Dada. They were gone for some time and my mind was withdrawn, so

I didn't notice Jing return. After the prospective buyers had left, and we had begun to walk toward the horses for the ride home, Jing asked me, "Shu, what is wrong with you? You are absent these days. I speak and you don't hear me. You don't see me coming. You don't remember our appointments. You don't seem to take an interest in what is transpiring with our properties. It is as if you are in another world, far away."

"Forgive me, Jing. My mind is elsewhere, but I will try to do better. Did they agree to buy the winery?"

He nodded. "But you haven't even asked what price they offered."

"Jing, I have to leave the family's financial matters to you. I am in no state now to deal with them."

"Are you upset with Bai that he has been gone for so long?"

"How could I not be upset? It's almost a year. It couldn't take that long to find some property for us."

"You know your husband. Don't be upset with him."

"I've begun to wonder if he really cares for me." My voice began to crack.

Jing stopped walking and put his arm around me. "Shu, how can you say that? You really are angry at him this time."

"I don't know if its anger, Jing, or just feeling abandoned."

"Don't doubt his love for you, Shu. He is just being Bai."

I sighed without responding. I myself didn't understand this rising dissatisfaction with my husband. At night I found myself whispering tearfully into my pillow, "It is not right for you to treat me this way, to be gone for so long with hardly a word. This is not how a husband should be." My mind would respond, *But you know this is Bai. It does not mean that he doesn't love you.* Yet still, the ache of resentment persisted.

We had been walking for weeks and the landscape had changed greatly. Often at night when the elders would sit together, they would question my mother, wondering whether we were lost. How did we know we were heading in the right direction? She would assure everyone that Dada was guiding her. He came to her in dreams and indicated the way forward.

I had been greatly grieved when Dada died, but my mother told me I must not think of my own needs but of what would be best for the clan. Dada knew we had to move on, and he also knew he would not last the journey, and so he had chosen to depart his body in the place he had known with Muni Baba. "Don't cry over loss or death, Sundari," she said to me. "They are part of the natural cycle of life. Those you love, you will meet again."

As we came close to our journey's end, my mother was wounded, and I had to search for help. My brother and I had been running for quite some time when we met a man coming toward us. He seemed already to know of our situation and asked to be taken to the one who had been wounded. By this time, it was midday and my mother was fading quickly. Asking us to leave him alone with her, he went into a deep meditation. The elders were befuddled. What was this stranger doing, sitting in mediation, when medicinal herbs were needed? But he had brought none. Somehow, I trusted him and after many, many hours my mother began to return to life as the poisonous substances slowly oozed out of her wound.

I handed him some food and for the first time took a close look at his appearance. He was tall with a strong torso and wore a simple white cloth tied around his waist, reaching the ground, a very different garment from the ones we wore. His clothing was not made out of the forest plant material that we used; I noticed its fine texture and couldn't help but stare at it. His hair was tied on top of his head, kept neatly together by a string of beads. By his controlled manner I took him to be some years older than I, but still quite young and attractive, very attractive in fact. I could not keep myself from staring at him.

When it became clear that Amma (Mother) would need some days to recover, , the man asked me to accompany him to the town with some others to help prepare for the clan's arrival.

I got up from my cultivation practice. I had been sitting in my room in the early morning hours. The visions I had seen of Sundari in the cave on Lushan Mountain were beginning to make sense. Clearly, I had fallen in love with this man and then there had been some difficulty. I didn't think I needed to see anything further. In fact, I didn't want to know any more. I decided to go out for a walk in the nearby park. Once there, I found a quiet place and sat down. Even with open eyes, however, the images kept coming. Regardless of what was happening externally, internally I was somewhere else, watching, listening, participating in another life.

"His name is Sachit and he must be a deva, or a rishi, because he healed you without any medicines." I was talking to my mother soon after the clan had arrived and settled into the few huts that had been assigned to us.

She shook her head. "He is a brahmin," she replied. "They are devoted to learning and to spiritual practices, and they perform the ceremonies in the temples. Their healings methods are different from ours. We rely on plants, while they rely on vibration, on sound, on what they call mantra. Dada knew how to use those sounds. He had even given a mantra to Prema to protect herself." My mother's voice became very quiet when she mentioned the name of my sister.

Sachit came to see us often, one day taking me to meet the great Saraswati River, which was so vast it looked almost like a sea. Our people loved the river, and we settled easily into this new world. Living by the river made us feel as if we had rediscovered something our ancestors had possessed, a closeness to the spirits of the water. Here they didn't speak about the forest spirits, but, rather, invoked the devas. I recollected what Dada had taught me about the difference between the lower nature spirits and the higher devas. We were now under their protection.

Months passed, and my sadness over the loss of Prema and Dada was gradually replaced by the joy of being with my newfound friend Sachit, who came to see us often under the pretext of checking on my mother, but who, I felt in my heart, was really coming to see me. My mother, sensing my attraction to him, cautioned me one day about his vow of celibacy as a brahmachari and student of one of the great sages of the community, but I cast aside her warning.

Sachit seemed amused by my ignorance of the customs in his society and was eager to teach me about the way they lived, but I could not change from the forest girl that I was. Wherever I went, I carried the spear that Dada had made for me and this caused him to laugh every time.

"You don't need that in Brahmavarta," he said to me one day with a chuckle. "You are quite safe here."

I looked down, embarrassed, and replied quietly, "My grandfather made this for me. Actually, I don't know how to use it, but it is the only thing I have from him and it helps me feel that he is with me." An awkward silence followed, and I lifted my eyes to look at him, thinking: *Why don't you understand me, Sachit? Why do you think me ignorant?*

When he first brought me to meet the river, he took my hand and dipped it into the rushing waves and blessed me with the water. On another visit, he pressed his lips to my head. He helped me find my sister, who had fallen in love with a naga prince and gone to live in their world. He was clearly beginning to feel the same affection for me as I felt for him.

According to our tradition, such intimate signs were an indication that we were now to be mates. This brought me great happiness and I thought of nothing else but the time when I could approach him, because in our clan it was the woman who was to openly state her feelings first. But it didn't work out as I had thought it would. I had gone to stay in the hermitage of a great woman sage, and for two years she had tried to awaken my spiritual interest, but my thoughts were only on Sachit. Her loving ways and wise counsel did not prevent me from pursuing him as soon I left her care. But when I shared the feelings in my heart, he turned cold and abruptly walked away, rejecting me, abandoning me by the side of the river, crying that I wanted to marry him and have his child.

Everything changed after that. Word had gotten out that I had inappropriately approached him. My mother grew distant and disturbed, claiming that both of her daughters were willful and neglectful of the good of the clan, putting their own desires first. I was now the cause of humiliation and trouble for my clan. I didn't understand. What had I done wrong? He had taken a vow of celibacy, but why couldn't he break it? There was nobody to speak for me, nobody to guide me. I had thought our feelings were mutual. How could I have been so wrong? My wounds were deep. They didn't bleed, but they festered; the silent aching grew until I couldn't stand it anymore, and I didn't know how to quell my throbbing heart.

The harsh words of my mother rang in my mind: "Do you think yourself fit to be his wife?" We were a forest clan not yet assimilated into their society, not yet understanding their ways. How could I be so brash?

Slowly I wound my way back to the waking world. I looked at the scene before me in the park, somewhat dazed. I had forgotten where I was. Couples were walking arm in arm, and I felt the sadness of Sundari, compounded by my own sadness at Bai's absence. *I know that Sachit, the one who abandoned me by the river, was you, Bai. But why must you still stay away now, sending hardly a word of news? Is your love so feeble? Do you feel no responsibility to me?* I wanted to cry but I didn't. Instead, I watered the seeds of anger and insecurity.

As I sat there, the words of Sundari's mother continued to haunt me, "Do you think yourself fit to be his wife . . . do you think yourself fit?" I couldn't erase them from my mind. Finally, getting up, I whispered, "I can no longer stay home hoping for your return. I can no longer just be your support, waiting and wondering while you wander the world. My life means more than that." Returning to the house, I wrote a brief note to Bai asking him to come home immediately, saying I needed to see him urgently. Lui sent a messenger to Xuan Town to deliver the letter. The days passed and my anxiety grew. I waited impatiently for a response, but none came.

"Are you sure the message reached his cousin's house?" I asked Lui several times.

Each time she replied, "It reached there. His cousin assured me he will deliver it to him." A darkness settled over my mind, the darkness of doubt and victimhood, and gradually I began to feel that Bai was once again abandoning me. *His love for the world is greater than his love for me*, I told myself. After several weeks of waiting I said to Lui one morning, "Arrange for two horses for tomorrow. You and I are leaving first thing, but please don't say anything to the family. I will leave a note for Jing.

"Where are we going, Shu?"

"To Lushan Mountain."

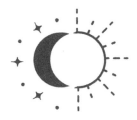

Chapter Seventeen

RESOLVING THE PAST

Once we arrived at Lushan Mountain, I left Lui at a local inn and told her to wait until I returned to pick her up. "Shu, where are you going? I cannot leave you." Her voice betrayed deep concern. Lui had known me since I was a child and had always shown great care for me. Over the last many weeks, she had seen how little I was eating, how often I was secluding myself in my room, and again and again she had expressed her concern. Now her fears were multiplied.

"Don't worry about me, Lui. I am going a bit further up the mountain to visit my dear friend Master Li Tengkong. I would take you with me but . . . well, it's a Daoist hermitage and it may not be appropriate. Rest here until I return for you. It won't be long." Reluctantly she agreed to part with me.

When I arrived at the hermitage, Ying came to the door and was surprised to see me as I had sent no advance notice. "Shu! We were not expecting you. Shifu is not here."

"Can I stay here for a time, Ying? I desperately needed to get away from my family and Bai is traveling. I need time alone."

"Of course. You are part of our family, but, Shu, all our beds are taken." She paused and then added, "I will bring an extra sleeping mat into my room and you can share with me."

"No need, Ying. Is anyone staying in the cave?" She shook her head. "That is where I most want to be now."

"Alright, let me make arrangements. But Shu, you don't look well. Why do I see such sadness in your eyes?" I turned my face away and didn't respond. I was afraid that if I spoke, I would release the tears I was struggling to suppress. They would flow once I was alone in the cave, but I didn't want anyone to see what I was experiencing internally. Ying knew me well and wouldn't let me go until I had unburdened my heart. Putting her arm around me, she sighed and asked, "Is it Bai?"

"I am leaving him," I replied quietly in a breaking voice.

"What? You can't be serious, Shu. Whatever the problem is, it can be worked out."

"I feel abandoned by him. He has been gone for over a year, and it is the same behavior. He abandoned me once before, long ago. I saw it. Why do I have to repeat this and feel this pain again? I deserve more from a husband, Ying. I do." I looked at her with tearful eyes.

She replied quietly, "Shifu will never let you leave Bai. Come, let's go to my room where we can speak undisturbed." Her room was behind Shifu's cottage. Once there, she sat me down. "Shu, is Bai's behavior any different now than when you first met him? Hasn't he always been a traveler? Hasn't Shifu made this clear to you? This wandering is not a reflection of a lack of love. Why are you so insecure? Each one of us has our own path to follow, and once we set expectations of another, we are bound to be disappointed. There is something else at the bottom of this, I think. Perhaps you have stirred the mud of old memories and are bringing up feelings that have not been resolved. Now is the time to resolve them. Here, change into this robe and go to the cave, but it won't be like the other times, Shu, because Shifu is not sending you there. You are going of your own accord. So, stay in the cave as much as you need to, but you can also come out when you want, if you want to walk among the trees or wish to join us for a meal." I nodded.

Once in the cave I didn't enter cultivation. Rather I went to the sitting area, propped myself up against the cold cave wall, drew up my knees, and rested my head on them. Releasing myself into the waves of memory, I let go of my identity as Shu as the waters of Sundari's life rolled over me, scene upon scene, and I let myself sink into their depths.

Many scenes from the life of Sundari passed quickly before me. I saw my unwilling and painful departure from my family and clan, the humiliation in which I left, my sad goodbye to the sacred river that I had come to love greatly, the sense of unworthiness that had stayed with me as my mother's words burned deep into my mind, my marriage to a man I didn't love, the day in the forest when the naga cursed me, the fire ceremony performed by a sage called Kapila, throwing my beloved string of tulsi beads into another sacred river called the Ganga, the vow I had taken, Sage Gayatri's visitation as I sat in despair by the river, and her submerging the vow I had made into the deep cavity of my mind. I remembered the years when I had stayed in her hermitage, soon after my arrival from the forest. I recollected the stories she had told me, but now with new understanding. Scenes of those moments flew before my inner eyes, and then the scenes slowed down and my awareness once again entered Sundari's body and the ordinary flow of her life.

Several months had passed since the day of the yagna and several weeks since Sage Gayatri had come to me by the Ganga. I remembered that Kapila had said that he would explain how his grandmother maintained such a youthful appearance. He had been much on my mind since I had made my sacrifice and had thrown my most precious tulsi beads into the river, but I had not felt brave enough to pay him a visit. One day, I gathered my courage and went to the temple. I was told that he was not there and, as I turned away in disappointment, the young brahmin told me that if I needed to, I could visit Kapila at his home.

"Would he mind?" I asked in surprise.

"Not at all. He is readily available to all who need to speak with him. He lives in a small cottage at the edge of the forest. Anyone can point you in the direction."

As I walked along the path, I thought to enter the forest and gather some wild berries to offer to Kapila.. I knew exactly where the bushes of sweet berries were and easily filled the basket I had brought with me. Then I continued on to Kapila's modest cottage, which I found without much difficulty. Hesitant to disturb him, I stood a short distance from the doorway, wondering if I really had the courage to knock. As I stood there wavering, he came out and, noticing me, greeted me warmly.

For the first time, I took note of his tall and elegant figure. During the yagna I had been too disturbed to take in his appearance. Now I saw that he had the same nobility of bearing that his grandmother had, and that there was a deep humility and kindness that shone on his face.

"I came to thank you for performing the yagna for me," I stammered.

"No need to thank me, Sundari. It is always an honor to perform a fire ceremony."

I was quiet for a few moments and then said, "After the ceremony I went to the river and made a vow." My voice fell off and then I continued, "I don't remember what my vow was." My hands naturally went to my neck to touch the now-absent tulsi beads. "It was about my tulsi beads, I guess . . . Your grandmother came, and a calm and peace descended over me that I haven't felt since leaving the forest. She subdued a pain that had been ravaging my heart. I am so grateful to both of you." I looked away shyly.

"The pain of separation, of leaving the forest—I have also felt that. This pain was also part of your suffering, as well as the losses of your sister and your grandfather. It wasn't just Sachit. It was a compounded pain. I understand." He looked at me caringly. For the first time I realized how true those words were. I had poured all my feelings into Sachit, blaming him for what I had undergone, but it was more than just him: it was the loss of a way of life and those I had held dear, and it was the distance that had grown between my mother and me, and, in fact, between myself and all of the clan.

"You have brought my favorite berries," he remarked with a broad smile as I handed him the basket. "I often go to the forest to collect them myself." It was then that he noticed the spear I was carrying. "Do you mind if I look more closely at your spear?" he asked with a curious expression. I handed it to him and watched as he ran his fingers over the smooth wood and then closed his eyes. "A very special spear," he murmured. "Do you carry it with you always?" I nodded. "Someone has surrounded you with the protection of many mantras. It is good that you have kept this with you."

"What do you mean?"

He smiled. "I can hear the mantras that were chanted while carving this spear. Someone took great care in creating this for you. I imagine it was someone very special."

"My grandfather," I replied in amazement. "That was so long ago. I never knew he chanted mantras while making it."

"Do you want to hear them?"

I nodded enthusiastically.

"Come, let us sit on that boulder." After we seated ourselves, he instructed me to close my eyes and concentrate at the point between my eyebrows. "I will try to transmit what I hear." He gently held the spear and asked me to do the same.

I closed my eyes, and all became still, very still. The whisperings of birds, the swirl of the breezes in the trees, every sound ceased, and out of the deep silence emerged my grandfather's voice, quietly chanting mantras. I listened and felt his presence near. When the chanting stopped, I opened my eyes and saw Kapila still engaged in meditation, a beautiful radiance emerging from him.

After a while he opened his eyes and smiled at me.

"That was my grandfather's voice," I murmured. "And all these years I didn't know. I followed his counsel and kept the spear with me at all times, although nobody understood why." My voice fell away. How persistently my mother and family had tried to take it away from me, thinking it a useless remnant of our forest life.

"Everything happens at the right moment, Sundari. Come, let us go into the cottage and I will tell you about my grandmother."

He led me into his cottage, and I carefully placed my spear by the door. Then he guided me to a low table with woven mats arranged around it. Motioning me to sit, he began. "I have to go back in time to explain. The story begins with Rishi Bhrigu. Have you ever heard of him?"

I nodded. "When I lived in the forest as a young girl, my grandfather told me about him. He said that Rishi Bhrigu had taught our Muni Baba to read the stars and planets."

He closed his eyes and sat in silence for some time while I waited. "So, you are from one of the clans under the guidance of Muni Baba? That must be how your grandfather came to know those powerful mantras."

"You have heard of him?"

"Who does not know of Muni Baba, one the great sages of our time? But let me get back to my story." Kapila reclined slightly, resting his back against the wall, and began his narrative.

"Rishi Bhrigu had two wives, Sage Khyati and Sage Puloma. It was Puloma who gave birth to a son called Chyavana. When he grew older, Chyavana spread the teachings of his father—the understanding of the science of reading the stars and planets and of predicting the future through their movements. But when he was a young man, Chyavana had fallen in love with a beautiful young girl who lived in the forest, as your clan did. They were planning to marry, but, before they could, she died suddenly and mysteriously, and he fell into profound despair. His father, being the great Rishi Bhrigu, counseled him to devote himself to a deep meditation practice. He did so, establishing a hermitage in a forest near where he had met this young girl, and he spent many, many years absorbed in meditation, until he grew quite old.

"Meanwhile the young girl he had loved was born again as Sukanya, the daughter of Raja Sharyati. Father and daughter were riding through the forest one day with their retinue when the raja became thirsty and hungry. They soon came upon the hermitage of Sage Chyavana. The young brahmins of the hermitage fed the raja and his entourage and gave them fresh water. Before departing, the raja said he would like to thank Sage Chyavana, who he had heard so much about due to his devoted meditation practices. The brahmins were quiet. None of them had seen the sage for many years, and yet they didn't want to offend the king.

"Sukanya also felt an intense desire to meet the sage, and she began to look for him all around the hermitage. As she was searching, she came upon a very large ant hill. At the top of the hill were two beams of light, shining out through the structure. She realized that the sage must be meditating there and so, lovingly began picking off the dirt and insects from his body. As she was cleaning away the ants, memories of her past birth began to arise in her mind. When she had patiently cleared away the mountain of ants and the sage sat before her, she recognized him as the one she had once loved. Even though she was now a young woman and he an aged man, her feelings had not wavered.

"The sage, seeing the young girl before him, recognized Sukanya as his departed beloved. They went to Sukanya's father and announced they wanted to get married. The king was glad to meet the sage, but hesitant about the marriage. He took his daughter aside and said, 'He is a great seer, no doubt, but are you sure you want to marry this old man?' She was a very wise woman and pleaded with her father, and so they were married.

"But now Sage Chyavana wanted his youth back. He wanted to enjoy his time with his young wife, and he felt very badly that she had to put up with an old man. The sage began to pray to the Ashvins."

Kapila paused in his tale. "Do you know who they are?" I shook my head.

"They are twin devas who possess great healing powers and transmit celestial knowledge of healing. Sage Chyavana prayed to them to have his youth restored. His *tapasya* (spiritual practice) had been so intense for so many years that he was due a blessing from the devas, so they granted his desire. Appearing before him, they manifested several very rare herbs and told him to mix them together and put them in a pool of water. For seven days he was to bathe himself in that water, submerging himself completely.

"When he emerged from the bath, his youth had been restored. But his wife was not pleased. She saw that her sage husband had been deluded into thinking too much of his physical appearance. Now, Sukanya was not an ordinary woman. She was a sage in her own right and had mystical powers. She cast an illusion upon him so that he would see her as an old woman. In essence, he became young and she became old. When she approached him, his love was unwavering. He laughed when he saw her and said, 'Whether you are young or old, wear a youthful body or an aged one, does not matter to me. My love for you is the same.'

"She responded, 'That is wise of you, my dear, but why do you not ascribe the same wisdom to me?' Immediately he realized his mistake and begged her forgiveness.

"At that moment the Ashvin devas appeared and said their blessing could not be revoked. Then they asked Chyavana, 'You now have the means of reversing age, what will you do with this knowledge, sage?' He looked at his wife and she replied for him, 'We will destroy this formula. If it spreads, humans will focus only on their outer forms and not on gaining spiritual wisdom, and it will disrupt the cycle of death and rebirth, which is designed to help humanity grow in spiritual knowledge through many different experiences.'

"Sage Chyavana was thoughtful and replied to his wife, 'I understand your concern. I think it is best to hide away what is left of this water. It is useful for the rishis and sages to extend their life, as their only desire is to bring benefit to humanity, not personal gain.' She consented. The Ashvins were so pleased that they granted to both of them powerful methods of healing, which have been handed down to us today.

"After the Ashvins had departed, the two sages put the remaining celestial formula into jugs and hid them in remote caves. Many years ago, my grandmother, Sage Gayatri, was in a long retreat in one of those caves. When she came out of meditation, she was very thirsty. She wondered where to get a drink of water and noticed an urn tucked away in one of the crevices. Lifting the lid, she discovered a cool, sparkling liquid and took a long drink, leaving the rest for another sage to find. At that moment, the appearance of her body froze at the age she then was, and this is why her body is that of a woman in midlife, even though we think she has passed two hundred years. We are not even sure about her age. My grandfather, on the other hand, is even older, but has not retained his young body. In fact, my grandmother often laughs about this, because she says it was her husband who sent her to this particular cave. Clearly, he wanted a young-looking wife." Kapila chuckled as he finished his story.

I sat there as still as could be, in utter amazement. Not since my time with Sage Gayatri had I been so enthralled by a story. "So that explains it. Never would I have imagined that Sage Gayatri had a grandchild your age. Is Sage Chyavana, then, known for his knowledge of medicinal plants?" I asked.

He nodded and replied, "And more than that. He is known in particular for his devotion to Surya Dev."

"Is it he who taught us to worship the sun god?"

The sage smiled and was quiet for a few minutes before responding, his voice full of reverence. "He knew Surya Dev to be far more than the power that gives life to our sun, but realized him rather to be the universal force that brings light into being, the consciousness behind this light. This universe could not come into being without light, not just physical light, but subtle spiritual light as well. The force that brings this light into manifestation is the one we call Surya."

"Oh," I replied quietly, not quite able to grasp what he was saying. "My grandfather told me that our clans have a special relationship with Surya Dev because of the ice melting and our migration, but he never explained it as you have. I was young then and perhaps he thought I wouldn't understand." My voice tapered off as I added, "Actually, I still don't understand." A woman then entered the room, and Kapila introduced me to his wife, Amala.

"Please stay for our afternoon meal. I will prepare it while you chat with my wife."

"It would be my honor," I replied. After he left, I asked his wife in surprise, "Does your husband often prepare the meals?"

"Most often. My husband does not like to receive service from anyone, even me. He lived alone in the forest for so long that he is used to gathering and preparing his food." I was surprised to hear this as I would have thought that Sage Gayatri's grandson would have been brought up in one of the hermitages, with many students to serve him. "You don't know his past?" Amala asked. I shook my head.

"I am sure he wouldn't mind me telling you. His father was the only child of Sage Gayatri. Soon after his marriage, he was sent into the forest to help teach the forest clans the wisdom of the rishis. But while traveling with his family through a wild area, his father was killed by rakshasas, leaving his wife and their one child, Kapila, who was very young at the time. After his father was killed, his mother found a small abandoned hut and she and Kapila began to live there. A few years later, the mother died of a poisonous snake bite. Kapila was eight years old then. Can you imagine such a young child having to perform his mother's cremation all alone?" She shook her head, as I opened my eyes wide in astonishment.

"Where were his grandparents?" I asked.

"He knew nothing of his mother's family; he knew his father's parents had hermitages but didn't know how to find them. So, he lived alone in the hut, gathering forest foods as he had when his parents were alive. He struggled with hunger, sickness and fear, fear of the thunder at night, of unfamiliar forest sounds, fear of the rakshasas who had killed his father. I don't know many who could have survived."

Kapila entered, carrying several varieties of cooked foods. His three children ran in, and everyone eagerly enjoyed what he had prepared. As I ate, I recognized some of the foods. "I remember these plants from my childhood. Where did you find them?"

"They also grow in this region, but one has to walk quite deep into the forest to find them. Most of our food comes from there. Kapila still likes to gather wild food," replied Amala.

After the meal was finished, Kapila said he would walk me down to the river, and from there I could find my way back home. We walked at first in silence, and then I asked him about his childhood. Since I had heard the story from Amala, I had not been able to settle my mind. During the meal, while engaged in conversation, I could only see a child alone in the thick forest.

"Do you mind if we sit for while by the river," I asked him. He nodded his assent

Turning to look at me with the clearest eyes I had ever seen, he began. "You are wondering how I survived in the forest by myself? Each day I didn't know if I would be alive to see the next day. Each day I would get up and thank Surya Dev for allowing me to meet the day once again. Every night I would search for the moon and ask the deities there to see me through the night.

"Many months after my mother died, while searching for food I found a small statue of a devi hidden in the brush. I took it home and wondered how to pray to her for help, for guidance. That night my grandmother came to me in a dream. I had not met her before, but I recognized her instantly as my grandmother, and in the dream, I sank onto my knees to touch her feet. Lifting me, she said, 'I have sent you this statue of Shri Devi, a very powerful and loving devi. Pray to her in the language of your heart and she will protect you.' Then she gave me a mantra and taught me how to use it. It was that statue and mantra that saved my life and saw me through those hard years. From time to time, especially when there was a need, when I was ill or very frightened, my grandmother would come to me in dreams." He turned his eyes from me and quietly looked out over the river.

"I learned very valuable lessons during those years. Never did I feel sorry for myself, even though I didn't know if I would ever be able to find my way out of the forest. Every day I was grateful simply to be alive, and I learned not to let personal losses wound me too deeply. When I had to cremate my mother, that was perhaps the most difficult moment, but what could I do? I had to look tragedy in the face and encounter it head on. I learned to be like a lake without ripples, to temper my emotions, to see my struggles as a gift." His voice was as gentle as an undulating stream and as he spoke, I felt his peacefulness wash over me.

"Did your grandmother never come looking for you?" I asked meekly. I knew how loving she was and wondered why she would not search for him.

"I was to learn later that this was her greatest test," he replied quietly.

"Was it a test sent by Indra Dev?" I inquired, remembering all the stories she had told me of sages being tested by Indra. He nodded. Recalling how I had heard her sing so lovingly to Indra Dev by the river in the early dawn, I murmured, "How could she continue to love him, when he gave her such a difficult test?"

"She will have to tell you that story." Then turning to me he asked, "Does a test diminish one's love, Sundari? You know the answer to that. Your love has also been tested."

I blushed and didn't respond. After a few quiet moments I asked, "How did you find your way to Kashi?"

"When I was eighteen, a wandering brahmin passed by and asked to spend the night. He was on his way to the Sarasvati River and when he heard my story, he offered to take me with him. There I found my grandparents, and some years later my grandmother sent me here. But when I left the forest, an unexpected sadness came over me. It was due to my separation from all the animals and plants I had come to love. I had felt myself as part of them, and suddenly they were no longer there. It was a transition I had to make, as did you.

"Kapila, I am so moved by your story."

"Next time you come I will show you the statue of Shri Devi, my most precious possession."

"Next time?"

"Surely you must come visit my wife and me again. Sundari, you and I share a memory of and love for the forest life. Not many here have that. I came to know the animals and plant life as my family and cared for them as I would for a brother or sister, and that knowledge is more valuable to me than anything I have learned since. I suspect it is the same for you." With those words he stood up and indicated that he would now leave me as the path to my home was straight ahead.

As I walked home, the thought entered my mind: *If I was not worthy to be Sachit's wife, was I fit to regard Kapila as a friend?* He was also highly regarded in the community. Was he just being polite, or did he really mean for me to visit again? I wasn't sure and so I decided not to disturb him unless I could find a reason.

Kapila was on my mind when I arrived home and all through the evening. Before going to bed that night, I went to touch my grandfather's spear as I did every night, but it was nowhere to be found. I realized, then, that I had been so distracted by Kapila's story that I had left it in his cottage. *That will give me a reason to return*, I thought to myself. But still I put off a return visit.

As the days passed, I could not get Kapila out of my mind. He was the grandson of two great sages, yet he was so humble, so unassuming. His story stayed with me for weeks. For years, I had felt so sorry for myself over a relatively minor trauma, the rejection of a love, and yet he had experienced real tragedy and didn't feel any self-pity. More than anything else, his story served to change my attitude toward my life. Sachit and I had both been young and inexperienced when we met. Why was I still holding on to something that happened so long ago? Why could I not release it? I had admired

Sachit so much in my youth, but the man I really admired and wanted to emulate now was Kapila. He had the strength to endure anything that might come his way. He might not know how to heal with mantra or be able to show me the world of the nagas, but he knew how to endure with grace, and that was an ability I envied: to resist the temptation to be undone by sadness or to fall into a pit of self-pity.

He had spoken to me of Shri Devi, the devi my mother and clan loved and honored; I had not often thought of her since leaving the forest. Kapila had retained so much of the simplicity and joy of forest life, and I wanted to regain that for myself. After arriving in Brahmavarta, I had tried so hard to be like the others, to fit in, all for the sake of Sachit's approval, so that he would accept me. But fitting in meant stifling my real nature, and in the end, all of my efforts had failed in any case. Although I loved our town, I was still very much a child of the trees, and was happiest when I could retreat to any little remnant of forest I could find. Meeting Kapila awakened a longing for a treasure deep within myself that I had nearly lost.

Although I very much wanted to retrieve my spear, one thing and another prevented me from returning to Kapila's cottage so quickly. After many weeks, I finally made my way back.

"I was expecting you," said Kapila, when he saw me approach. "You have come for the spear, haven't you?"

I nodded. "I don't understand how I could have left it. I have carried that spear with me everywhere since leaving the forest."

"You left it for a good purpose."

"What is that?"

"You no longer need it, Sundari. It has been withdrawn." He spoke quietly as he looked at me carefully, as if to gauge my reaction.

"Withdrawn?" I asked confused.

He nodded.

"You mean it is gone?" Again, he nodded, watching that sink in.

"What happened to it?" I asked in a shaky voice.

"When I saw that you had left it, I wanted to return it to you, but then I sat with it in mediation and I realized that it was meant to be with you only until you no longer needed it and then it would disappear. The next day, it was gone. It had disappeared into the ethers."

"Like Muni Baba," I murmured. For a moment my mind grew quiet and then, for reasons I couldn't explain, I smiled and said, "That is okay. If it is to disappear, I am glad it did so here, with you. You enabled me to hear my grandfather's voice again, and perhaps that was the spear's purpose all along." Walking on the river path back home, I remembered that my grandfather had foretold that the spear would one day leave me.

Several weeks later I again wanted to visit Kapila, but I felt that I had to find an excuse to do so. I wasn't confident that I could just casually appear at his door. Finally, a reason came to me—a question about the fire ceremony—and then some months later I found another excuse and made another visit. It went on like this for quite a while. I was happiest when I could be in his company, so I was always looking for something to ask him about. One day he said to me with a smile, "You don't need a reason to come here, Sundari. I meant it when I said that you remind me of the precious days of my simple forest life. You are more than welcome here any time.

As the years passed, I saw Kapila and his family with some frequency. Sometimes I would bring them food from the market, but they preferred the forest foods, as did I. Kapila had become a dear friend. I found that I could speak with him more openly than with anyone else. I never shied away from sharing my feelings with him. One day I said to him, "Your grandmother has been one of the most important people in my life, but I didn't fully appreciate her when I lived in the hermitage. I was so young then, and my mind was filled with passionate yearnings. It would mean so much to me to see her once again."

"I will let her know," he replied. I didn't ask how he would do that, how such a meeting might be arranged, or how she would travel, and truly, I put this thought out of my mind.

Several years later, I was walking alone by the Ganga when I saw a woman in the distance who seemed to be waiting for me. As I drew closer, I saw that the woman was Sage Gayatri, looking exactly as she had when I had left her so many years earlier. Standing before her, I immediately sank to my knees and rested my hands and forehead on her feet, not rising until I felt her hands lifting me. She led me to place where we could sit comfortably by the river. "You are looking much better, Sundari, than when I saw you last."

"The last time we met?" I asked, perplexed, and then remembered. "That was when I threw my tulsi beads into the Ganga and made a vow, although I still don't remember the vow that I made."

"It's not important. The vow will be fulfilled."

At the mention of the vow, the thought of my sister entered my mind. "Ammaji, it is my greatest wish to be reborn with Prema when that curse she received comes to fruition. That is still on my mind."

She nodded. "I understand. It is a noble desire and can be fulfilled."

I was quiet for a few moments and then said, "Ammaji, you have always been so kind to me, more caring than my own mother." Even now, she had come all this way in response to my request to see her again. I didn't take this visit lightly and wanted to express my appreciation. "I . . . I am so grateful to you, beyond what I can express."

She smiled. "When you first came to me, you reminded me a great deal of my grandson. I had not been able to show him love when he was growing up, or tell him stories about the rishis, as I would have liked to have done, but I fulfilled this desire with you. When I learned that you had been sent away, I was happy to hear you had gone to Kashi, where my grandson was living. It was my hope that the two of you would meet."

I was quiet, wanting, but not daring, to ask her why she didn't search for Kapila after the death of his parents. She seemed to read my mind.

"You may know his story. After his parents died, Kapila was left alone in the forest. I had not met him yet and didn't hear the news of my son's death when it happened, as I was far away, deep in meditation. Then one day, I had a vision in which I saw a young boy crying after the death of his mother, and I knew it was my grandson and that now both of his parents had been taken from him This was my greatest test. I was on retreat in a mountain cave and after this vision I tried to leave to search for Kapila, but every time I attempted to exit the cave, an invisible barrier would be erected, impossible to break through; I was prevented from leaving and had no choice but to return to my meditation."

"Who would do that?" I asked in consternation, wondering who would prevent a grandmother from going to her grandchild left alone and defenseless in the jungle.

Her eyes softened, and a most loving look came over her face as she replied in the gentlest of voices, "The most radiant one, the most beautiful, the most luminous. It was he, who rules the domain of the radiant mind. I have told you much about him. It was his test of me. I knew this and was torn between my love and yearning for him, for that state of being, and my love for this child I had not yet met. For so long, I had been expecting this Deva's approach, listening for those unheard footsteps, waiting for the lifting of the veil of separation, and that state was now so near, within my reach. I knew that if I broke my concentration, it might recede from me, and so I struggled for months, years really. I would get up from my meditation and try to leave, but the barrier was there. I would struggle with that invisible wall that stood between me and the outer world and then fall down in tears. Eventually, I would return to my meditation seat, where I would experience just a tiny taste of his joy, and so it went on like this.

"It was three years before I could leave that cave, before Indra Dev awakened the light-filled world of the higher mind, where the bliss of being resides, the all fulfilling Soma, the nectar of immortality. In that time, many things were shown to me about my grandson, and I was able to reach him through his dreams. Many years later, when I actually met my grandson and saw who he was, the simplicity and nobility of his character, I realized that had I left my meditation and gone to find him, to bring him to Brahmavarta, he would not have become who he is today. My beloved Indra Dev was helping me to help my grandson grow into his potential. That was the gift he gave in return for my sacrifice, my inner struggle."

I was quiet for several minutes and then I asked in confusion, "You have spoken to me so much about Indra Dev and still I don't understand. Who is he? Is he the higher mind you speak of, or is he a being?"

"Both," she replied with a smile. "He is a vast cosmic force who rules the light-filled domains of the higher mental worlds, impossible to grasp with the limited mind, which is such a weak instrument of perception. Only the superconscious can grasp that reality, and yet that vast force can assume a very personal form. It is the intensity of one's love and devotion that evokes a form out of the vastness that he is. But no need, Sundari, for you to concern yourself with these matters. It takes much discipline and long years of meditation to reach those states, which will come to you in the distant future."

As she spoke, the sound of her voice singing to her beloved Indra Dev by the side of the Saraswati River came back to me, and I said, "Once, I went down to the Sarasvati River at dawn and heard your song. It was the most beautiful of all the poems I had heard of the rishis. Why did we not learn it at the hermitage? Why do others not know it?"

She smiled. "So, you heard me?"

I nodded and she chuckled. "We are all poets, Sundari. When the heart is filled with love, we cannot help but sing, but I am not a great rishi, not nearly as accomplished as those seers." Then she leaned close to me. "But I will tell you a secret, my dear: the devas see the heart of a person and love can carry one just as far as the deepest spiritual practices, but that love must be all encompassing. You must be ready to sacrifice everything for that love."

"Even after all the trials Indra Dev put you through, you still have love." I was amazed and baffled by this.

"True love is strengthened by trials, not weakened. That is the purpose of the trials: they free one from limitation and misperception." I was still unconvinced but dared not question more. After a pause, she asked, "What else do you want to know, Sundari?"

"Ammaji, when I was living at the hermitage, you told me that one day you would tell me something about Sarasvati Devi."

She smiled. "You remember that?"

"I haven't forgotten anything you have told me, although I can't say I understand it all. I have the same question, actually. Is she a river or a devi?"

"She is far more than a river. She is the active creative power, that within us which inspires, transmits knowledge, and seeks to express itself through song. It is said that she rests on the tongue of the poet, and that it is she who breathes words into the poet's mind. But she is not only within us; the force we know as Saraswati is also bringing into being new stars, new planets, new life. She is the flower unfolding, the seed within you that bears life. She is that great creative force that moves through the universe bringing the unmanifest into manifestation."

"She is all of that?" I exclaimed.

"Now I will tell you of her relationship to the river. For ages, the seers had been in meditation high in the sacred mountains where the water was locked in ice. They were also there when the ice began to melt and the rivers began to form. Perhaps they even aided that process. Some of the seers say they heard the Devi's footsteps guiding the river in her downward flow through unmarked mountain passes. Some saw her hand caressing the river to stir her waters and generate life. Some saw her light body emerge from the watery depths, and so the river was given her name. She imbued it with creative power, and for millennia poets and sages have gained their inspiration from that river, seated in meditation on her banks. That is why so many are drawn to gather by her side. Devi is also here in the Ganga. She is in all the rivers, but the Sarasvati River holds a special place in the hearts of our poets because so many of their songs were inspired by her outer flow, which led them to the inner Sarasvati, the inner flow of life, which in turn carried them to the oceanic mysteries of the universe."

"That is a lot for me to understand, but I am sure your words will remain with me for a long time."

She nodded. "What I am explaining cannot be grasped with the mind alone. It must be experienced, and that is the purpose of meditation, to give you that inner experience. Each one of us can attune ourselves with the same creative power that gives rise to the poetry sung by the seers. The sages are able to hear the words emerge out of the silence. We can do the same, if we truly set our hearts and minds to it. Now, Sundari, before I leave you, is there anything else you would like to ask?"

I was quiet. Sage Gayatri looked at me inquiringly. "I do have another desire," I replied meekly. She nodded, indicating that I should ask. "You have done so much for me." I breathed in deeply before asking, "If I could . . . it is my greatest wish to serve you in my next three births."

"Serve me? That is not necessary, Sundari, not at all."

I felt myself blushing, as if I had asked for something completely inappropriate, and so I added quietly, "In our clan, it is a tradition that when one has received knowledge or something of value, one gives something back in return. The only thing I have to give you is my service, and it will certainly take me more than one lifetime to make a sufficient offering."

Smiling, she replied, "The only requirement here is love. There is no need for anything else because love is the greatest gift."

Folding my hands, I lowered my head and replied, "Service is a way for me to express that love. It is my deepest desire, but if it is inappropriate for me to ask this, then please forgive me and ignore my plea." She entered meditation and rested in silence for a long time while I sat with folded hands and bent head, inwardly pleading with her to accept me as her servant in the future. I knew that I was far from being ready to engage in the strict spiritual practices her students underwent, but if I could be near her, that would be enough—just to feel her radiating love.

Finally, she emerged from meditation and looking into my eyes, replied firmly, "All right, Sundari, I take your request as a sign from above. So be it, with Ganga Devi as our witness. As you have requested, for three births you will serve and during one of those lifetimes the curse of the naga will come into effect." Not until much later did I realize that by making this request, I might have caused Sage Gayatri to commit to taking rebirth.

Peace settled into my heart after this visit. For so long I had suffered with the unfulfilled desire to serve Sachit. All I had wanted to do was be by his side, supporting him in any way he needed, but that desire was now released. Instead, my future would lead me into service for Sage Gayatri.

It was some months later when I was visiting Kapila and his family that he took me aside and handed me an object wrapped in a cloth. "This is a gift for you," he said. Unwrapping the object, I saw that it was his statue of Shri Devi.

"Kapila, this is most precious to you!" I exclaimed. "How can I accept it?"

"It is not polite to refuse a gift," he replied with a smile. Looking up into those eyes, clear as pure still water, I opened my mouth to speak but could not. Finally, I just repeated, "Kapila."

"It is not from me. It is from the devi herself. Will you then accept it?"

"But why are you parting with this?"

"Some years ago, you gave something precious of yours to the Ganga, and so something precious is to be returned. That is the way the universe works, Sundari. Nothing is taken without something being given." After a pause he added, "It is the same with love, Sundari. There is no shortage of love in this universe. If it doesn't flow to you from one source, it will come from another, and more important than receiving love is giving it. That is a lesson I learned in the forest. The more I gave love to the animals around me, the happier I was."

I drew the statue to my chest and held it tight. "You don't know what it means to have her statue and to have it come from you."

He started to say something else but then stopped himself.

"What is it Kapila?" I asked.

He was quiet for a few minutes and then replied, "Sundari, I know you have suffered a lot because of Sachit. That was your trial. Don't let bitterness enter your heart. I have no doubt that one day your love for him will be fulfilled." He laughed and then said, "The trick is to see the gifts we are given, which often come in the most unexpected way."

When I got home that afternoon, I placed the statue in a special spot and decided I would spend a few minutes every day reflecting on the deity. As I arranged the area, the thought came to my mind, "Kapila, since the day we met I knew we had a special bond, and now Shri Devi has confirmed it."

My dear, most humble friend Kapila didn't live long after that. In the few years of life that I had left, I would often find myself sitting by the Ganga speaking to him as if he were there with me. "It was you," I said to him one day, "who taught me about love. I spent so many years aching for Sachit, feeling rejected, abandoned and unloved, pitying myself, but in the end, you taught me that the love I was seeking already exists within me. There was never any need to search for it."

As the end of my life approached, I knew there was an unfinished matter between me and Sachit, and I died feeling sure that sometime in the future we would meet again, when we would be able to embrace each other, not out of need or insufficiency, but in order to mutually share the love that lives within.

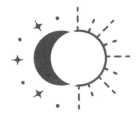

Chapter Eighteen

SHIFU'S TEACHING ON LOVE AND SACRIFICE

I had been in the cave for five days, not engaged in cultivation, but rather reclining, resting, walking, and reliving portions of my past birth as Sundari, which I realized had taken place in ancient *Tianzhu* (India). As the scenes of Sundari's life came before me, and I heard her mother's cutting words about her daughter's unworthiness, I cringed as I recognized that those feelings still lingered inside me so many millennia later. Hadn't that been the reason for my reserve when Bai proposed marriage? Hadn't I secretly felt unworthy to be the wife of such an eminent poet? As I made this connection, I slowly picked up the jeweled dagger that rested by the meditation seat in the cave and began slashing the air, crying out, "I will destroy forever these seeds of unworthiness that were planted so long ago, unknowingly, by a mother I am sure I have long ago forgiven." When thought-seeds sink into an unformed mind, they cannot easily be dispersed but must be grabbed by the root, so that is what I did.

As scenes of the later years of that life came clear to me, the pain Sundari had felt over the rejection by and separation from Sachit was replaced by a sense of deep gratitude for the precious friendship with Kapila and the wise kindness of Sage Gayatri. How much I had learned in these few days during my stay in the cave. The time had deepened my understanding of my relationship with Bai. Any anger I felt toward him, any sense of abandonment, dissolved. The words of my friend Kapila and of Sage Gayatri resounded in my head: "Don't let bitterness enter your heart" and "True love is strengthened by trials, not weakened"—words spoken millennia ago but so relevant to my current life.

From the beginning of my relationship with Bai, I had been clear with myself that I didn't want to judge his failings, just as I didn't want him to judge mine, but I had slipped into being angry at him for something that was part of his nature. He wasn't ignoring me. He was simply being the wandering poet. I had idealized Sachit and I had also idealized Bai, despite the fact that Jing had cautioned me that he was a great poet but perhaps would not be the greatest of husbands, at least not in the conventional sense. I had said to myself that I was not a conventional person and didn't care about such things, because he understood my spiritual yearnings. Hadn't I said that was my only requirement for a husband? Yet, I had not fully uprooted my anger toward Sachit until now. In my remembering, I felt again the intense love I had had for Sachit, which was stronger than any anger, and it was the same love I now felt for Bai. I could not be by Sachit's side to support him in life, but I could do that now with Bai.

Standing up and slowly circling the small cave, I said out loud, "Foolish girl, you cursed both yourself and him to wait so long. You made him wait almost ten thousand years and now you are complaining when he stays away for a single year. Perhaps it is payback." I smiled. If only Bai knew. Then my thoughts turned to Sage Gayatri's words about sacrifice. She had sacrificed her attachment to her grandson for higher knowledge, and it was done out of love, not anger. She had given up her own will for the Deva she loved so much, and he had returned that gift a thousand-fold. What love was between them, this sage and her Deva! That was a true love story.

Sundari's sacrifice was made out of anger, for her sister as well, but really, I thought, it was misguided. Who benefited from it? What was the true meaning and purpose of this sacrifice, I began to wonder? I would have to ask Shifu about this.

I looked around the cave and could not help but speak to the stone walls: "How I treasure the days I have spent with you. You have witnessed my suffering but also my growth in understanding and the peace that has come into my heart." As I spoke, I ran my hands along the walls. Then resting my head against the stone, I whispered, "You are surely a mystical cave, holding many secrets, and I will be forever grateful to you."

I came out into the dappled sunshine. Remembering the words of Kapila, I closed my eyes and internally spoke to the sun deities. *You were my ancestors once. I bow down to you and express my love and gratitude.* Then I walked along the nearby trails for a while, stopping every now and then to observe the rock structures, those benevolent towering figures, and the lush greenery, the mists hanging low over distant peaks. For some time I stood still, observing and listening to the squawking and tweeting of birds, and then I returned and sat on a rock cliff near the cave. Closing my eyes, I entered deep cultivation and lost track of time. When I opened my eyes, I found Shifu seated beside me. I began to rise but she placed her hand on my arm. "No need for formalities now, Shu."

"Shifu, I am so sorry I didn't give any notice before my arrival."

"Do you think I didn't know you were coming?" I looked at her, thinking that her words would never cease to amaze me. "What pattern have you seen in the behavior of Sundari, Chunhua, and Meihua?"

After reflecting, I shook my head and replied, "I don't see any pattern, Shifu. They were such different lives."

"Look more deeply."

Silently I reviewed the three lives I had experienced, and suddenly I saw the connecting thread. "Sundari didn't defend herself and share what had truly happened with Sachit, how their affection had been mutual. In effect, she allowed herself to be exiled. Chunhua was falsely accused by her husband and family but instead of standing up to them and defending the truth, she ran away and chose exile. Meihua also was falsely accused and didn't defend herself and was put away. They had no confidence in themselves, no voice, no courage really."

"It is a pattern of thinking and behaving that was set in you long ago and that has never been fully undone. So, while this behavior has not emerged in every life that you have had since Sundari, when the conditions were ripe, when you were put to this particular test, you fell into that old pattern. You are only becoming aware of it in this life. Patterns repeat themselves and we keep suffering until something makes us change."

"Shifu, I realize now that these feelings of being unworthy and unloved by Bai and my fear of him abandoning me . . . these feelings are unwanted leftovers from a much earlier time. I have no use for them anymore."

"You cut them to pieces, didn't you, with the dagger? That is why the dagger is there, to destroy harmful patterns of thought."

"Shifu, there is no keeping anything from you."

"The first time I sent you to the cave, you guessed right: that naga was a magical creature who had come to bless you, to unlock your memories so that you could put to rest the residue of your life as Sundari."

"But he wasn't the same being as the dreadful naga that I had killed, was he?"

"Indeed, he was."

"How can that be, Shifu? One had dark intent, but the other was full of light. I could tell the difference in their eyes and even in their hissing sound."

She smiled. "Do you really want to know?" I nodded. "There are those few who know how to transform negative energies into positive ones, demons into benevolent beings. You have learned about the creative force in the universe; there is also a transformative, regenerative force that works to transmute these dark entities. As long as there is creation, there will be polarities, tugging and pulling at each other. The third universal force is the one that preserves the balance between these polarities. This balance, this harmony that the universe is ever in the process of re-establishing is called the Dao, and that is what we must seek to align ourselves with.

"Who could have transformed that evil naga?" She didn't answer. I reflected and then murmured to myself. "Was it Muni Baba?"

She nodded. "Your clan was under his protection. He allowed your grandfather to give the mantra to your sister, which enabled her to enter the naga world, creating some disturbance among the ruling classes there, and so he had some responsibility in this matter. That naga was out to destroy her and you were a means to get to her. He was very powerful, and after you killed him he was about to take birth again in the naga world, which would have repeated the cycle. Muni Baba saw this and worked to transmute the darkness in him, and he eventually became a very benevolent being. In the cave that day, he blessed you. Can you perceive what that blessing was? He fulfilled a great desire of yours."

"To have a child," I said quietly. The words came out of my mouth, as my desire for a child had become more urgent.

"You will now have Bai's child. Shu, there is another meaning hidden in this story. In the way that powerful beings can transform negative entities, each of us must transform the negative feelings within ourselves—our anger, greed, selfishness, and self-pity, our sense of being the victim. This sense of victimhood is also a pattern you have repeated. You must end it now. The process is both an inner and outer one. The more we transmute our own darkness, the less darkness there will be in the world around us."

"Shifu, the life my clan lived when I was Sundari was much like the life we tried to recapture in Hanning, but couldn't. In ancient Tianzhu they lived in the Dao without even knowing to seek it or what to call it."

"Life back then was an earlier stage in what we call human development, but one in which there was greater harmony with spiritual truths. The Dao was natural to them. They didn't have to name it. They were living naturally in that state. We have fallen far from that, despite our many developments. The great sages Lao Tzu and Zhang Daoling tried to recapture that state, but on a personal level. They showed a way for each one of us to regain our harmony with the Dao, but now we must make an effort. It is not the way we are used to living.

I reflected on what she had said and then added, "I am so grateful I was able to see the life of Sundari, for now I remember what it is to live in the Dao, although she certainly broke away from that harmonious way of living."

"You have not quite understood something."

"What is that, Shifu?"

"You have not understood Wu Wei."

I smiled. "You are right. I certainly don't have a good grasp of that."

"When you saw Sundari begin to step into the great river, you thought she was not acting in harmony with the Dao, that she didn't know about the strong currents. But had she not tried to step into the water, Sachit would not have put his hands on hers and begun a whole train of thoughts and actions. That was when the spark of attraction really took hold between them. Perhaps she was in the Dao after all." Her eyes sparkled as she looked at me with a slight grin.

"Shifu, it is far more complex than I imagined. It is like the unending unfolding of a lotus, revealing mystery within mystery, within mystery . . . endlessly."

"You have just described the universe."

"Shifu, I have one regret."

"What is that, Shu?"

"That woman sage, Sage Gayatri, she was so patient with me. When I was in her hermitage, I was the worst of students, not even a student really. I didn't understand her stories at all, and yet she spoke such wisdom. I didn't make any effort, yet she never gave up on me. Later she came to me when I was in great need after the fire ceremony and took away the pain of the vow I had made. She did so much for me, and I never was able to fully express my gratitude; no, it was more than gratitude, it was love. I had forgotten her for so many millennia, and now that I have remembered her, I wish so much to show my appreciation for who she is . . . for showing me that there is such an unselfish love in this world."

Shifu was quiet for a few moments and then replied in a gentle tone, "I am sure she knows your feelings. Remember, thoughts and words travel. When the heart speaks, it crosses all barriers of time and space. I have told you that the Dao is nothing but universal love. That is the foundation of all that is. When you are in harmony with this all embracing, all-inclusive love, you are in the Dao."

"Shifu, if I hadn't been sent away, I would not have met Kapila, who was such an inspiration for me, so dear to my heart. The cause of my suffering turned out to be a great blessing. I think Sage Gayatri knew it would be that way."

"You could not have been sent away without her consent," she replied quietly. "She had taken responsibility for you."

I was quiet but my thoughts were not. I was reflecting on the quality of love of that great sage, who had shown such consideration and care for me, who had been such an undeserving student. Then I thought of Shifu. Her love was the same. Hadn't she come to me whenever I was in great need. And Shifu's love was not just for me, but she showed the same care for each and every one of us. I gazed over at Shifu and saw her smile and knew that she was aware of my thoughts. Embarrassed, I changed the subject.

"But, Shifu, what is this sacrifice that Sage Gayatri spoke of so often ?"

"Life is a sacrifice," she replied slowly. "Every day, every moment, we are sacrificing the higher good, the enlightened knowledge, for the lower desires. At some point in our journey we must turn this around and sacrifice the lower pleasures for the higher ones. Sacrifice is an offering we make to the universal forces, which are working to awaken the immortal within us. When we understand sacrifice properly, we realize it is nothing more than a love offering. What could Sage Gayatri offer to the deva she loved so much? Only her last attachment, the one that tugged so painfully at her heart. She asked for no return, but there is always a return. That is a universal law. In return for her sacrifice, she received the transcendent bliss of the celestial world and a grandson who was able to come into his higher being. That is the secret of sacrifice, but it must be done with the proper intention, seeking nothing in return.

"When you took a vow to postpone the fulfillment of your love for Sachit for such a long period of time, you made a sacrifice, and in return, you were given the gift of your friendship with Kapila.

"Over time, the true meaning of sacrifice has been lost, just as the true understanding of the gods has been lost as people began to project human qualities onto them—petty jealousies and the like—and as people came to fear them, thinking that if they didn't perform certain ceremonies they would be punished. This is childish thinking. The gods and goddesses are benevolent cosmic forces working unceasingly to awaken the immortal in the mortal being, to bestow higher wisdom. Their sacrifice on our behalf is the greatest of all sacrifices, for they could remain in their eternal bliss and needn't work so diligently and patiently on our behalf, but such is their love."

I pondered her words and then replied quietly. "I am so much better able to understand this than Sundari was. She had not much intelligence at all!"

She laughed. "You have traveled far in ten thousand years! Surely now you understand a great deal more."

"Shifu, I have come to see that it is our perception of events, rather than the events themselves, that shape our thinking and our destiny. Sundari never considered Sachit's feelings, what he might have been going through. She saw everything from her own narrow perspective, and that caused her to take the actions that she did."

Shifu looked at me intently without responding.

"Am I doing the same now?" I asked somewhat shamefully. "I came here this time, out of anger toward Bai, out of feelings of abandonment, without thinking of his needs."

"Abandonment? Anger toward Bai, whatever for?" She smiled mysteriously and I understood that she knew everything.

"Honestly, I thought I would leave him, but that anger is gone, completely. I love that man and would never leave him."

"Then I think I should explain, to clear things up: Bai never received your letter. I actually went to find him. When the letter arrived at Xuan town, he had already left and gone to Yangzhou. Then I heard he was in Nanjing. I carried the letter, disguised myself as a Daoist priest, and went to meet him. My friendship is not with you alone, but also with him."

She began to speak in a low tone, and I could see her concern. "I want him to stop taking those immortality pills that are so popular now among some of the hermits. They are filled with all sorts of metals that are not good for the body. They are harming him, but he has such faith in them that I am not sure he will comply with my advice. I didn't think he would listen to you or even me, but I thought if he met a Daoist priest with knowledge of these matters, he might listen, so I presented myself as an experienced alchemist. That husband of yours is very stubborn, so I don't know if he will stop taking the pills. I also wanted him to know not to tarry much longer because the empire is on the verge of collapse, and Xuan town is not a safe place of refuge. I suggested that he head south of the Yangtze, where it will be safer."

"Here I was, angry at him, while you were trying to help."

"It was a repressed anger that you had long hidden," she replied. "I am glad you are free of it. He never saw the letter, because I knew once you had gone through your experience, you wouldn't want him to. But, Shu, you must return home immediately. Soon it won't be safe on the roads. I will get you to the inn tomorrow, where your attendant is staying, and you must take horses home, not a carriage. It will be faster. Shu, you didn't defend yourself in those previous births, but there may come a time when you will have to defend your husband. Make sure you have the strength to do so. He will need you." I nodded.

"Your old room is available for you tonight. The woman who has been occupying it has left for her home, so you may go there and rest."

Shifu rose and I also got up to leave. I was about to say something and then paused.

"What is it?" she asked.

"Nothing, Shifu." She looked at me with a strange expression and I looked away. "It's just . . . I never found out whether Sachit ever married in that life." My voice trailed off. I turned my eyes to her again.

"Does it really matter, Shu?"

"No, but I would like to know," I replied meekly. It didn't occur to me to question why I thought Shifu would be able to answer, because I had come to believe she knew the answer to any question I might have.

"He never married." She sighed and then her voice became stern. "That you even think to ask shows you are still doubtful of Bai's love for you, carrying over insecurities from the past. Get over it. The one who loved you then still loves you now. As Sundari, you had wanted Sachit to break his vow and choose between you and his teacher. He couldn't do that. Now you silently seek to make Bai choose between you and life on the road, which is the inspiration for his poetry. Don't do it. Don't repeat the pattern. Stop looking to the external world for that which lies within you." Abruptly turning away, she began walking back to her cottage, leaving me speechless. I think it was her words and the harshness of her tone that finally broke the insecurity with which I had been living.

That night I went to my writing table and just sat there. "This may be the last time I write in this hermitage," I said quietly. "But what should I write? I wish I could remember that beautiful song Sage Gayatri sang by the banks of the sacred river, so full of love and longing. At that time, it had uplifted me so, but I don't recall the words. I will write about her and the god she loved."

Gayatri's Song
You hurled me with thunderous force
Into the depths of the cave,
Where seed thoughts battle
And vie to take root,
Where obstacles blossom.

Like a howling child,
I resisted your touch
As you swept away

The remnants of clinging,
The remains of separation,
Pursuing desire,
And relentless thought.

If I cannot climb
To your distant abode
My love will draw you
And on your rays I will ascend
Out of this darkness.

I long for your approach,
Oh radiant One,
Oh gracious Indra, lord and revealer
Of the luminous mind,
Lift me out of myself
And into your light-filled world.

The next morning, I went to see Ying and once again thanked her. "You are not leaving Bai, are you?" she asked hesitantly with a downcast face.

I shook my head. "How could I ever leave him? My love is only stronger now." Then I turned serious and added, "I just hope those delusions don't come over me again."

"I think you have resolved what needed to be worked out, Shu." I nodded. Taking her leave, I then went say goodbye to Shifu.

"On your way home, stop briefly at the side of the Yangtze River and perform a ceremony. It will help bring closure to your memories."

"What kind of ceremony, Shifu?"

"Anything will do. Here, take this packet. I have put in some ink, a brush, and some paper. You may want to write something to transform the pain you have felt."

"Shifu . . ." I looked at her gratefully as I took the small packet.

"No need to say anything more." She turned and left me to reflect on what kind of ceremony I might perform.

Another nun accompanied me to the inn where Lui was staying. She had been anxiously awaiting my return. When we approached the river, we stopped. I left her with the horses and walked alone along the bank. After a few minutes I sat and reflected on what to do. Then I took out the writing materials and recorded my feelings.

Releasing Ancient Memories
I lifted these ancient lives of mine
And set them on a ship to sail down the Yangtze River
Into the dark distance.
"I can't hold you any longer," I whispered,
"Your weight is too great.
But find a safe place to be
And every now and then
I will come visit."

I watched many faces drift away
But those I loved lingered.
And as a breeze brushed my ear
I heard the words:
"Love cannot be forgotten
For it does not know time."
I smiled and nodded.

Your faces are engraved
In my heart.

I wrote the poem twice, kept one sheet of paper and rolled the other one up, then I placed inside the rolled paper a small bit of my hair that I instinctively felt to cut before leaving the hermitage, thinking that something of my current life should go as well. Then I closed my eyes and thought of all the people I had remembered from lives past, knowing there were so many more I had not recalled. Placing the rolled paper into the water, I set it adrift and watched as the waves took hold of it, washing it downstream. I saw it sink from my sight. I sighed and whispered, "Now there is completion."

That night we stayed at an inn and I was inspired to write another poem, hoping to preserve my precious memories.

Song to Goddess Sarasvati
You are the inspirer, the one who grants knowledge,
The yearning for wisdom and wisdom itself.
You are the song of all things.
You open the eye of the poet
And whisper rhythms into the ear.
You dance through our bodies,
Lifting us into your joy.

You are the creative urge
That causes rivers to sway
Through the land.

You are the unfolding lotus
Unraveling mystery within mystery

Without end.
You are both within and without,
Sarasvati, the sacred goddess of creative life.

The next morning, at the first light of dawn, we resumed our journey home. As we rode further and further north, I saw streams of people walking with bundles on their backs. Halting the horse, I climbed down and tried to stop some of the people to ask what had happened. Nobody would speak. I looked into their tired and frightened faces and knew that war had broken out.

Chapter Nineteen

CIVIL WAR

The journey home took several days, and I was sure that Bai would reach home before me, but when I arrived, I couldn't find him anywhere. Disappointment overcame me, and I was about to leave for a nearby tavern to see if he was there, when I thought to check a small back room where he sometimes went for cultivation. Quietly pushing aside the door, I found him seated on a cushion, reading, his back facing me. For a few moments I stood there, my heart pounding. *Why this surge of feeling?* Approaching him, I slid down onto the floor behind him, and resting my face against his back, I placed my arms around him.

"Bai, I am home."

For a moment he was silent. Then he turned and embraced me. "When I got here and didn't find you, I was worried. Then Jing told me you had gone to Mount Lu, and I was afraid you were angry with me, Little Phoenix, for staying away for so long. Are you angry?"

Lifting my face to look into his eyes, I replied, "No, Bai, I am not angry anymore, but I have missed you terribly, and I was hurt, very hurt that you didn't return sooner. That is why I went to the hermitage."

He tightened his grip on me. "I am sorry. I never wanted to cause you any pain, never, Little Phoenix. I am here with you now and will stay with you for a long time. We have to leave in the next few days before the roads become unsafe. Jing and the family left this morning. They wanted to wait for you, but I told them to leave and that they could always find us through Li Tengkong. She will know where we are.

"Where are we going, Bai?"

"A Daoist priest I met told me to go south of the Yangtze, but I think Nanjing will be safe. We will head in that direction, but we should take as little as possible with us." Bai had many acquaintances in Nanjing, who I am sure he was thinking would help us get re-settled.

"On the way home, I saw many people walking with parcels, leaving the cities. What exactly has happened?" I asked in a concerned tone.

"General An Lushan has gathered a very large army and has launched a rebellion against the central government. They started from Hebei and have captured one prefecture after another. I have even seen some of his troops here on the outskirts of Liang Park. We must leave as soon as you can get ready. Gather whatever possessions you need."

His worry cast a pall over the last days at our home, but as always, whenever we came together after a long separation, his passion was great during the quiet night hours and we both found much comfort and pleasure in our intimacy. I was glad that my experiences of the last many months had been put to rest and I could focus on Bai and the crisis at hand. During his time away, Bai had not found a place for us to relocate. He had not been happy at Xuan town and there were lingering questions about Nanjing, so we had to leave our home without knowing exactly where the winds of fortune would take us.

The roads were now filled with many more people trying to escape. Bai could not help but stop to talk with some of them. They told harrowing tales of the brutality of General An Lushan's army, which was conducting killings, rapes, and thefts on a massive scale, burning whole villages. They told stories of dead bodies lining the streets, loyal citizens turned into beggars overnight. We stopped to spend the night at an inn and, while I went to rest, Bai went into the streets to gather more information from the refugees who, like us, were trying to flee the war. When he finally came to bed he couldn't sleep, so troubled was he by the accounts of atrocities he had heard.

"Such cruelty," I cried out to Bai as he shared some of the stories with me the next morning. "Where does this brutality come from?"

"An Lushan is a beast, not a man, but even beasts don't behave this way," he replied soberly, putting his arm around me. "We can't go to Nanjing. His army is heading there, and people will start to flee the city. We will get on a boat and head upriver on the Yangtze toward the capital, where surely it will be safe."

"But Bai, this is not only the General, it is also the army, our men of the Tang Empire. They are torturing their own people. This is not an invasion from a foreign force. It is our own people killing us."

"I can't explain it, Little Phoenix," he said quietly, looking away. "It was the emperor's folly to fall under the influence of his consort Lady Yang and for so many years now to be wasting the empire's resources, ignoring his governing responsibilities and passing his time in frivolities."

When we reached the river, I was shocked at how the scene had changed. I thought about the peaceful Yangtze of a short time earlier, when I had set my poem into the calm waters and had watched the rolled paper drift downstream. Now there was dread and panic everywhere. Even the roiling river seemed to reflect the fear that was engulfing everyone. We found a boat to board, and headed west, stopping along the way to find acquaintances of Bai who could inform us about the situation.

At one stop, we learned that the emperor, now quite aged and feeble, had asked four of his many sons to take charge of the armed forces, sending them in different directions and dividing the authority among them. The rebels had captured Luoyang City in the east, not far from our home, and set up a government there. General An Lushan had declared himself the emperor of Great Yan and was now heading to Chang'an, the capital city in the west. Receiving word of the General's approach, the emperor and the court were getting ready to flee the capital. We were deeply shaken when we heard this news and knew that we could not continue our journey west.

"The territory north of the Yangtze is already gone," said Bai's friend. "You must head south."

"Bai, let's go to Lushan Mountain. I am sure we will be safe there." His friend concurred. "That area is too remote for the rebels to bother about. The emperor sent his son Prince Yong to defend the southern area and he is gathering an army."

A short time later we heard that the emperor and the court had fled to Sichuan. The royal guards had killed Chancellor Yang Guozhong, a relative of the famed Consort Yang, who they blamed for empowering General An Lushan years earlier. They also killed Consort Yang's sisters and forced the emperor to allow the hanging of his greatly beloved Consort herself. It was a desperate time. Truly, it seemed the country could not escape total turmoil. The capture of the capital would shatter the empire.

The region around the Yangtze River no longer seemed safe. We headed to Lushan Mountain, the place I so dearly loved and had visited such a short time ago under very different circumstances. We found a place to settle not far from Shifu's hermitage, but I was not able to visit her as Bai was much depressed at the situation and I had to pour all of my efforts into him. Despite the brokenness of the world around us, the next few months were ones of relative stability for Bai and me. This was the life I had hoped for with Bai, one of retreat into the remote countryside. We heard little news of what was happening around the country, although we knew that the fighting was fierce and that the emperor's son Prince Li Heng was seeking to quell the northern area. He had declared himself as the new Emperor Suzong of the Tang Empire, with his father's blessing.

It was during these months that I realized I was pregnant. Despite Bai's depression, and the raging war, this was a happy time for us. We made several trips to visit Shifu, but each time, she was away. Ying told me she was traveling through the villages as there was much hunger and despair, and it was likely that she would not return for many months. "Most of the women here have gone home to their families," she explained, "leaving only those of us who permanently live here." Bai and I were sitting with her outside of Shifu's cottage.

"At least Bai is here with me and we have time alone in the country-side. It is what I have long desired," I said as I took hold of Bai's hand.

"Here, Shu, take this food from our garden." She handed me a large basket of vegetables.

"Are you sure you have enough?"

"With only a few of us left, we have more than enough. We are even supplying some of the villagers. Further north, so many farms have been burned and destroyed. People have nothing to eat. The rebels are ruthless. They will destroy everything and be left with only a broken and impoverished land to rule." She shook her head.

"How quickly things can change, Ying."

"Overnight, everything can turn upside down."

"This is a result of all the corruption," Bai said. "It has been building for a long time and could have been corrected, but it was allowed to fester and grow. If you tend to a wound early you can heal it, but if you ignore it, the wound can kill you."

Bai had been listening to my conversation with Ying until then without speaking, but he could not help but show his disdain for the corruption that had taken over the court. I had told Ying how depressed he was over the situation in the nation, and she urged me to practice cultivation with him. However, he was not able to focus his mind, so I had to think of other ways to distract him. A few days after the visit with Ying, I went outside our cottage into the cool autumn air and sat in the sun. It was a bright afternoon, and the sun felt good on my body. As I closed my eyes, I reflected back on my life in the ancient time when we expressed love for the sun deity. I was engrossed in these memories when I felt Bai place a blanket over my shoulders.

"It's cool out here. I don't want you to catch a chill," he said as he sat beside me. I smiled and extended the blanket to cover him as well. We sat in silence for a while and then I asked him, "Bai, are you still taking those immortality pills?"

"Why do you ask?"

"The thought occurred to me."

"I'm not taking them anymore. Before returning home, I met a Daoist priest who knew a great deal about alchemy. He discouraged me from taking the pills. When I assured him that I myself was very good at alchemy and told him the ingredients, he warned me that the metals involved were harmful to the internal organs. I believed him and so I stopped."

I hit him playfully. "So, you listened to the priest and not to me. How long have I been telling you this?"

He took my hand. "I should have listened to you about many things."

"Can I tell you a story, Bai?" He nodded. "Once in ancient Tianzhu, there was a sage named Chyavana, who was the son of a very great sage." I proceeded to tell the story I had heard from Sage Gayatri's grandson, and then ended by saying, "His wife was very wise. Together, they hid the formula from people because they knew that it is not the human body that is immortal, but the spirit. Surely you know this, Bai."

He smiled, "Yes, but just like that sage, I have a young and beautiful wife and want to stay young for her."

"All the more you should learn from Sage Chyavana," I chuckled. Then I added, "You know, the people of Tianzhu believe they are descended from the deities of the sun, or at least that those deities have played a great role in guiding them. But our people, Bai, have a special relationship with the moon goddess. Why do you think that is?"

He was thoughtful. "We have to look far into the past."

"To the Yellow Emperor? It is said that he had many magical powers."

"Well before that. His ancestor was Shennong, who brought the knowledge of how to cultivate the land, save seeds, and bring water to the fields. Before Shennong, our ancestors lived off the foods of the forest, which were plentiful. He also brought knowledge of healing, of the medicinal arts. But even before him were Fuxi, the earliest of the wise leaders, and his sister Nuwa, who populated these lands. Those early communities were matriarchal, and it may have been then that we came into relationship with the moon deities. There is a feminine energy that comes from the moon, and perhaps it was *Chang'e* (the moon goddess) who guided our people at the beginning of our civilization. Even today, she holds great importance for us."

I nodded. "We still worship her during the mid-autumn festival. I used to think those were myths, but now I wonder . . ."

"What are myths but ancient memories that have been distorted and reduced to folklore over time. Don't forget that for many millennia our history was relayed orally from generation to generation, as there was no need for writing at the time. There is always a kernel of truth to these legends, but the popular telling brings the stories down to a level that can be understood by the common people and often the truth is lost. Every great civilization must have had a deep relationship with one of the deities."

"So, it must have been like that," I mused. "In ancient Tianzhu, there were many sages who had great knowledge, who could see the deities. It must have been the same here."

"No doubt the ancient sages here also had great powers, and that is why the common people deified them. All advances in civilization were made by such people." Turning to look at me suddenly, he asked, "How do you know so much about ancient Tianzhu?" I looked down and didn't answer. "Did you learn all of this from Shifu or are these your memories?" he asked quietly.

"My memories," I replied just as quietly.

"Such ancient memories. It is quite extraordinary, Little Phoenix."

I turned to look at him and thought, do you really remember nothing from that time, Bai, nothing at all? Changing the subject, I then added, "Bai, people in those ancient societies lived in the Dao. It was their natural way of being. We see them as primitive but spiritually they may have been more advanced. We strive so hard to be in harmony with nature, but for them it was their way of life." My voice fell off as I became silent.

After a few minutes, Bai said, "It is getting chilly. Let's go inside." He began to get up, but I put my hand on his arm.

"Wait, Bai, I have something to tell you." He sat back down and looked at me expectantly.

"What is it, Little Phoenix?" I suddenly felt shy before him. Suppose he wasn't happy about the news, after all we were in the middle of a brutal rebellion. It might be difficult to think of bringing new life into the world at this time.

"Bai, I am with child," I said quietly, looking into his eyes to gauge his reaction. He was getting on in age, already in his late fifties, and I didn't know if he truly wanted to have a child so late in life.

"Are you serious?" he asked and then immediately said, "Of course you are. You wouldn't joke about such a matter, but we are in the middle of war." Then his face softened. "It is right to bring in new life when there is so much death. I am happy, Little Phoenix, truly happy with this news."

I was relieved that he seemed to be sincerely happy. On the boat I had been nauseous several times, and he had been worried about me. Since arriving at Lushan Mountain, I had also felt unwell, but now we knew the reason. While I had been worried about Bai's mental state, he now became worried about my physical condition and tended to my every need. Finally, I thought, we will have the life together I have been hoping for.

The months passed and one day an old acquaintance of Bai's from Chang'an arrived with a request. Prince Yong, who the emperor had put in charge of defending the area south of the Yangtze River, was asking Bai to accept a position as an official advisor to his campaign. I could tell how honored Bai was; he saw the offer as another chance to serve the country. Placing a large bag of gold on the table, the man added, "There is much money and the chance of a high court position for you if you accept."

Turning to Bai, I shook my head and said quietly, "You know you can't leave me now."

The man did his best to convince him, but finally Bai said it would soon be spring festival, a time when families must be together. "I am sorry, but I can't leave my wife at this time." I thought I detected a note of sadness in his voice.

"I understand. I will return at a later date."

Many discussions followed between Bai and me. He was convinced this was an opportunity for him to fulfill his need to serve. I saw how the opportunity lifted his spirits, but I also feared for him, for us, thinking of the dangers.

"We have been isolated here and don't know the situation. You may be stepping into a trap." He was quiet and didn't respond. After the spring festival ended, the man returned again with great fanfare and flattery, telling him of the prince's eagerness to meet him.

I had begun to feel better, no longer overcome by feelings of faintness or stomach upset, but I was reluctant to let this uprising disrupt my family life yet again. Bai saw my determination and consoled me, "I will only meet the Prince and see what I can do to advise him. It was the emperor himself who gave him the task of defending the south. I won't stay. I won't engage in any fighting. I am doing this for the little one yet to be born. We want a stable country for the child."

"Do you promise you won't engage in any fighting, that you will only go meet him and then return?" He nodded. I had no choice then but to give my consent; after all it was the Prince, the son of the emperor, calling him.

Bai left. A few weeks later, Ying came to visit me. We had a nice chat and I told her about the baby growing inside of me. She was pleased. "You have wanted a child with him for so long and I am glad that this desire can now be fulfilled. By the way, where is Bai? I would like to congratulate him."

"He has gone to meet Prince Yong, who has asked him to advise his campaign." Her face turned pale and a look of concern came over her. "What is wrong, Ying? He promised not to engage in any fighting."

"Haven't you heard?" she asked in an agitated voice.

"Heard what?"

"General An Lushan has been killed by one of his own men and Prince Li Heng has become the new Emperor Suzong. He has been trying to unite the country. All of his brothers are supporting him except Prince Yong, who has been called to Szechuan to meet with their father. But Prince Yong refuses and wants to create his own state. The people have already recognized Emperor Suzong. If Prince Yong doesn't recognize him, he will be considered a traitor. Most of the prominent advisors to Prince Yong are abandoning him, so clearly, they want someone of Bai's reputation by his side. Quickly call your husband back."

"Are you sure of this, Ying?" I asked fearfully. She nodded. "Bai must have found this out by now." I tried to hide my distress, since I suspected Bai would not leave Prince Yong on his own. The opportunity of a future court appointment was too enticing.

"There is an old karma coming into play, Shu. The real reason Shifu went to meet Bai several months ago when you were last at the hermitage is that she saw the potential of this karma to unfold now; she warned him not to get involved with any of the royal family. She couldn't see clearly what the old dynamic had been, but she suspected that when he was a ruler, there was some competition between the ones we know as Princes Heng and Yong, and that Bai had taken one side and imprisoned the other one. Shifu couldn't see the details and so warned him to stay away."

"Ying, I suspect they are lavishly honoring him and that is why he has not returned. He loves that kind of thing. I will go find him."

"You are pregnant, Shu. You shouldn't leave here. Write a letter and send someone to find him." I nodded.

After Ying left, I took refuge in my room and whispered to my absent husband. "I understand now that we are not meant to lead a peaceful life, but please, Bai, if you can hear my heart, please come home."

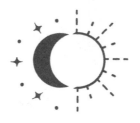

Chapter Twenty

BANISHMENT

"Bai has been imprisoned," Jing said in a gentle but disturbed tone. This was his third repetition of the statement, and I was having a hard time comprehending his words. "Imprisoned, Shu. It is true." Jing had arrived just a few minutes before with this news. He placed his hands on my shoulders and shook me gently as if to bring me out of a daze.

"Imprisoned? What on earth for?"

"For treason."

"Treason!" I cried. "That is ridiculous. Nobody is more loyal to the empire than Bai."

"Sit down, Shu, and I will explain." He led me to a pair of low chairs, and we sat face to face. I stared at him in disbelief. "The army of Prince Yong has been destroyed by the forces of Emperor Suzong. The soldiers who weren't killed have fled and the ships have been burned. All the prominent people had abandoned the Prince, except for Bai. He finally tried to flee and return here but was caught and imprisoned."

"Jing, I still don't understand. Bai has been gone only a few weeks. He went to meet with Prince Yong. He hadn't consented to be part of any campaign, any government."

"Shu, he was a pawn, a ploy of the Prince, who was looking for prominent people to bolster him. The Prince was killed by an officer in the new Emperor's army, without the order of the Emperor, and now everything is in disarray. The Emperor wanted to capture his brother, not kill him, but all of those who assisted the Prince are now considered traitors."

"Where is Bai now? I must go see him."

"He is in jail outside of Jiujiang."

"Let's go, Jing. Take me to him." I rose from my seat. Until now I had been able to hold back my tears, but the thought of Bai, my brilliant poet husband, locked up was too much to bear. Jing suddenly noticed my stomach, which had started to protrude, and seemed stunned for a moment.

"You're pregnant?"

I nodded. "Come, let's go quickly."

He placed his hand on my arm and sat me down again. "Shu. You can't go anywhere in your condition. I will go to the jail."

Pushing away his hand, I looked at him and replied with utmost determination. "Nothing on earth will prevent me from going to my husband and from petitioning every official in the new government. I will kneel outside the Emperor's quarters if I must and in my pregnant state beg for the release of my husband."

"Think of how Bai will feel to know you have traveled in this condition, and to see him locked up. Your husband is a man of great pride. Don't do this to him."

I sank down onto the chair and let his words sink in. "You are right, Jing. I hadn't considered his feelings. I am well enough to travel, so I will go with you to Jiujiang, but I won't go into the prison. I will send some books with you while I wait outside. The last thing I want to do is to hurt his pride."

"That is reasonable. Let us leave first thing in the morning."

Asking Lui to accompany us, I locked up the cottage. After Bai had left for the encampment of Prince Yong, I had bought the cottage, using some of the gold he had been given by the Prince's messenger, with the thought that it was the perfect place to raise our child. Now I brought the rest of the gold with me, in case I needed to purchase Bai's freedom. Passing through a nearby village as we began the journey through the mountains, I stopped at the home of a couple I had come to know, students of Shifu, and left the key so they could look after our cottage, as I had no way of knowing how long I would be gone. They were more than happy to assist.

We stopped often along the way to ease my discomfort in traveling, so it took several days to reach Jiujiang. Once there, Jing took two rooms at an inn. He left Lui and me there while he went to the prison to meet Bai. Before he left, I asked him to have Bai make a list of all the officials who had been admirers of his poetry, as I would start my pleading with them. I handed him the books on Daoism that I had brought. "Give Bai these books. He will know they are from me," I said quietly. "And here is some money in case you need to buy your way in to see him."

He shook his head. "I have plenty of money, Shu, for that purpose. You hang on to this. We will need it when we go to petition his old acquaintances. I am sure things haven't changed much in the Tang Empire."

Jing returned a few hours later. "How is he?" I rushed to ask. Jing didn't answer. "Did you see him? Were you able to buy your way in?" He nodded.

"Shu, he teared up when I handed him the books. He asked me how you were and if you were still at the cottage. I told him that you are here at an inn and eager to come to him. At first, he insisted that he didn't want you to see him in his current condition, but then, his feelings got the better of him and he agreed."

A feeling of distress came over me.

"He is fine, the same old Bai, but his pride is crushed. This is truly the sad story of an innocent man, one of the great minds of our time, who thought he was helping his country and got caught in the rivalry of opposing princes. He gave me this list of names. I will go with you to meet each one to enlist their support. Meanwhile Bai is writing a petition that he wants you to hand to them. He mentioned Gao Shi, a poet and prominent official in the Emperor's court. He admires Bai very much and can certainly get him released.

The next morning, Jing took me to see Bai. I was saddened to see his condition but did my best not to show it. Reproach was far from my mind, as my only thought was how to get him out of there.

"You should not have come, Little Phoenix. It is not good to be distressed in your condition."

"How can I not be distressed when my husband has been falsely accused? I will fight for you, Bai, with all my strength. It seems this little baby inside of me will need to learn to be a fighter. That is the only way to survive in this world."

Thus began my journey to secure my husband's life. With a child growing in my womb, I entreated and offered bribes to many powerful officials to facilitate the release of my husband, only to find myself turned away again and again. Sending an advance letter pleading for his assistance, I traveled to meet Gao Shi, but he wouldn't receive me. He had helped other poets who had found themselves in difficult straits, but they were all supporters of Emperor Suzong. Bai had fallen for the inducement of Prince Yong and thus was considered a traitor.

The only consolation I had was knowing that this was some karmic entanglement and that Bai was reaping the result of actions taken long ago. "Perhaps this will free him from that past," I whispered to myself one night. It was then that I remembered the words of Shifu about my needing to defend my husband in a way that I had never defended myself. *I have done that now, Shifu. I am doing all I can.*

Finally, I found one official who would help. His name was Song Ruosi and he, like so many others, was a great admirer of Bai's poetry. Unlike the others, he saw the injustice in what had taken place and was ready to plead on his behalf. He knew that Bai was no traitor to his country. With the help of his efforts and another official, Bai finally was released from prison. Song Ruosi went even further and offered him a position on his staff, but our worries weren't over. Although Bai thought he was exonerated and was hopeful of an official position in the new government, Jing informed me that a judgment on his case had not yet been made, so his release was merely temporary.

It was now summer, and I was approaching the time of delivery. Bai wanted me to return to Henan with Jing, who had taken the family back to our home there, but I wanted to deliver the child in our cottage on Lushan Mountain. We went back and forth about this. Finally, he agreed that I could return to the cottage, but insisted that after the birth I should go to Henan, while he stayed in the employ of Song Ruosi, awaiting a decision on our future.

I fully expected that our new Emperor would see the injustice of Bai's plight and would exonerate him, so I returned to Lushan Mountain for the last months of the pregnancy. Ying came to see me often and found a woman in the nearby village to deliver the baby. As soon as I began having pains, Ying came to be with me and stayed throughout the delivery. Even a blood sister would not have been more devoted. A few weeks after my daughter was born, I awoke to a knock on the door. Ying quietly entered and came over to peek at the baby, who was sleeping beside me.

She smiled and said, "Shifu returned to the hermitage late last night and will be here soon to visit you. Don't try to get out of bed," she cautioned. "Prop yourself up and I will bring you some food."

"Ying, I must get up to wash and greet her properly. I have not seen Shifu in so long." Hesitantly, she helped me rise and eat a little of the soup Lui had prepared, and then she helped me get ready to meet Shifu. When Shifu arrived, I rose to bow to her. Acknowledging my greeting with a nod of her head, she went over to the bed and lifted the infant in her arms. Placing her hand on the little head, she closed her own eyes, and I knew she was blessing this new life. That was the reason I had wanted to give birth on Lushan Mountain. I had had a feeling Shifu would come.

"Shu, what a beautiful child!" She exclaimed after placing her back down on the bed. "Have you given her a name yet?"

"Chang'e. It's the name that Bai has chosen." I was so happy to see Shifu after so many months.

"The moon goddess, very appropriate. I am told she was born on a full moon night." Then speaking quietly to the infant, she whispered, "So, you finally found your mother again."

"Shifu, the delivery was difficult. It went on for hours and hours, but we are both fine now and I am glad it is over."

"And Bai?"

"He is waiting for the judgement, assisted by Song Ruosi, who helped secure his release from prison. Nobody else would help us. Shifu, what karma is this from his past? The accusations against him are most unjust. He only went to meet the Prince, to hear him out, not to support him, and yet he is accused of treason. It is a crime, the way they are treating him."

Shifu looked thoughtful. "I couldn't see clearly, but I believe he is reaping the effects of his actions during a time that I suspect was the Warring States Period. His thinking is very much from that era, and since he was young, he has not been able to disassociate himself from political matters because that karma was not finished. Your husband is a brilliant man. I warned him of the dangers, yet he believed he could help the country in this way. He still sees himself as a statesman, and in the past, he was just that."

"Shifu, will you stay at the hermitage now?"

She shook her head. "The condition is very bad all around the country, especially in the north. Millions of people have died and millions more have been displaced. There are still pockets of rebellion, and the foreign troops that the new Emperor has enlisted to help suppress the rebellion are now conducting their own looting. He has not gained control of the country, no matter what is being stated publicly. I have been traveling to tend to basic needs. I returned here because the travel was getting to be too much for Changying; when I leave, I will take one of the younger nuns with me. We are needed in the villages, where there is much hunger and disease. If you remain here, Ying will look after you. We have enough vegetables in the garden and the forests are full of food."

"Shifu, I want to stay here, but Bai made me promise to return to Henan."

"That is also good," she replied. "You will have family to help you with Chang'e. There is a Daoist couple here in the village that I know quite well. If you like, you can offer for them to stay here and look after the cottage while you are gone. Their son and family are now living with them, and their cottage is quite small. I think they would welcome the opportunity to be caretakers here."

"They looked after the cottage when I went to meet Bai after his imprisonment. That is a good solution. I like them very much."

Shifu was thoughtful for a few minutes and then added, "Shu, I told you once that you and Bai have separate paths. You have come together for this brief time and to have the child you have long wanted, but your path is different from his. Don't forget that." I nodded. Shifu could see that I was tiring, and she took her leave. I saw Shifu on two more brief occasions before she departed again.

As autumn came to Lushan Mountain, I was gaining in strength but kept postponing my departure. Finally, I decided it was time to leave, before the weather turned. As I was making preparations, I received a message from Jing asking me to meet him, saying that we would travel together to see Bai and wait for the judgment, which was soon expected.

When we reached Bai, we found him quite depressed. Even the sight of his infant daughter did little to lift his spirits; although she brought temporary smiles and laughter to his face, I could see through appearances. I pressed him, and it was then that he informed us that the judgment had come. He was to be banished to the far southeastern reaches of the empire, to Yelang, for three years. I burst into tears. He was meeting his daughter for the first time and now he was to be banished. It seemed too cruel.

Turning to me, Jing said, "This is not a bad outcome. There were some who were pressing for execution, others for life banishment. Surely, Shu, you and Chang'e can wait three years."

I turned and said to Bai, "We are coming with you." For the first time, my husband looked old and haggard, and I worried for his qi. The thought occurred to me that if he were not taken care of, he might not survive the banishment. Nothing he could say would dissuade me from following. Finally, he conceded.

"Let me go first and see what the situation is. If it is acceptable, I will send for you and Chang'e. Little Phoenix, know that wherever I am, I will wait for you. Remember that." He looked me in the eyes as he spoke these words. I nodded and dried my tears.

"I know that, Bai. You will wait for me, as I will wait for you. While I am waiting, I will take a cottage in Yuzhang. It is much closer to Lushan Mountain and away from the rebel strongholds in the north. Send for me there." He nodded and said that would be a better place for me and Chang'e.

Jing and I stayed with Bai until the time of his departure. In that short time, I implanted in my mind the memory of our brief time together as a family, taking note of every time he held his daughter and drew her close, every time he pressed his lips to her head. Those were precious days. Then Jing, Lui, the baby and I accompanied Bai south to Jiujiang, where he got on a boat to sail up the Yangtze River to Sichuan; from there he would proceed south on foot. Jing helped me to find a suitable cottage in Yuzhang and then returned to Henan, where he had received a minor official position in the local government.

Many months later, I received word that as soon as he had reached Sichuan, Bai had been pardoned and recalled from banishment. He was now heading back to us. Famine stalked the central lands and the Emperor had decreed a general amnesty in an effort to unify the country, but there was still sporadic fighting and the economic and social conditions were desperate. Despite the despair that continued to engulf the empire, my hope was lit again. I knew Bai was heading home.

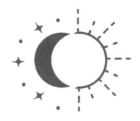

Chapter Twenty-One

PASSAGE: AN ENDING

The roads to Yuzhang were blocked by the military, and it took Bai some time before he could reach me. In the many months since we had seen each other, we both had aged considerably, due to the conditions under which we were living. It had been a daily struggle for Lui and I to find food, and I had also had an infant to care for. When I saw Bai's stooped form silhouetted in the cottage doorway, I was truly shocked. I hid my concern, as I was so happy that he was alive and that we were together again. Soon after his arrival, I received a message from Shifu, asking us to come to Lushan Mountain as the food situation was better there, so we made the journey to our cottage.

The couple who had been living there and looking after it had built a small hut for themselves adjacent to our living space. Bai and I were able to have some time alone as a family, along with Lui, who had cared for me like a mother all this while. I could see the damage done to Bai's spirit from his imprisonment and brief exile, and from the destruction of the empire, and I could tell it would not be easily repaired. He was ill and old now, perhaps too old to recover. It tore my heart to see him like this.

After a few weeks, Bai seemed to improve, and my hope was renewed. Maybe it would be possible for us to begin a new life in the mountains, where we could focus on our cultivation practice and raise our child together. One night he called me to him, motioning for me to sit beside him. "Come, Little Phoenix. I want to talk to you."

"What is it, Bai?" I asked, seating myself on the cushion next to him. He had been reading but now he put his papers aside.

He looked at me quietly, and then placing his hand on my check, he said, "Shu, after I am gone, I want you to remain here and raise our daughter in this cottage. She will have a good life here, and I will take comfort knowing you are close to your Shifu." Rarely did he call me by my given name—only when he had something serious to say.

"Don't speak like that, Bai," I replied, looking into his eyes. "We will have many more years together."

Moving his hand to caress my hair, he continued to look at me, as if studying me. "My life has been difficult, but I have no regrets, except one. Do you know what that is, Shu?" I shook my head. "I regret that so often I have kept you waiting, that I could not always be with you when you needed me." After a long pause, he asked, in a voice that revealed his emotion, "Do you forgive me, Little Phoenix?"

"Bai, there is nothing to forgive." Realizing it was both Bai and Sachit speaking, I rested my head on his chest and replied quietly, "It is I who should ask forgiveness for not always understanding you."

"You are the only one who has understood me." He suddenly changed the subject. "How much gold do we have left?"

"Not much, Bai."

"And food?"

"I am able to gather much of what we need from the forest."

"It should not be like this," he replied quietly as he looked away. "I should be able to provide for my family."

"I like gathering food from the forest, Bai."

"I know you hide from me how difficult our situation is. When I am not here, how will you manage?"

Placing my fingers over his lips, I replied, "Don't think that way. You are here with me now and will be for a long time. Besides, I am perfectly capable of managing, you know that. All my time alone has prepared me . . ." I didn't finish the sentence, as I didn't want to admit that I sensed the time was coming when I would have to manage alone.

I tried my best to distract Bai, often by asking him philosophical questions, as he always loved to show his knowledge about such matters. One day he saw me reading the teachings of Laozi and came to sit beside me. Turning to him, I asked, "Explain this to me, Bai. What do you think it means?" I read the lines from Laozi:

The spirit of the center is called the mysterious feminine.
Its doorway is called the source of heaven and earth."

He smiled and replied, "I think you should ask your Shifu. She will know the meaning."

"I want to know what you think."

He was thoughtful for a few minutes and then replied, "Laozi also refers to the source of the ten thousand things as the mother. The creative power is the feminine and it is the source of all—mysterious, hidden, at the center of everything. It is this creative feminine power that is the essence of the Dao. That is what I think it means." He was quiet again and then added, "It is this creative power that inspires the poet, but she can manifest in so many ways. She can take the form of a common person, a simple act—the drinking of wine at a tavern, the flight of a bird, anything in fact—and such everyday occurrences can inspire a poem. That is how I see the mysterious feminine at the center of all things."

"That is what I love about you, Bai. You are able to bring the loftiest thoughts down to everyday life."

"Is that all you love about me?"

I smiled and leaned over to embrace him. "There is nothing about you that I don't love. I love your mind, your insight, your wisdom, and most of all your heart." I became thoughtful as the image of the mother I knew in my life as Sundari came to my mind. How strong she was, what leadership she displayed, and yet how I had misunderstood her. In our clan, she would never allow a child to go hungry or any person to be uncared for. All her decisions were based on what was best for the clan. Never did she allow her personal desires to interfere. She was the mother at the center of it all, just as Laozi described, only on the human level.

"What are you thinking?" Bai asked.

"I'm thinking . . . I'm thinking how difficult it is for women today to find their voice, to be heard. But it wasn't always like that. Not at all," I replied quietly.

"I've never heard you express such sentiments." I didn't respond. "I hear your voice, Shu. Isn't that enough?" I nodded and didn't say anything further, since my feelings were unclear, and I could not adequately express them.

As I lay in bed that night, I looked over at my sleeping husband lying beside me. How dear he was to me, how close I felt to him, and yet even he did not understand how difficult it was to awaken confidence in myself, how so often in my mind I belittled myself in comparison to him. "No, Bai," I whispered quietly. "It is not enough that you hear me. I feel the pain of so many women. I still know the sorrow of so many lives when I lived as a woman without a voice, without any say over the course of my life. It is only Shifu who has helped me find my strength, find myself. But I do not fault you for not understanding. How many men do?" Lovingly, I lay my hand on his cheek and fell asleep that way.

For days after, as I read and re-read the lines on the feminine by Laozi, I was struck by the similarity between his words and the teachings of Sage Gayatri about the goddess she called Sarasvati, only the principles were expressed so differently, according to very different times and cultural settings. Laozi didn't give a name to the mysterious center of all things because he refrained from using human language to name that which cannot be named. During the time of Sage Gayatri, when the word was so revered, the high and the mysterious were named, but there was a very different use of language then. Since emerging from my last stay in the cave, I found myself often comparing the teachings of the Dao with the teachings of what I had learned of the Veda; they appeared to be but different ways of expressing the same insight, a shared wisdom.

I had managed to lift Bai's spirit for a time, but it was not long before he was sulking around again, feeling locked in by his inability to move about and meet with people. I suggested he go to a tavern in the nearby village, and he readily agreed. When he returned, there was a certain glow on his face that I recognized. He told me that he had met someone at the tavern who said that life was coming back to Nanjing. There was social activity again, and he suspected that some of his old friends might have returned. If he went, surely he would be able to earn commissions. Prominent people often paid Bai to write essays and poems about them, and nothing would bring him back to life more readily than being among his admirers. His desire for this stimulation had been awakened and this filled me with both relief and fear. Something of the old Bai had returned, but he was not well, and I questioned whether he could endure any more hardship, even the difficulties of travel.

Nanjing was a city Bai loved and I thought being there might help revive his spirit. On the other hand, who would care for him? At home, I was so conscientious about his eating and made sure he drank the medicinal soups I prepared. The forests were filled with plant medicines of all kinds, and I took care to see that he ingested them every day. But I also knew that the isolation and his idleness were taking a toll, so I wavered.

Sitting outside alone one evening, I remembered how Shifu had so often cautioned me not to try to change his nature or interfere with his destiny. "You will never be able to keep him from continually leaving, so don't even try. It will only frustrate you. You must accept your life with him as it is, and don't cling to an image of what you want him to be." As I remembered her words, I sighed and knew that I had no choice but to let him leave once again, so I consented. One of Bai's great assets was the many friends he had cultivated through his extensive travels. Even though they didn't come to his aid during his imprisonment, I knew they would once again gather around him, value his poetry, and welcome him into their circles.

My parting from him this time was less tearful than past partings. It was a parting of submission, a complete surrendering to what his fate held in store for him and what mine held for me. I didn't cling to him as I had so many times in the past. I didn't try to dissuade him at the last minute. I watched as he held his daughter and kissed her on the head. Then he held me tight, and I whispered, "Take good care of yourself, Bai, and return to me when you can." Then, he was gone.

Soon after Bai left, the news spread that the old Emperor Xuanzong had died, as had his son, the new Emperor Suzong. Chaos once again ruled in the court and factional fighting paralyzed the government. Finally, Suzong's son, Daizong, was enthroned, but during this time rebel fighting surged in the north and the country was again thrown into disarray. Refugees continued to pour south of the Yangtze, and Shifu was overwhelmed with caring for the many people in need. She traveled most of the time, leaving Ying to care for the women at the hermitage, whose numbers now swelled beyond capacity. I spent as much time as possible helping Ying.

One day, Shifu returned and told me that a message had been left for me months ago in a nearby village. The letter was from a relative of Bai's saying that Bai was with him at his home in Dangtu County, very ill, and that his son was looking after him.

"Leave Chang'e and go immediately," counseled Shifu.

"You say the message was left months ago. Perhaps he has died, Shifu," I said, as tears filled my eyes and I felt my whole body become weak.

Shaking her head, she quietly consoled me. "He would not leave without first seeing you, I am sure of that. But Shu, you must be strong now. Draw upon your years of cultivation. Don't let Bai see your sorrow."

Taking my horse, I hurried to Dangtu County. When I arrived at the cottage where Bai was staying, for the first time I met Boqin, his beloved son by his first wife. I was grateful that the young man had been there to nurse him.

Bai was drifting in and out of consciousness, but when I leaned close and whispered, "Bai, I am here," he opened his eyes and tried to smile, whispering "Little Phoenix." The thought entered my mind that I might never hear that name again, and with a heavy heart I lay my head on his chest and said, "How precious that name is to me, Bai. I remember when you first called me that."

He was awake enough to stroke my head, resting his hand there as he drifted to sleep. With sorrowing eyes, I looked at my husband, who was now a shadow of the man I had known. His skin was sallow and drawn, dark hollows hung beneath his eyes, and he bore the look of a man nearing death, but I would not accept this. I said silently to him, *I fought to get you released from prison, and I will fight to keep you alive. I won't let you die.*

Lowering myself onto the floor, I slept with my head against his bed, clinging to his hand all night. For the next two days, I barely left his side. I imagined that he was looking better and soon would be able to move to Lushan Mountain. At one moment, he whispered that he was at peace now that I had arrived. I whispered back, "Bai, we have many years ahead of us. Rest and get well so that I can take you home." He didn't answer. That night I climbed into his bed and lay myself beside his warm body. Resting my head on his chest, I felt him try to put his arms around me, but they were weak and fell back onto the bed.

I lay that way throughout the night, listening to his shallow breathing. I tried to stay awake, as I wanted to keep careful watch over him, but sometime in the early morning hours I fell into a semi-sleep. Dreaming, I found myself on the back of a flaming red phoenix, with Bai seated in front of me. I held on tightly to him as the phoenix flew through the air at great speed. It had been so long since I had flown on one of these magical birds, and now I was doing it with Bai. We flew higher and higher, and soon the radiant full moon came into sight. I realized that this was where the phoenix was taking us. When the phoenix landed on the moon, Bai stepped down, and I could feel his joy. Before us lay a wondrous landscape of mountains and rivers, enclosed in a subtle, magical light. There to greet us was the goddess herself, looking as she had when she came to me in the cave. Still astride the phoenix, I bowed to her, then turned and said to Bai, "I have to go back to our Chang'e."

Facing me with a smile, he replied, "I will wait for you." Then the phoenix turned around, and I flew back to earth. It was a beautiful elevating dream, and I awoke feeling a deep calm within me. I wanted to share the dream with Bai, and so I began to describe as many details as I could: "We flew together on a phoenix, Bai. It was a beautiful one, flaming red. I am so glad you got to fly. Bai . . .?" My voice trailed off as I became aware of the coldness of his body. There was no sound coming from his chest. His shallow breathing had stopped.

Lifting myself from his body, I realized that my Bai had slipped away. At that moment, I didn't know what was real: the phoenix I had envisioned or this moment when Bai was no longer inhabiting his body. Moving as if in a trance, I went to find Boqin, who was reading one of his father's poems. After I told him that Bai had died, he recited the last lines of the poem he had been reading, "Song for Accompanying Uncle Hua on Xie Tiao's Tower":

"Ah, life is such a sad thing that tomorrow
I will undo my hair and sail away in a little boat."

"My father is finally free of his sorrow," he said and burst into tears. I couldn't console him. I couldn't cry. Numb with disbelief, I left all decisions regarding the disposing of the body to him. After the ceremony was over, I was at a loss as to where to go. I wanted to be alone and rode to our little cottage in Yuzhang. It was there that the emptiness hit me. I couldn't remain in the cottage alone and so, for the first time in my life, I went on my own to a tavern, a place that Bai used to frequent when he was with me. I drank and drank, thinking that wine would bring him back or at the very least help me feel close to him, but it did neither. The tavern owner saw my despair and came over to me.

"Lady Zong, why are you here alone? Where is your husband?"

Looking up at him with empty eyes, I replied with slurred words, "My husband, yes, where is my husband? Oh, I remember, I took him to the moon the other night. He is waiting there for me." My head was spinning and unable to control my movements, my head fell onto the table. I heard him say, "Let me take you home." I felt him lift me onto wobbly legs and

369

steady me as I stumbled home alongside him. As we stood at my door, he asked, "Are you all right, Lady Zong?"

I reached into my purse for some money, but he refused it. He opened the door for me, and then left. The cottage was cold and dark, and I couldn't see anything. After taking a few steps I bumped into a chair, then walking further I knocked over one object and then another. It was at first light of day that I opened my eyes and found myself lying on the floor. I didn't remember how I had gotten there, but several pieces of furniture were knocked over, so I assumed I had fallen after getting drunk. My head was throbbing, and I felt a great bump on one side.

My only thought at that moment was to get back to Lushan Mountain. Without giving myself time to recover, I mounted the horse and headed home. The peace I had felt on my last night with Bai, the joy of riding the red phoenix with him, all of that was eclipsed by the reality of what I now had to face. I tried to imagine what my life would be like without waiting for Bai anymore. It seemed that so many of my days had been taken up with expecting his return, but there would be no more of that now. It was he who would have to wait for me.

I hadn't cried when I lifted myself from Bai's chest and realized he had died. I hadn't cried as his son and I placed what remained of him into the waiting arms of earth. I didn't cry as I rode home. It was as if I were paralyzed and couldn't accept the reality of his death, or else my pain was too deep, beyond the realm of tears. When I arrived home, I shut myself away and took to my bed, refusing to see anyone, even my daughter, and also refusing all food. I heard Lui tell Chang'e that I was ill, and she should let me rest until I recovered. Turning over to face the wall, I stared blankly at the vastness of the gaping hole into which I had fallen. All I could see was gloom swirling around me, the darkness of losing Bai.

I don't know how many days passed like this, but one day I heard

Ying's voice outside my room. Lui was telling her that I had refused to see anyone and was taking little food. "She will see me," insisted Ying. I was lying in bed, as I had been for days. She entered the room and came over to me. "Shu." I turned to stare at her with empty eyes. I hadn't spoken since my return, and even now no words would come. "Shu."

I allowed her to lift me to a seated position, but still I stared at her without speaking. Tears began to well up in her eyes. "I have seen you go through so much, but I have never seen you like this." I didn't answer. "Speak to me, Shu. Speak to me, say anything. I have come to cry with you, to share your pain."

Struggling, I finally managed to murmur in a breaking voice, "I can't cry, Ying. I have no tears. All I have is emptiness. There is nothing left inside of me."

"That's not true, Shu. You have a world inside of you. You still have so much to give, poetry to write, people to love. Little Chang'e to raise. You are not alone."

"I feel so alone. Why did he leave me like this?"

"Shifu told you that Bai and you were traveling on different roads, meeting at this crossroad for a brief moment in time, and that you mustn't cling to him. Do you remember?" I didn't respond. I don't think her words sank in. "That is the way life is. We come together with our loved ones and then part, and then we come together again. That is the Dao. You have years of cultivation practice. Use what you have gained to help you now." I didn't respond. My years of cultivation seemed like a distant memory. "I am not leaving until you eat. Changying has prepared a special soup of medicinal herbs. It will calm your mind and help you sleep."

"I'm not hungry."

"Hungry or not, you have to eat." When she entered the room, Ying had brought with her a small bowl of soup, and now she started to spoon feed it to me. I allowed her to do so and then fell back on my bed and heard her quietly slip out of the room. Every few days Ying would come with a different preparation of medicinal soups. By the third time I no longer allowed her to feed me and would take the food on my own. Then I would fall back down on my bed in the hope that I could escape into the forgetfulness of sleep.

After several weeks, I knew Ying was growing disturbed by my lack of progress, but there was not much I could do. She kept prodding me to get up, so one day I did. From that time on, I would get out of bed and spend the day in the corner of the room, hugging my knees and resting my head on them, dreaming of Bai. Instead of reliving a past life, I was reliving my life with him, all of our tender moments, and I didn't want to emerge from those memories.

Often, I took myself back to the time when Jing first brought him home, drunk, in the early hours of the morning. I remembered the next day how shocked I had been when Jing told me who he was—the much-esteemed poet Li Bai! I remembered each time he came to call on me, walking together in the park or in a nearby forest, always seeking time with nature. I remembered lying down on the forest floor while he would talk and talk, relaying his many experiences with prominent people. And then I remembered his marriage proposal and my inability to commit, his departure, and his return after his dream of me flying on a phoenix. I relived all those moments and so many more: the days we spent by the lake after he came to get me from the hermitage, my second return from the hermitage after he had gone looking for a place in Xuan town, his passion the night of his return, when I conceived after so many years of trying to have a child, and then our few happy months in the cottage, where our daughter and I now lived. My whole life with Bai passed before my mind again and again, as I clung to the memories. In between, I began to be able to spend some time with Chang'e, but I couldn't laugh, I couldn't smile, I couldn't cry. I was paralyzed, stuck in a world between life and death.

Finally one day, Shifu arrived. I was sitting in my usual spot on the floor when, unannounced, she entered my room. My hair was undone, I was not dressed properly, but there nothing I could do about it. This was the way I was now. I looked up at her with empty eyes and couldn't even rise to greet her properly. She sighed when she saw me. Seating herself beside me on the floor, she looked at me with concern. "Shu, you have grown so thin, and your qi is completely blocked, knotted in so many places, preventing you from even breathing properly. Your heart has been frozen. You must unfreeze it now. You have mourned enough. Months have passed since Bai's death. It is time for you to return to life. Lui tells me little Chang'e cries for her mother at night. She has lost her father; do you want her to lose her mother as well? Long ago, when you lived in Hanning, you left a daughter behind. Recall that moment now when you were forced to separate. Do you remember her clinging to you as her father pulled her away? From then on, she lived with a broken heart. When she came of age, she secretly left her father's house in search of you, never to return. She would not believe that you were not also searching for her. She never found you in that life but vowed she would not give up until she did. It took her a long time, but finally she has come to you. Will you again turn your heart from her?"

"Shifu," I exclaimed. "Is Chang'e that daughter?" She nodded. "Shifu, in this one lifetime I have had to bear the sorrow of so many lives. How many more must I bear?"

"As many as come. Think back to your ancient life by the sacred river.

Did your friend Kapila ever fall into the trap of self-pity?"

"Kapila. He suffered greatly but was always grateful. He never allowed himself to be a victim."

"Remember now why his grandmother didn't come for him when he was alone in the forest. She knew that his parents had died and that he was a mere boy. Do you recall why she couldn't leave the cave and go to find him?"

"I don't remember, Shifu."

Shifu looked at me with clear, steady eyes. "Her only son had been killed, and the wife had died. He was the only one left to her, this grandson, yet she let him be alone in the forest for ten long years, living within the reaches of death. At any moment he could have been taken from her. Don't you think she desperately wanted to go to him?"

"It must have been very difficult, Shifu."

"She suffered greatly, and so many times wanted to search for him, to see whether he was alive, but she was always stopped. It broke her heart, and this was without doubt the greatest trial she had to go through."

"I remember her telling me it was the god she loved who stopped her, the one who comes to test the sages. This was her great test," I replied, now recalling that part of the story.

"The god she loved did this for her out of love," Shifu replied softly. "He was helping her become who she came to be, and he was helping Kapila become who he came to be. Had she gone to rescue him, none of that would have come to pass. At a certain point, she realized this, but it did not stop the pain. Every time that poor boy cried out, she felt his cries fall like spears striking her chest, but she was helpless. She had to endure this for ten years, but through this suffering she found peace and attained the highest knowledge."

"It worked out well in the end," I said quietly. "They finally were able to meet."

"And it will work out well for you and Bai in the end. This is not the end, Shu. You must have patience to endure this time of separation, and if you quiet your heart, you will be able to feel him near. He has not gone very far away. It is only your thoughts that have created the distance."

I looked at her gratefully. Only Shifu could pull me out of this deepest despair. "Shifu, Sundari lived in pain because she couldn't have the one she loved. I had the one I love but still I have this pain. I don't know which suffering is worse."

She smiled and replied in a gentle tone, "That is the nature of life, my dear. One only surmounts suffering when one lives in the changeless, unattached to the passing shadows of life. Love is not dependent on any outer circumstance. Love is the nature of the Dao; when you are in harmony with the Dao, you recognize love as the very essence of your being and of life. There is no having it or not having it. Bai left you the beautiful gift of your daughter, the one who has been searching so long for you. You must tend to her now. The empire lies in tatters. Children have lost all family members. Disease and famine roam everywhere. The ravages of war are unremitting. You must pull yourself together so that you can serve. Sit up straight," she said firmly, "and breathe deeply."

I saw Shifu make a series of hand movements to unlock the blockages in my qi. Suddenly spinning me around, she struck me on my back with such force that I nearly fell forward. I cried out in great pain, and then came the release, the breaking of the dam, and all the bottled-up emotions rushed forth. The grief that I had been holding so tightly finally exploded, and I burst into a torrent of tears. She held me while I cried for the first time since Bai's death.

"It's good to cry. Let these tears clear the channels of your qi," she said quietly. "It's important to mourn, but you must also recover. I want you to start writing again." There was firmness in her voice. "And I want you to come to the hermitage and help Ying care for the women. Spend time with Chang'e reciting Bai's poetry to her, telling her stories of her father. Help her to know him. That is the way you will come back to life."

I nodded. "I will do my best, Shifu." In fact, the process had already started. Somewhere deep inside, I felt Bai pushing me away, and for the first time I realized that perhaps I was holding him back. As long as I clung to him, he would not be able to move on.

A few days later I began to write:

Losing the Dao
I never knew the sky could empty itself of stars,
That the moon would abandon course
And drift away from the earth,
Leaving a well of darkness.

I endured our many separations
Knowing you would always return,
But this separation I cannot bear.
The distance you have flown
Is well beyond my reach.

My dear husband,
Extend a branch of sympathy
That I may climb to you.
Even the Dao once so bright
Has dimmed to my sight.

Some weeks later, I wrote another poem. As the words emerged, I knew I was beginning to recover. I was able to perceive the Dao within my sadness.

On the Death of Bai

In the middle of a warm summer day
Snow blankets the sky.
Flowering branches become bare.
Not a bird in sight.

Sadness sweeps my world.
This too is the Dao.

It was around this time that I began to feel a presence, one that was palpable, but hard to describe. I would feel it most especially when I would find myself falling again into the pit of sorrow. At those times, the presence would lift me up and prevent me from sinking back. Often, I thought it was this presence that was bringing me back to life, with its calming, gentle energy that brought peace to my heart and guided my slow healing process.

A year after Bai's passing, I was back to performing most of my daily activities. Sadness still shadowed me, but I was able to function within it. Some days, I felt that I was hanging onto this aching feeling because it seemed to keep me close to Bai, but I actually knew that to be an illusion. *Joy will also keep him close,* I told myself, but how to find that joy again? I didn't know. I wondered if I would ever again feel my spirit lift when the sun warmed my body, when summer breezes brushed across my face, when I watched the animals prance between the trees, or when I stared back at the moon glancing down at me.

One day, when I was helping Ying at the hermitage, she told me that Shifu had returned. I asked if I could see her, and she told me that Shifu was waiting for both of us in her cottage. I tried my best to put on a cheerful face as we entered the room. She motioned us to be seated and asked that tea be served. She told us about the conditions of the country villages she had visited and the continuing desperation of so many. Then, suddenly turning to me, she asked, "Do you know what rumor about Bai's death is spreading among the villagers?" I shook my head. With an enigmatic smile and a glimmer in her eyes, she continued. "It is said that the great poet Li Bai was drunk one night and went out in a small boat. Looking down, he saw the reflection of the moon on the river, or maybe it was a lake, and thinking it to be the moon herself, he reached out to embrace her, fell in the river, and drowned."

I burst into laughter, and Shifu and Ying looked at one another, smiling. "Shu, I haven't seen you laugh since Bai's death," exclaimed Ying with great pleasure. Then I looked from one to the other:

"Shifu, is it you who has started that story?"

"Me?" she exclaimed, assuming a look of shock.

"Shifu, I like it. Let it be that Bai died while seeking to embrace the moon. It is a perfectly appropriate way for him to have died."

Before leaving, I asked Shifu why, after so many years of cultivation, I had fallen into such despair. "How could I lose overnight what had taken me so many years to gain?"

"Because you are human," she replied. "And because of your love for your husband. It is natural, Shu. It was your greatest test, and at one time or another, in one way or another, we are all tested. Shu, you tried for many years to have a child but couldn't. Think what a wonderful gift it was for you to have your child before Bai left this world. Life always presents us with hidden gifts, and we must be grateful for those."

"That is true, Shifu. But after losing Bai, I lost sight of the Dao and couldn't find my way back for such a long time."

"You have now, and that is what is important. Besides, you haven't lost Bai. He is in another place now, and you will meet again before too long. In fact, every story has a beautiful ending, though most of the time we can't see it."

Laughter came back into my life, and I was able to find joy with my child, the most precious gift Bai had left me. One day, Ying asked me if I was still feeling so lonely. I shook my head. "For some time, I have felt a presence with me, particularly when I am missing Bai the most, and this has brought me a great sense of peace. Sometimes I feel the presence sitting by my bed throughout the night, but I can't see who it is. Do you think it is Bai, Ying?"

"Only you can tell that, Shu. Does it feel like Bai?"

I shook my head. "No, but I can't imagine who it else might be. Unless it is a dear one from the past coming to console me."

One day, Jing came to visit. He was bemoaning the conditions under which Bai had died and asked whether I had seen him before he passed. I nodded. "I was fortunate, Jing, to be with him when he took his last breath."

"A great figure like him should not have died in such poverty."

"That is my sadness, Jing. Nobody loved this country more that Bai, and in the end, his country abandoned him. It was his imprisonment and banishment that broke his spirit. I think he would have survived had that not happened, despite his ill health from drinking and taking those alchemical pills."

"But the country has recognized him now, Shu. That should give you some comfort."

"What do you mean?"

"Have you not heard?"

I shook my head.

"Last year, by court decree, Bai was appointed counselor to the emperor, an honorary title. The emperor summoned him to the capital, not realizing he had already died. At the same time, a friend of his published his collected works. Now there are several such collections. His reputation has been restored. Bai will finally be recognized as one of the great poets of the Tang Empire."

"That does give me some relief. I was beginning to think of going to pound on the doors of those corrupt officials so that he could receive the public recognition he deserves."

"No need for that now. It is done."

Some eight years later, a night came when I couldn't sleep. The bright light of the moon was streaming into my room, and I tossed and turned for hours. Finally, I got up and went outside. Looking into the sky, I began to address the moon. "What exactly is your relationship to us, the people of this land? The Daoists know you. Our poets write about you. We celebrate you every year during the autumn festival. Are you really our ancestor?"

My words were met with silence.

After a while, when the moon crossed the sky and faded behind the trees, I went inside and fell asleep as morning approached. When I awoke, I decided to walk to the hermitage and visit the cave, which I hadn't done in so many years. I didn't know exactly why I had stayed away for so long, but I had felt no calling, no reason to go there. On this day, I felt a pull too strong to ignore. I knew Shifu was away, and Ying was not expecting me. Without stopping to greet her or the other women, I walked past the hermitage and up the hill to the cave. I stopped for a few minutes and then continued walking until I found an overhang where I could sit and look out at the vast expanse before me, the cloud-tipped mountains and empty sky. Looking up, I saw the faint outline of the daytime moon. I greeted her and sank into silence.

Suddenly, I found myself peering deep into the ancient past, watching scenes unfold before my inner eye. A moon goddess wanted to experience life on earth as a human. For many years, the ice had been melting and oceans rising. New rivers formed as rains drenched the land. During the era of the frozen water, the number of humans had remained small, but now it grew and grew. The goddess saw her chance, the opportunity to help humanity take a leap forward, and so she took birth.

Tall and slender, she moved with much grace. She exerted her powers, helping to guide the people to settle where the land was fertile by the newly formed rivers. Inspired by her wisdom, women began to follow her, and to hold together communities of families. She taught the elders how to use the vibration of sound to control the weather patterns and manage the flow of water. Often, she used music to calm the waters when it rained too heavily and the rivers overflowed. She could be heard playing a melodious instrument in the forest, as sounds that people had not heard before floated in the breezes, sounds that seemed to have magical effects and kept nature in balance.

The moon goddess remained for many centuries before returning to her sky world, but she kept close to her descendants, guiding them in dreams and visions. One such descendant was the great seer, Shennong, who brought much knowledge, including how to plant according to the stages of the moon, helping to develop successful agricultural practices. The physical moon exerts its pull on water: when the moon is full, groundwater is more readily available to hydrate plants and seeds. The spiritual moon guides creative energy through the power of vibration: the spiritual life of the land is lifted by the beautiful sounds of music and poetry. That is why the moon is such an inspiration for so many poets.

An inner voice described all of this with great clarity.

"So, it's not merely a legend, it is true," I whispered. "It is as Bai once described to me: 'A solar deity came to populate and guide the people in ancient Tianzhu, and a moon deity came to seed our civilization. The memory of the goddess has remained in our country, although only in distorted fragments.'"

Then my mind took a different course. *If the goddess, the feminine energy, helped to seed our civilization, why do women have such a difficult time coming forward, finding their voice? Why do we not bring that feminine energy into the center of our society, and why must we women so often do our work in the shadows, in the unseen places?*

Then, internally, I heard the response: *The physical universe moves in cycles, and this part of the cycle will pass. The universe continually seeks to balance itself, and the male and female energies will again find their equilibrium. When enough individuals reach that state, it will manifest on a grander scale. You must think not only in earth years, but also in long cycles of time.*

Someone was speaking to me, sending these thoughts to my mind, but who was it? I was alone on this ridge. Suddenly I felt an urge to turn around and when I did, I saw a man, who looked to be a hermit, gazing down at me from a higher ridge. Instinctively, I knew it was he who had transmitted these thoughts. I quickly got up and began to climb toward him, but I could not close the distance between us. My steps brought me no nearer to him, although he did not move, and he remained as far away as when I was seated on the overhang. Realizing that I would not be able to approach him, I stopped and stared. I was able to discern his features, but mostly it was his benevolent presence that I felt.

There was something vaguely familiar about him, but I couldn't identify when or where we might have met. As I stood there, a large flock of birds flew by, making a great squawking sound. For a split second, I turned my head to see what was causing such a commotion, and when I looked back, the hermit was gone. Now able to climb the rocks that had stood between us, I searched the whole area, but he was nowhere to be found. Try though I might, I could not identify him. He was not Dada, not Yeye, not Sage Gayatri, so who was he? It was a mystery I couldn't solve.

I came home that afternoon and wrote a poem:

The Silent Sage

He covers me with subtle light
And whisperings of joyful thought
To bring me comfort in the night,
The one I have not met
But who watches me
With the care of a beloved.

The distance of a world
Separates us,
But I feel him as close
As my heartbeat.

I began to wonder if I hadn't imagined the incident. I did not have the luxury of time to dwell on it or to investigate during cultivation, as I had a child to raise, but I took comfort in the thought that there was a benevolent being watching over me, someone to whom I was deeply connected and who one day perhaps I might meet.

As Chang'e grew older, I started to read Bai's poetry to her. Soon she was reciting her favorites. One day she returned with Lui from the village, where she had many friends among the local children, and was busying herself outside while I was helping Lui prepare food for the evening meal. A song drifted through the open door and reached my ears. In her sweet voice, my daughter was singing over and over:

> *"Seeing moonlight here at my bed,*
> *and thinking it's frost on the ground,*
>
> *I look up, gaze at the mountain moon,*
> *then back, dreaming of my old home."*

It was Bai's poem, "Thoughts in Night Quiet," but I had never read that poem to her. Putting aside the vegetables I was chopping, I went outside. "Chang'e, where did you learn that poem?"

"One of the village children taught me."

"Do you know who wrote that poem?"

She nodded. "Baba. All the village children sing it. I have learned many of his poems from them." Her words brought tears to my eyes.

"Is it true, Chang'e, that village children sing his poetry?"

She nodded. "But Mama, Lui told me you also write poems. Why haven't you read them to me?"

"My poems are different," I replied. "When you get older, I will share them." And years later, I did. When Chang'e was around 18 years old, she decided she wanted to become a Daoist nun. I was very pleased and knew that Bai would be too. It was then that I shared with her my times in the cave and let her read my poetry. I wondered if my poems about Hanning would awaken memories in her, but they didn't.

Chang'e had spent her growing-up years running through the hermitage grounds, bringing laughter to all the women there. She loved working alongside Ying in the garden, visiting the cave, where she believed magical animals dwelt, and watching the wildlife, her companions. She was a gentle, loving child, and I liked to think she was the gift of Sachit and Bai to me, bringing back the daughter I had lost in Hanning. Here on Lushan Mountain, I was able to give her the life that I couldn't give her in Hanning. I told her stories of that time and repeated the tales I remembered about Yeye until she came to feel that he was indeed her grandfather. When I ran out of stories about Yeye, I made up more, so she would continue to feel his presence.

As Chang'e grew older, I began recounting the stories I remembered from my time with Sage Gayatri, stories about the sages of old. And I told her of the young forest girl who grew up in a world of trees and wildlife, but who one day came out of the forest and fell in love with a man who taught her the secret power of words and inspired in her a love of poetry. I said, "They had to separate and wait nearly ten thousand years to meet again."

"How did they find each other?" she asked in amazement. "Did they remember their love?"

"How they found each other is still a mystery, but love is not forgotten, not when it is true love. When they met the first time, she so wanted to have his child, but she couldn't. When they met again after so many thousands of years, this desire was fulfilled, and they became a loving family."

"That is a beautiful love story," she said. "To wait ten thousand years and then find each other again."

"There are so many love stories. In fact, Chang'e, life is one big love story. I have told you about the love between the deities of the sun and moon. That is a story most people have forgotten, but the ancient ones knew it. After all, it was the sun that sent the moon to us to reflect light during the dark hours. What greater gift could there be?"

"My father loved the moon, didn't he?" she asked quietly. "He refers to it so often in his poetry."

I nodded. "And your father was very much loved by the moon goddess. It was he who named you after her. I would often feel her come and listen to his poetry, so I knew how much she adored him. One night as I was sleeping, she whispered to me, asking that I bring him to her moon world so that she could hear him recite throughout the night, and so I did. I flew with him on a flaming red phoenix. It was the first time for him, but I had flown on a phoenix before. The moon world is very beautiful, not like what we see when we look up at the moon from here. It is a magical place, and I wanted to stay with him there, but I had to return to take care of you. I will go to him when the time is right, because, as I have told you, love never ends."

"Now I know you are teasing," she said. "How could you ride a phoenix?"

"It's true, Chang'e. Look up at the moon during the night and you will see your father there, reciting poetry to the moon goddess. Sometimes I get up in the dark and listen. If you get very quiet and listen very attentively, you can hear him. His poetry floats on moon breezes and brings joy to all the beings there who love him dearly."

She smiled. "You are not only a poet, Ma, you are the best storyteller."

Some time later I wrote a poem about my daughter:

To My Daughter
I hid all remnants of war and famine,
And the iniquities of our time
In a cloak of silence,
So they would not sadden you.
Instead I surrounded you
With the beauty of the flowering moon,
Goddesses emerging from rivers in the sky,
and magical creatures who whisked you away.
But I could not keep the world
From creeping into our mountain hideout.
And so now I must give you
The strength of a towering tree
To withstand the winds that will blow.

From an early age, Chang'e had shown a keen intelligence and the gift of a sharp memory, very much like her father. Her penetrating gaze was also reminiscent of his. Every summer, Jing would send his wife and children to stay with us through the warmer months, and Chang'e would ask them to please bring books, always more books. She could not quench her thirst for knowledge. They would supply us with books of poetry, history, and philosophy, and she would fully engross herself in studying them. I thought to myself one day that she had the best of both worlds—the beauty of the untamed natural world as well as great intellectual stimulation. She especially loved to hear myths and legends of olden times.

One day she came to me and said in an inquiring tone, "You have told me about Fuxi and Nuwa, the ancient ancestors who established the early matriarchal societies. They are often shown as being half-human and half-serpent. Could they have been from the race of nagas that you once told me about? You said they had great intelligence."

I was thoughtful. "I have never made the association, but you are right, they are described as being half-serpent, which I assume means they had the power to shift their appearance, perhaps assuming the form of a serpent every now and then. We only have remnants of our ancient history and must use our imagination to fill in the blanks. That is the role of the poets and storytellers." It was then that I realized that Chang'e had her own well-developed thought processes and was now able to function in the world without my guidance.

More time passed, and I felt myself nearing the end of my life. I asked Chang'e to come with me on a journey. She had not left Lushan Mountain before and so was very curious. When she asked where we were going, I wouldn't reveal our destination. We took two horses and rode through the mountain paths to the Yangtze River, to the very spot where so many years earlier I had set a poem adrift in the gentle current. As we sat there, I said, "Chang'e, many lifetimes ago I used to live by a very sacred river. I learned to love that river as I would the goddess; indeed, it is said that the goddesses caused the waters to flow when the ice melted so long ago. This vast Yangtze River is the sacred river given to us, to our people, and I hope never to forget to express gratitude for that. You must come here every now and then and sit by the river in cultivation. I have seen the Yangtze in the most peaceful of times and also during the ravages of war. It is peaceful again, and I pray that it stays this way."

We both entered cultivation for some time. Before we got up to leave, I took out a sheaf of all the poems I had written over the years and tied it together with a bamboo string. I made a motion to set them in the river, but Chang'e lurched forward and stopped me, placing her hand on my arm. "What are you doing?" she asked in dismay.

"Saying goodbye to my poems," I replied quietly.

"You can't do that, Ma. Your poems don't belong to you alone. They belong to the world." I looked at her in surprise. Those were almost the very words Bai had spoken to me when I had burned my earliest poems. I understood that it was Bai speaking through our daughter, and so I withdrew my arm. She said, "If you are done with them, Ma, leave your poems with me. I will treasure them."

As she spoke these words, another image came before me. It was of Sundari as she neared the end of her life, carrying her precious statue of the goddess to the bank of the river, intending to offer it into the water, when her daughter placed her hand on her arm and asked her to please leave the statue in her care.

"I will leave my poems with you, Chang'e, and you will then have a record of my spiritual life."

I looked out over the water and thought of Sachit and Bai; as their images came before me, tears moistened my eyes, clouding my sight as my mind returned to long ago. Leaning over, Chang'e hugged me. "Are you sad, Ma, because you are thinking of Baba?"

I replied gently, "I am not sad, Chang'e. These are tears of gratitude. I am remembering how your father first introduced me so long ago to the beauty of poetry. Through him, I fell in love with the sound of words. The cadence of his voice would uplift me and carry me into a faraway world, more beautiful than this one. It is those sounds I am remembering now, and my heart is filled with gratitude." Then I added, "I owe my ability to write to Shifu, who helped me find my voice, but it was your father who led me to poetry and who has always been my inspiration." I turned to face her and smiled, "That is the legacy I leave you, my child."

"It is one I will treasure."

I took one last long look at the river, thinking that I might not see her again. The trip through the mountains was getting difficult as I was getting older, and I intuitively felt my time now was limited.

A few months later, perhaps inspired by her first trip down the mountain to the river, Chang'e announced one day that she wanted to go in search of her brother.

"Your brother?" I asked in surprise.

"Didn't Baba have a son? You once told me that his daughter from his first wife had died, but his son was still alive, and you had met him. I would like to find that part of my family."

"Chang'e, Jing and Yue and their children—they are your family."

"I want to know my father's family," she said firmly.

"Alright, I will come with you."

She shook her head. "I must do this alone."

"It is not safe for a young woman to travel alone," I protested, but she insisted. I went to seek Ying's counsel.

"Let me talk to her. I will send one of the nuns with her."

She got Chang'e to agree to that arrangement, and she and an older nun departed for their journey while I prayed that she would find the brother she was seeking. It was several months before they returned. She wouldn't say much about her trip, except that she had found her brother and had spent several days with him and his family. There was a smile on her face as she spoke about Boqin. "I knew that Baba loved him, and now I know why. He shared so many memories of Baba with me, and now I feel I know my father better."

H er return marked an ending for me. I now felt at ease, knowing that Chang'e could manage her life on her own. I didn't live many years longer. Shifu had already been gone for quite a long while. Some said she had died, but Ying said she simply had returned to where she had come from. It wasn't until after Shifu had passed that I began to question who she truly was and how she could have known so much about my past life experiences. How could she have known the details of Sage Gayatri and her trials, known about Yeye? It was as if Shifu had blocked these questions from arising in my mind when I was with her; once she was gone, it was no longer possible to ask, so I had to leave those questions unanswered.

Ying once told me that Shifu was able to attune her mind with the minds of her students and to experience what they did. But how could that be, I wondered? When I would reflect on these matters, I would hear the words she spoke to me so often, "Shu, you are too much in the thinking mind, occupying yourself with the ten thousand things. Free yourself from these encumbrances. They are like shadows in the wind, with no real substance, so why dwell on them?" Once I had asked her how to free myself; her response was "inner cultivation."

"But, Shifu," I had protested, "my cultivation is not deep."

She had smiled and replied simply, "One day it will be if you keep at it."

That day didn't come for me. I was never able to go deep in my cultivation practice and I also was unable to overcome the thinking mind, but somehow, I came to believe it didn't matter. Perhaps that would be left to the future.

Whenever I had met with Shifu, she would always ask to see the poems I had written since our last meeting. She liked to read them out loud. Then she would inevitably put them aside, close her eyes, and smile, saying, "Very good, Shu, very good." Her words meant as much to me as those of

Bai. He was my poetry mentor, but she was the mentor of my spirit. I had never written of my feelings for Shifu, but suddenly I felt the desire and did so. Afterwards I went to sit outside the cave where she and I had often sat together. I imagined that she was seated beside me, and with closed eyes I recited the poem to her, knowing the words would reach her and that she would smile and say, "Very good, Shu, very good."

Shifu

I think I have known you for eternity
Yet, how can I truly know you,
Who are as mysterious as the Dao
As near and as far.
You speak of the joy of empty Being,
Unfettered by the ten thousand things.
I could never find that place
Yet I know that is where
I will find you.

Like the Dao,
My love for you
Cannot be named
Or spoken,
But it is more real
Than the ten thousand things
That disappear
With the flicker of an eye.

A year or so later, I sat down to write a poem to Bai, thinking that while we had brought to completion something from the past that had been left unfinished, there was no ending to the love I felt for him. It was to be my last poem.

To Bai

You and I are now free from an ancient decree.
The stars no longer circle and bind us
To a past we barely remember.
Now we can wander together at will.
So prepare the way and wait for me.
When the bright moon rises
And embraces the sun,
Then we will meet.

Passage: A Beginning

I awoke in a rather confused state. Sitting up, I looked around and saw that I was in the same forest where Satya had found me, but how long ago I didn't know. How much time had passed since then? For a brief moment I had to think who I was. Then it came to me. I was Shu, still identified with that form, still wrapped in the memories of the life I had just come from. I had returned to the place I had been before taking that birth, but in between, I had experienced another life on earth. I heard the words "Little Phoenix," but I couldn't tell if those words were coming from an external or internal source. Turning, I saw Shifu seated a short distance away, but it was not her voice I had heard. She rose and came to sit beside me.

"Shifu," I murmured. "You are here." She nodded. Then I watched as her appearance changed into that of Sage Gayatri, and I stared at her in disbelief. "Ammaji? It was you?" Again, she nodded. Shifu had also been Sage Gayatri? I tried to let this sink in, as her form changed back into that of Shifu. "It was you who trained me and enabled me to recall all of those memories?"

"Satya had unlocked your memories before you took birth, but he was concerned about what might emerge. He knew that if he took birth to guide you, it would confuse you, and so he asked me to take a human birth. Also, I had some responsibility for what had come to pass and was happy to give you the training you could not undergo in your previous births. In unlocking your memory of Sachit, we didn't know what else would be released. At your level of cultivation, it would have been overwhelming if the memories of all your lifetimes were to flood you. As it was, you experienced plenty of difficulty just with the recollection of those few lives."

"If Satya had taken birth, I would have been torn." I murmured.

"You would not have been able to fulfill this long-held, buried desire, and it was time for Sachit to fulfill his desire, his love for you. The conditions of your vow had been fulfilled. I told you once I would help you bring that vow to completion."

I looked at her lovingly. How much she had done for me over the course of time. "You did not forget me," I whispered.

She smiled. "Forgetting is only a temporary state. When one awakens, all things remain within one's sight."

"Shifu, why did I return here to this sacred forest?"

"Because he is here. He was drawn to this forest to revive his memories of his life as Bai, his memories of you, which have dimmed with the passing of time. He is here to fulfil his word, his promise that he would wait for you."

I didn't respond right away but then said quietly, "I thought I heard Bai call my name, his special name for me."

"He is by the stream." She helped me up, and I looked around at the beautiful scene before me, the trees draped in flowering branches of so many colors, the soft moss-clad ground that spread between the trees, the stream rippling over light- reflecting stones as it curved through the forest. This world was now so real and the world of earth was receding into the form of dream.

"Go to him," she said. "He has been waiting for you. I will leave you now."

"Shifu," I murmured as she began to fade from view. I reached out to her, but she was gone. I didn't want to let her leave so quickly. There was so much I wanted to say to her; I had so much gratitude, but I felt Bai silently calling me. I walked over to where he stood. As my eyes took in the sight of him, I saw the imprint of Sachit's form faintly flicker within his form, but it quickly faded, and I realized he was answering my question as to whether he truly was the one I had known as Sachit. He now appeared as a younger form of the Bai I had known, younger even than when I had first met him, but he was the same Bai, only the shadow of inner struggles no longer clung to him.

For as long as I had known him, Bai had held within himself a longing to be acknowledged for who he truly was, but this was never realized during the lifetime we shared. It was a longing I hadn't fully understood, but one look at him told me that that shadow was gone, completely dissipated, and how glad I was to see him shining with a clarity and joyfulness that he had never found when I had known him on earth. His field of energy was now more light-filled. As I stood looking at him, I thought about what an extraordinary man he had been; here it was even more evident. Then, I remembered the despair I had fallen into when he had died and how difficult it had been to pull myself out of that dark hole. The expression on his face indicated that he was aware of my thoughts. What words could be found? We continued our wordless exchange. We stood both within the boundaries of time and outside of them: seeing the past, taking in the present moment, and knowing that our future could, in an instant, pull us forward into another embodiment, but none of that mattered. We were here together now.

He hadn't left behind his identity as Bai. He hadn't taken rebirth, he hadn't wandered into a faraway realm; he had waited for me as he said he would. What greater sign of love? The thought of our daughter came before me, and I desired to share with him my memories of her, and so I allowed images of the many stages of her life to pass through my mind so that he could know them too. A smile crossed his face as I showed him the life of his daughter.

I then saw his thoughts reflecting on how needlessly he had been troubled about worldly affairs and how he had been unable to devote himself to deep cultivation, but I also saw that now he had let go, releasing so many things that seemed important on earth, but not from this vantage point. *It all passes*, he conveyed, *so quickly. That life is like a dream now, which appeared real when we were in it, but, upon awakening, became nothing more than a mental imprint.*

Our identities were not confined to Bai and Shu. We were two souls who had a deep connection, a long and charged history behind us, and a path before us that we could not yet see, but one that likely we would each have to walk alone. We didn't know whether we would come together in the future or not, but it didn't matter. A deep connection once made never dissipates, because it does not operate in the field of time and space.

My mind flew back to the time when he had first come to get me from Lushan Mountain, when we had suspended all our outer duties and together enjoyed the beauty of the natural world. I looked around. This world was even more awe inspiring. As this thought came to me, he took my hand and, with a smile, led me out of the forest.

I heard the whisperings: *Love does not die, Little Phoenix, it is carried from one life into the next until it expands and embraces all, and then it becomes an experience beyond feelings and attachments—a most joyful expansion—and that is why we are here. A celebration within this grand universe is taking place, and we are meant to be there.*

A celebration?

He was glowing. *A union between a goddess of the moon and a deity of the sun, for the purpose of pouring love into the physical world. It does not happen often, but for centuries this courtship has been building and now the union will take place.*

A union?

A rare union between the inner worlds of the sun and the moon. It will be celebrated far and wide and will unleash such a bounty of love that many living beings will benefit. This joy will spread not only through the inner worlds but also in the physical one and relieve some of the suffering there. It is still a dark time on earth, but this union, this love, will help accelerate the movement toward greater awakening.

As we walked, I saw many, many light beings moving with such gracefulness through the valleys and mountains around us. Joy filled the air, and as I looked around in astonishment, I remembered that this was the place to which I had come before I had taken birth as Shu. When I died as Meihua, I had awakened in this field and then was drawn to the forest, where I found Satya. I had sensed a celebration then but was told it was not yet time. Perhaps that is why I took another birth so quickly after my last return. I was meant to be here with the one I knew as Bai.

My heart was so open that I turned to Bai and wanted to express myself, but thought was gone, no words were there. I looked at him and smiled, and he smiled back. We walked and sat and walked again, exchanging fewer and fewer thoughts, as slowly all clinging to my life on earth lifted away like mist dissolving in sunlight. I was here, and earth was far away, speeding with the spin of years and decades and centuries. Earth time was not our time, and there was no urgency or limitation to our span of life. A millennia of earth time could pass, and we would hardly notice.

After some time, he asked in thought, *Do you feel the deep exchange between the deities of the sun and moon?*

I nodded. How could one not feel it? It was like being in a rushing river with waters flowing all around you. From a distance we could perceive beings emanating beautiful light: some were gathering in the air, some on the ground, some on the distant mountain peaks, some in the waters that fell from the mountains. Everywhere, forms were emerging from beams of light.

We walked to the mountains to see the light beings up close, and then to the rivers, where we sat among the beings for a long time, listening as their songs arose in exquisite harmony. We sat in cultivation, and after a while I could no longer distinguish between beings radiating different qualities. They were like many facets of a single gem, multiple reflections of a single beam that seemed to have merged into one radiance. They were separate, each emanating their own identity, and yet in some mysterious way they were unified, a single emergence of light. Turning to Bai, I sought to see if he was experiencing the same. I saw that he was; no exchange was needed. For some time, we rested in the thoughtless realm, beyond where the mind can travel, where true being can emerge.

As I was sinking deeper into that place of unity, something tugged at my awareness; a thought arose, an image of the hermit I had seen but briefly toward the end of my life as Shu. I looked around and saw his form standing by the edge of the forest we had come from, not so far from where we now rested. He was gazing at me and I stared back, but he was at a distance and I couldn't quite make out his features. I knew him by his presence, which was drawing me very intensely. Bai looked up and saw me gazing into the distance at the figure by the forest.

"Bai, I have to go find someone."

He nodded, "Yes, you must go." We both rose, and I took one long, last look at Bai, imprinting his image in my mind. He took my hand and held it for a while; as he released it, I turned and began to walk toward the forest. The figure had now disappeared, but I was determined to discover the identity of the one whose presence had meant so much to me in the last years of Shu's life.

Entering the forest, I walked some distance at a hurried pace, until, emerging from the crowd of trees, I found myself in a very familiar place, by a large body of sparkling, crystalline water that I knew so well, that I had tended for so long. I was home. Walking closer to the clear waters, which shone with a blueish-green hue, I found Satya seated in meditation, his back turned toward me. Surely, he would know the identity of that hermit who so mysteriously had disappeared into the forest. I knew that I had to calm all the ripples of my mind and heart before greeting him and so I stood there for a while. When I felt as still as the waters before me, I whispered, "Satya, I am back." I saw the faint outline of a movement and knew he was emerging from meditation. After waiting a few moments, I began to describe very slowly the scene I had come from. "Satya, it was such a celebration, beyond description, beyond words. Why were you not there?"

"I was," he replied, still not facing me. "Did you not recognize me?"

"I didn't see you," I replied. And then I watched him assume another form, though I still couldn't see his face. "You are changing your appearance."

"Aren't we always changing our appearance?"

It was true. I was no longer Shu. My form had become that of Usha again. Slowly he turned and I recognized the hermit I had seen on the ridge that day in my life as Shu, the one who had just appeared to me at the edge of the forest. "It was your projection!" I exclaimed. "How could I not have recognized you?" He smiled, and then his appearance changed again, and Kapila sat before me. "And he was also you! How could I not have known this until now?" Again, he smiled. Then his form became that of my beloved Satya. I couldn't speak, but my thoughts were not quiet. Silently I whispered, *You felt my pain when I was in mourning over Bai and you came, just as you came to me when I was mourning the loss of Sachit.*

How could I not, he silently replied. *Both times you were unable to get over your despair. When we met as Kapila and Sundari, you had not yet gained discernment and your emotions were so unsettled. It has taken you a long time, but you have gained patience and composure. In your last birth, Bai taught you forbearance.*

Only then did I realize that it was all our separations, all of Bai's absences, that had taught me to endure. How different everything looked from here. Still in the realm of silence, I asked, *Satya, why did I not realize before now that you were my dear friend Kapila? All the times that we have been together here, how could I not have known this? How could I have forgotten you, who are so dear to me?*

Those memories were locked, and it was not yet time to release them, he replied in thought.

When I died as Meihua, you came to me in the sacred grove and unlocked my memory. You released the memories of Sundari's life that had been long put away. You opened that door but were cautious, not knowing what other memories would be released.

In reply, I heard his thoughts. *You didn't want to return to birth so soon, and there was the possibility that you would miss the opportunity to fulfill your desire, to meet him again. When your memories returned, that love was awakened and you couldn't resist the pull that drew you into another birth, but other memories managed to sneak through the door, those that were relevant to the life of Shu. Do you remember, Usha, that before you met Bai you were on the verge of marrying another man your parents had chosen? Then you had a nightmare that dissuaded you from that marriage, which made possible your reunion with the one you had known as Sachit.*

I had forgotten that. *So, your presence was there all along.* As we exchanged these thoughts, I found myself embraced by the clear, still eyes of Satya, and I was struck by the quality of his love, of a different order entirely from the conditional and possessive love expressed on earth. But why should I be surprised? This was the character of the one I knew as Kapila, now even more refined.

I was thoughtful. *Will I retain my memories then?*

You know that when you assume a human birth, all that came before is submerged in the ocean of the mind so that you can begin as if anew. But there may be people or events that awaken memories in you. That remains to be seen. Perhaps that door will never fully close.

F alling into a deep reflection, I expressed to him that I now knew that it must have been he who had lifted many years from my vowed separation from Sachit. He had taken those years upon himself, and thus he and I had not been able to meet again on earth for many millennia after our meeting as Kapila and Sundari.

Usha, your life as Sundari has now been fully resolved. The emotions and desires set into motion then have now been entirely put to rest. You have fulfilled your desire with Sachit. The love between the two of you has completed itself. Your love of the sacred hymns led you not only to marry one of the great poets of the time, but also to become a poet yourself, so you could express your deepest spiritual yearnings and insights. Several lifetimes after your life as Sundari, you were born into a cursed family and had to live with some degree of misfortune, fulfilling the curse of the naga. Then, lifetimes later, you also met Sundari's mother again, the one who you had rejected, and in that life, you tended to her, bringing her peace in her last days. During that same lifetime, Sundari's sister Prema took birth and had to endure much suffering in order to fulfill the naga's curse. You were there to ease her pain, just as Sage Gayatri had promised. And most importantly, you have now received proper training from Sage Gayatri, who you knew as your Shifu, training that you were not ready to undergo in your life as Sundari, or in the subsequent lives when you served her. The training you received from Shifu will now shape the course of your future.

It took nearly ten thousand years to fulfill all of that, I mused.

You know that one year in earth time is one day here, and so ten thou-

sand years is less than thirty years here . . . not much time at all.

My thoughts now turned into spoken words, and I asked, "Satya, who is Shifu? Who is Sage Gayatri truly? Such a magnificent being. Never has she had a thought of herself."

He closed his eyes without answering, and I understood that he would not be able to describe her through words and was instead transmitting a vision. It was not until I closed my eyes and sat quietly for some time that I was able to see her true form as the beloved of Indra Dev, the god who rules these light-filled mental worlds. "She has become one with that deva she so loved," I whispered quietly. I heard Satya's mental response. *Even when she takes physical form, she is not apart from that luminous one. Separateness is only an appearance. The earth world is filled with appearances; what seems to be, but is not. It is nothing but that.*

When I opened my eyes and found Satya gazing lovingly at me, I could not help but try to express what could not be expressed. "The most high comes into a lowly human form to help those of us who may not even be aware that we are seeking."

"The cosmic forces are continually working for the awakening of the world, for the union of all beings with the illumined consciousness. Didn't she once tell you this?" he asked.

"The mysteries she revealed could not be understood by me at that time. It is only now that I can begin to grasp them."

"When in human form, we do not truly know who anyone is, and the great ones usually come in a well-hidden disguise. Come, let us walk," he said. Taking my hand, he led me through beautiful landscapes so familiar and treasured by me.

Sometime later, when we sat to rest, I said, "Satya, the thoughts and desires set in motion in one life find their end results over the course of so many lives, spread over vast expanses of time. How that comes to be is one of the wonders of the universe."

He nodded.

I continued: "How often you have told me this, and how true it is. The nature of cause and effect is a deep mystery that few can penetrate." I was quiet and then asked, "How much time has passed on earth since my life as Shu?"

"Over two hundred years."

"That long?" He nodded. Bai and I had finally had our time together, a good, long time. I felt full and satisfied, and I felt intuitively that Satya had arranged this. "I will stay here now with you for a long time."

"Will you?"

I nodded. "I hardly saw you after my life as Meihua, and now I have spent this time with Bai . . ."

He didn't let me finish. "During a sacred celebration, everyone receives a special blessing. What blessing, Usha, will you seek?"

"What blessing? I can't think of anything." He was quiet as I ruminated. The memories of the human life I had most recently left, and which had been put to rest, now re-emerged. "During my life as Shu I felt deeply the scars left by the terrible war but could do nothing to ease the suffering. I could only watch from my perch on the mountain while Shifu and other nuns traveled the country providing food and caring for the sick. Shifu spoke especially of what the women had to endure, women who had had no part in the battle but who were the greatest victims of the upheavals. She worked tirelessly to help them, but I had a child to raise and could not assist. That is my only regret from that life."

He nodded and asked again, "What blessing, Usha?"

"I can't think of anything, Satya. I would stay here with you if I could."

"Look deeply into your heart, Usha. Are you not being pulled again to earth?"

Images of the An Lushan Rebellion came before me. I didn't want to see them and tried to brush them away, but they wouldn't leave my mind. "When Bai and I were fleeing the war, we saw such terrible scenes and heard horrible stories of atrocities, which I don't think I will be able to forget entirely. Even if I don't remember the details, the suffering will stay engraved in my heart. Shifu once described to me how, when the rebels returned to their villages, there was such division and hatred, even though a general amnesty had been declared. How could the villagers and the rebels come together, when the villagers knew that their relatives had been killed by that rebel army? The people who fought alongside those brutal killers had been their neighbors. It would take a long time, a generation or more, to heal. I had wanted to assist Shifu but couldn't. She had done so much for me, but what could I give back? Satya, it was not the first birth in which I experienced the horrors of war. I remember all too well too many wars." As I spoke small waves of emotion passed through me.

"You are not done with earth, my dear."

I looked at him with surprise and asked, "What do you mean?"

Gazing steadily at me with those clear, still eyes that showed not a flicker of disturbance, he replied, "Shadows and light. It is all shadows and light, and the shadows are part of the light."

I understood what he was saying, but I could not contain myself. "In my life as Shu, as Meihua, as Chunhua, and in so many other lives, it was difficult for me to find my voice as a woman. I remember that, and I remember thinking how common it was for women to feel that way. We had no say over the course of our lives. Only as Shu did I begin to feel as if I had a voice, but it was Shifu who helped me. Had it not been for her . . . But Satya, it was you who put the thought into my mind that someday the balance between the male and female would be restored, that equilibrium would return. Is that time approaching, Satya?"

He didn't answer right away, but then he said quietly, "I think you know what blessing to seek, and I think you know what your return to earth will be."

"What blessing . . . I don't know," I murmured. "But I do hope that in some small way I can help to do the work that needs to be done."

"That is the blessing you will receive, and I will do my part to help you fulfill that desire," he replied tenderly.

"When will I take birth again, Satya?"

"The opportunity has arisen . . ."

"That noble warrior I once met long ago, the one to whom I owe a very great debt, he has taken birth again, hasn't he?"

Satya nodded. "It is not a debt, Usha, but a return of love and an expression of gratitude, a desire set in your heart at an earlier time, which has bound you to him. There are samskaras for you yet to work out. Let the past unravel itself. Your task now is to tend to the future, to observe with discernment so that new waves of desire do not emerge."

"To observe with discernment," I repeated quietly. "How will I remember that?" My life with Bai was over, but another life was soon to begin, and I would be leaving one love for another, a very different kind of love, one of a purely spiritual nature. The blueprint for that life was already unfolding. The image of the warrior from long ago came before my mind and suddenly the memory returned to me: *he was the son of Indra Dev.*

Satya nodded and replied in thought. *Now you understand.*

I nodded in response. To see him once more, the one who had been known as Arjuna, I would traverse universes. But I could not dwell on who he had been in the past for the future was calling me.

"How soon?"

"Within days."

"Days here are years there. Let us spend some time together, Satya." I was determined to be present and not let my mind wonder about what lay ahead in my next birth. Although I knew Bai would never depart from my heart, he was slowly fading from my mind, as I renewed my bond with Satya in the uplifting atmosphere that nourished me between my times on earth.

One day I turned to Satya and said, "Although my memories of Bai have grown quiet and may rest in some hidden place, my love for him will never die."

"And it should not. How can love die?" he responded.

We were sitting one day by the water when my mind drifted back to Kapila, the first meeting between me and Satya, and I remembered how dear he was to me, but it was a different kind of love than what I had felt for Sachit. It was a joyful, calming love that made no demands and was not in any way possessive, one that had grown over time, that supported and enabled any experience that would help me grow in knowledge and awaken to the true nature of things.

Responding to my thoughts, he said, "We met during an age of higher awareness on earth, when people understood the power of the word and of thought to shape the outer world, when they knew themselves to be the creators. You and I did not need to express our feelings then, because we understood the unspoken exchange of the heart."

"The creative power of Devi Sarasvati was so present then."

"Nothing has changed, Usha, except the perception of people. If they cannot perceive the deities, it is due to a dimming of perception. Even during the higher ages, there were internal struggles, as you well know. And during the darkest times, when there is war and famine, there are people of great wisdom and virtue to be found, as you also know."

"The universal laws are so complex."

"Actually, quite simple, but perhaps not grasped by the logical mind, which is only one of many vehicles for attaining knowledge."

I laughed. "It is still a mystery to me how people find one another, how they know when the circumstances are right."

"It is spontaneous knowing, an inner attunement. Isn't that the Dao?"

I looked at him curiously. "So, you know something of the Dao?"

"Do you think I have not also been a Daoist?"

I was quiet and then replied is a loving tone, "Since you know the Dao, Satya, then let me say this:

The Dao that can be spoken is not the eternal Dao.
The name that can be named is not the eternal name.

I will add another line: the love that can be expressed is not the eternal love." At that moment, my whole being radiated with love for him, the one who sat beside me, but it was not a limited or confining love, it was all-encompassing. How could I possibly find words to express that vastness?

He smiled and simply replied, "Still the poet."

We sat quietly for some time and then I asked, as much of myself as to him, "Will I ever tire of these rounds of rebirth?"

"It is what you have chosen, and yes, there will come a time when you will choose not to go."

The day came when I was called, and I watched Satya's form fade from my view, like so many times before, as my consciousness began to withdraw and contract and I entered the beginnings of another human body, far away from the place I had come to know as China, in the land of Normandy, under the rule of the one who would be known to the world as William the Conqueror.

Epilogue

On the day I finished writing this narrative, that night I had a dream of Bai. I could not help but be struck by the timing, as if he was sending some confirmation, some approval of what had been written. Though we take on new incarnations, each one leaves its imprint in our memory, and we can at any moment reconnect with someone from our past, no matter where that being is, because in the higher mental world, time and space are easily transcended. Now, as I sit before my desk, I may be appearing in someone's dream as Chunhua or Shu, because it is not the rational mind that controls this process. It is the higher Self, which can assume any shape at any moment. After the dream, I wrote a last poem to Bai.

Knowing Bai Again

The last word was written,
My computer put aside,
The story complete,
That night, you came in a dream
Over 1200 years after your death.
There was no mistaking your presence.

The story began with a jade phoenix in a lamp shop
And ended with a dream.
Both signs to confirm
I was not wandering aimlessly
In some imagined past,
But had touched upon the truth
Of a past birth and the reality
That love reaches across time.
The dream, another gift from you,
My far and near beloved,
Revealing that as I was remembering you,
You were also remembering me.

Can I say with certainty that the memories I have recorded here are mine? Of course not. They may be those of another, channeled through me, but I have long known that my love for India stems from my memory of Vedic India, a time of far greater peace and the prevalence of wisdom, and this memory has never been fully erased from my mind. Whenever I travel to India, it is that India I am seeking, but I have come to realize over the years that the India I seek lies within me, in my memory, although remnants still remain in the outer world. It is those latent memories that over the incarnations have inspired my search for an idyllic community and for a more peaceful world. It was during that time in ancient India that I developed an intimate relationship with rivers, which remains with me to this day.

To those readers who have read my previous book, *The Untold Story of Sita,* and know of the servant in Sita's household called Meenakshi, you will recall that she was born into a cursed family. She was paying off the curse that she had received from the naga in her birth as Sundari, and it was Sage Gayatri who guided her to her birth as Meenakshi, where she could receive the blessings of being in Sita's household, to counteract the negative effects of the curse. When Sundari asked to take three births as a servant to Sage Gayatri, she did not realize the blessings that this request would yield. Sage Gayatri offered that last lifetime of service to Shri Devi, also known as Narayani, who took birth as Sita. In this way, actions begun in one life find fulfillment in another, often centuries and even millennia later, and it is the awakened ones who seek to alleviate our suffering and to ameliorate curses that cannot be retracted.

Throughout the writing of this book I have felt the presence of the one I call Bai. There is another history of him told through his biographies, but that is not the Bai I speak of. The Bai I know showed me a different face, not the one of an inebriated and proud poet seeking a place in the world, but rather of a man struggling to come to terms with the times in which he lived, who knew he had so much to offer but was too often neglected, a man of great intelligence and poetic genius, but most importantly, a seeker of truth. For a more complete biography of the poet Li Bai, I recommend the book *The Banished Immortal: A Life of Li Bai* by Ha Jin. From that book, I was able to fill in some of the blanks in my narrative, such as the name of the hermit friend from Bai's youth and the name of the man who helped get him released from prison, and sequence some of the events about which I wrote.

Images and scenes pass before my inner eye, often without names, and so some research is needed to fill in the empty places. The various biographies of Li Bai are ambiguous and sometimes contradictory with regard to his personal life, because the facts are sparse. In addition, what is left to us of Bai's poetry is only a small portion of what he wrote, so even that record of his inner life is paltry, but one can feel from his many poems his inner searching and spiritual longing. His style is remarkably modern and speaks to everyday experience, which is why Li Bai remains such a beloved poet today.

Li Bai's adoration of and frequent reference to the moon is an expression of the relationship that the moon has played in the unfolding of Chinese culture. In reading *The Selected Poems of Li Bai* by David Hinton, I came across the following statement in the introduction, which discusses this relationship:

> "It's difficult for us now to imagine what the moon was for T'ang intellectuals, but it was not in any sense the celestial body that we know. In a universe animated by the interaction of *yin* (female) and *yang* (male) energies, the moon is literally yin visible. Indeed, it was the very germ or source of yin, and the sun was its yang counterpart.... Hence, the moon was the heavenly incarnation of, was indeed the embryonic essence of the mysterious energy we call the spirit (yin spirit, with the sun being the source of yang spirit)."

What Hinton does not mention is the deities, the conscious forces, the spiritual energies within those worlds of sun and moon that are constantly working for the awakening of that which has not yet been awakened. I read these words long after I had the vision of the celestial marriage, which I describe in the opening pages of this book, but they helped me to better understand the celestial union I had witnessed.

History gives us a record of the outer events, but cannot provide us the inner narrative, the spiritual stories of the time. Without that narrative, there will always be an incomplete picture. While outer events are important, my interest has always been in the inner story, what was taking place in the inner field. As we look to our own personal past, it is our inner life as much as our outer that determines our future. Our thoughts, desires, and feelings are as much drivers of future events as our actions, as they hold tremendous power and are energies emitted into the universe. Every energy released must have a return.

Vedic India

Western scholars mistakenly assign the time of the Vedas to around 1500 BCE. They lock its creation to the time when the mystic hymns were compiled and written down, but it is commonly known that the Vedas were an oral tradition for many, millennia before they were written, and the writing of them was actually an indication of a decline in the mental capacity of people. Previously, the vast texts were held in memory; writing was not required to preserve them. Astronomical recordings in the Vedas, as well as tradition, indicate that the hymns go back at least ten thousand years and most likely longer. Many believe that what has come down to us is only a remnant of a far larger and earlier body of inspired poetry. Although I use the term Vedas in the description of the hymns chanted during Sundari's life, most likely that term was not even used until much later, when these sacred poems were compiled into a body of work by Sage Vyasa.

The poems in the Vedas were recited in an ancient form of Sanskrit, which makes them difficult to access. Even if we know the words, the meaning of their usage likely has changed. The best key to understanding the Vedas can be found in the work of the modern sage Sri Aurobindo, especially in his book *The Secret of the Veda*. In chapter 2 of that book, he describes the age in which these poems came into form:

> ". . . it is perhaps only the last testament of the Ages of the Intuition, the luminous Dawns of the Forefathers, to their descendants, to a human race already turning in spirit towards the lower levels and the more easy and secure gains—secure perhaps only in appearance—of the physical life and of the intellect and the logical reason."

He goes on to describe the Vedic era as the close of a period, not the beginning of one. He says: ". . . the system of the Vedic mystics was founded upon experiences difficult for ordinary mankind and proceeded by the aid of faculties which in most of us are rudimentary and imperfectly developed . . ." In the same chapter, Sri Aurobindo continues, ". . . for those hymns are couched in a language that was deliberately ambiguous." Then he adds that over the centuries and millennia ". . . the material aspects of Vedic worship had grown like a thick crust over the inner knowledge and were stifling what they once served to protect."

As the understanding of the profound symbolic references hidden in each sound of the words was lost, simpler interpretations became common; the power of mantra, of speech, was declining. In essence, hidden within the poems of the Vedas is the description of the process of awakening to one's immortal nature. The external forces, which manage the external world, known as the deities, are also internal ones, and the whole of human striving is to awaken the divine inner will, known as Agni, to guide the ascent; the higher luminous mind, known as Indra, comes to aid the internal process of realizing the state of the illumined or enlightened consciousness, known as Surya. Thus, the gods are both external and internal forces. We all know the adage "as within, so without"—we are a microcosm of the macrocosm. One needn't look to the outside world to come into relationship with these cosmic forces, for they reside subtly active within us.

The seers of the Vedas were highly advanced in spiritual understanding. They appeared at a time when earth herself was undergoing dramatic changes with the melting of the ice during the end of the last glacial period, around 11,000 BCE, and this was to reshape what we would now consider to be human society. It is said that the oceans rose 400 feet over the centuries, new rivers formed, and river-based communities were laying the groundwork for new civilizations to arise. This was called the Satya Yuga, the "age of truth," because life was lived in greater harmony with the spiritual laws. That doesn't mean that everyone had access to this higher knowledge, but the leaders of the society, the seers, did, and among the common people there was a deep connection to the world around them. They knew themselves to be part of the natural environment, and a sense of harmonious integration prevailed.

All traditions hold a memory of what they call the Golden Age, when life was simpler, more peaceful, and more in harmony with the natural world. All too often the modern mind ascribes this to myth or legend, but in India it is known to reflect a collective memory of an earlier age. I describe more about the *yugas* (cycles of time) in *The Untold Story of Sita*. As time moved on, there was an increase in individuation, the strengthening of ego consciousness, and people began to think less as a collective and more as individuals, seeking to satisfy their own desires and needs. The sense of self, with a lower case "s," became a more prominent part of the human psyche. This was the struggle we see in the life of Sundari. Perhaps it was a necessary step for the development of the rational, thinking mind. Previously people had lived more intuitively as part of a collective, not thinking of themselves as separate. The human population had been small, and there was plenty of wild food and little need for conflict. That changed with a growing population and an increase in individual needs and desires.

In recalling the life of Sundari, I caught a glimpse of what that "age of intuition" was like, when the rivers were known to be sacred, the forests plentiful, seers highly regarded, and the deities palpably near. As already mentioned, to the Vedic poets, the deities were cosmic forces, internal and external, attempting to awaken humanity to the higher truth, while maintaining balance within the created worlds, to awaken the immortal in the mortal. This understanding was lost over time, and to the general population the deities became personifications of natural forces, with very human traits, to be worshipped and feared. With the passage of time, so much understanding and knowledge was lost, but there were also gains in terms of the development of the material world; and even in dark times, there are always enlightened beings.

In the early stages of this development in India, people gravitated toward certain functions in the society according to their ability and interest. This was a fluid system that over the millennia became rigid, overly structured—less about ability, the qualities one sought to acquire in that life, and more about the family into which one was born. The *varnas* (later known as castes) over time came to function as guilds. In the early days there was no higher or lower; each sector of society was valued for its contribution. Sadly, over the millennia, so much distortion entered this way of ordering society, that a system that at one time had served the needs of society ceased to do so, evolving into a rigid caste system that has outlived its usefulness. In the attempt to rectify subsequent injustices, we should not forget the original intent and how much this system contributed to the flourishing of the great Indic civilization. We should also not forget that we all have passed through every category of society—we have been kings, warriors, merchants, artisans and servants—in order to learn the critical life lessons these stations were designed to transmit.

Tang China

Life had completely changed by the time of the Tang Empire. Within the cyclical view of history, this would have been during the Kali Yuga, an age when spiritual knowledge has decreased, the human mind is limited to the perception of the material world, and people strive after power and ego gratification. Even during the higher ages, there are personal internal conflicts that help the individual grow, and during the less-enlightened ages, there are those awakened sages who remind the human community of its higher purpose.

Early on, the Tang Empire was an oasis in a troubled world. On many continents at that time, there was political instability and social unrest. While Europe was in the throes of the Dark Ages, Tang China was experiencing a blossoming of cultural life. Great poetry, painting, woodblock printing, and music were lifting the spirits of the general population. During this time, China became the largest nation on earth, its capital city the most populous in the world. Also, at this time, the nation developed the first comprehensive criminal code and produced the first printed books. China was unified and there was general prosperity until the rebellion took hold and blew a great culture to pieces. It is said that at least thirteen million people died during the rebellion, which lasted a little over seven years. Some say it was far more, as many as thirty million. There was tremendous dislocation, with many fleeing the land north of the Yangtze River and moving south. The autonomous western region that had been held by the Tang Empire broke away. This wanton destruction was the heartbreak that Li Bai suffered—to see the land he loved, an empire so dear to him, break apart and leave desolation in its place. On the surface, with the quelling of the rebellion, the empire was pasted together and continued for about another 150 years. But it had lost its vitality, along with large areas of land, and its cultural life never reached the peaks it had known earlier.

Hidden within all of that violence and destruction were pockets of light—Daoist hermitages and Buddhist monasteries, where knowledge was preserved and passed on. Even centuries before the Tang Empire, the movement to create the Daoist state of Hanning was one such effort to regain what had been lost, to bring virtue and balance and love for the natural world back to society. Although this vision was not fully realized at the level of the state, it was preserved in small hermitages and mountain monasteries, where people found refuge from the troubles of the world.

The quotes that I use from the *Dao De Jing* are from the translation by Jeff Pepper and Xiao Hui Wang. Laozi, like the Buddha, did not speak of the deities, although he refers often to the heavenly worlds, which like the Buddha realms are inhabited by those higher light beings. Laozi and Buddha were from the same era, a time rife with superstition and fear, when the popular mind could not grasp the reality of these higher beings, and thus both of these masters spoke about the ultimate truth, the source of all, and did not dwell on the many realms of light within the manifest worlds.

In writing this book, I have peered into the ancient and still-living wisdom of both the Indic and Chinese civilizations, and I deeply revere and love both of these great cultures. If their knowledge can join, if the wisdom holders of these two traditions can come together, if we can see the beauty and depth of both, without competition but in a deep exchange, there is great hope and potential for our world to achieve what the seers have envisioned.

The Celestial Worlds

I must apologize to the reader for my inability to describe adequately what I have remembered of the celestial realms. I have searched for words and found none, and thus have been confronted by the limitations of speech. Thought transference, the transmission of images, is a far better means of communication and is the one frequently used in those higher realms.

Where are the celestial worlds? This is a common inquiry. Artists have depicted these worlds to be above the clouds, somewhere in the sky, but we know this to be a metaphor. They exist in another dimension of time and space, a subtle world of light that our senses are not programmed to perceive. Unless we attune ourselves with this higher vibration, we cannot hear the words spoken, the thoughts exchanged, or see the beautiful forms and landscapes of those worlds.

There is not only one celestial world, in the same way that there is not only one world in the denser universe of atoms. Our physical universe contains many planets with life, as humanity will one day discover. It is said that the celestial universe, the astral or subtle light world, is far larger even than the physical universe, but to access it, one must either leave the physical body, gain the capability to perceive this subtle reality, or awaken sleeping memories, which we all hold. Every individual can find some remnant of this memory.

Everyone's experience in what we call the "post-death" state is different. One's state of consciousness at the time of departing the body determines what one experiences. The length of time in that in-between state also varies greatly. It could be years, decades, centuries, or even millennia, depending on so many factors. In some traditions, it is said to be a mere matter of months or even weeks. We ourselves determine this—not our ego consciousness, but the higher Self, which knows when an opportunity arises to fulfil certain karmic conditions. Some people may experience their in-between life in a sleep state. Others may see people they have loved and lost. Others may go to subtler realms where the devas and devis do their work of maintaining the balance within the many universes and of helping these universes, and the individuals within them, to evolve. This process demands the efforts of a great number of awakened beings.

The word *deva* means "light being." When we speak of the many devas and devis, some think this is a denial of the existence of a single source for all that is. To the contrary, there is one pure, undifferentiated consciousness, but this consciousness projects itself as many and then further emerges into multitudes and so on. This is how creation comes into manifestation, through these projections. Different religions have various ways of expressing how the unmanifest comes into manifestation. To be "in the Dao" is to be in tune with these various processes of life. To "adhere to Dharma" is also to be in tune with them. But ultimately, words become useless, as do logical thoughts, because the reality being described exists beyond the realm of concept.

The universes are held together by a single radiant force of love, what scientists may call magnetism. The teachings and lives of the great ones manifest this love again and again on a very real level. Continually they come to earth to help us realize this.

In the writing of this narrative, I was often struck by the love shown to Sundari by Sage Gayatri and again to Shu by Shifu. This made very real to me the understanding of love as the central force in the universes. I understand that this love was shown not only to Sundari, but is also shown to every living being with whom those great ones came in contact. It was through Sundari's eyes that I experienced that time on earth, but how many more Sundaris were there? Each person has their own long history of stories and of connection with great beings, whether they are remembered or not. We all participate in that love.

When I first had the dream or vision of a union between two deities, I did not understand what I was seeing. It was only through the process of writing this book that I came to understand that there are subtle cosmic events, unseen by human eyes, that bring great benefit to all life, and we can attune ourselves to those events and participate. The universal love I speak of is inclusive, not an exclusive experience. By understanding that love is the foundation that holds the universes together, we can perhaps bring this wisdom to a world in desperate need of caring. What else can help us collectively evolve to a higher understanding and a more conscious way of living peacefully together with all life forms on our shared earth?

The last chapter of this book describes my memories of my time in the celestial world with the one I call Satya. During my time with him, I had begun to see my next incarnation, which would bring to completion desires that had been initiated in India millennia earlier during the time of the great

Mahabharata War. The details of that story can be found in my upcoming book, *Rukmini and the Turning of Time*.

Finally, my hope in sharing my personal memories and stories is to awaken some remembrance in you, my reader, some faint memory or acknowledgement of your long history, of your meetings with the great ones, your trials and successes, your loves, and your times of rest and renewal in the place that is truly home. Those memories may emerge in the shadows of a dream or in subtle intuitive knowings. They are surely there. Once we realize that our journey never ends, that we are immortal, that there is nothing to gain externally, since all is within us, we will have a new understanding of our time on earth.

As a final stroke of Shu's ink brush, these poems emerged:

When the Bright Moon Rises
When the bright moon rises and embraces the sun,
When the sacred waters of the Sarasvati and Yangtze meet,
When the wisdom of these ancient lands converges
And their sages again are heard,
All will be well with the world.

Sitting Among the Leaves
I sit among the leaves of my lives,
Watching them pile high,
Each telling its own story,
Stories I unknowingly cling to.

With one breath
I can blow them away
And see them dance into the distance.

But do I dare let them depart?

Do I dare call the winds of awakening
To free me,
So I can finally be
Who I am?

Acknowledgements

I want to express my gratitude to those who have helped bring this book to fruition:

To my editors, Parvati Markus and Shyama Chapin, who have read and re-read this story, re-living it with me;

To Heran Gao, who has tirelessly worked to translate my books into Mandarin and who has been one of the early readers of this book to check some of the Chinese references;

To Sri Aurobindo, who brought the sacred Vedas alive for me, for illuminating so many of the hymns and transmitting to me a deeper understanding of the deities;

To Sraddhalu Ranada, for the clarity of his insight into the teachings of Sri Aurobindo;

To Li Bai, whose poems have served to awaken memories;

To my Shifu of old, whose patience and loving care helped resolve lingering karma and set the foundation for my later meditation practice;

To my many friends and colleagues at The Global Peace Initiative of Women, who have patiently waited while I have wandered in faraway places and time periods, reliving lives that have long passed.

GLOSSARY

India

Agni Dev—the cosmic power that creates fire and heat and also manifests as the higher will; over time he came to be seen as the fire god

Amma—mother

Ammaji—respected mother

Apsaras—heavenly beings in beautiful female forms

Brahmachari—celibate

Brahmavarta—the name given to the region between the Sarasvati and Drishadwati Rivers, where the early Vedic people lived and where Indic civilization originated Brahmin(s)—the class of priests, teachers, and protectors of sacred learning

Dada—respectful address for elderly male, grandfather

Deva(s)—god(s), literally "light being"

Devi(s)—goddess(es)

Ganga—sacred Ganges River, and Ganga, the goddess

Indra Dev—the cosmic power that oversees the mental planes, known as the celestial world. This power is also the higher mind that works to advance the evolutionary process. Over time, Indra Dev came to be known as the king of the gods and of the celestial worlds.

Kashi—old name for Varanasi, Benares

Maharishis—great rishis, highest order of sages

Mantra—sacred words of power

Muni—silent self-realized sage

Nagas—a class of semidivine beings who can assume a human or serpent form

Prana—life force

Pranam—respectful salutation made with hands together in prayer position

Raja—king

Rakshasas—violent tribes, known to eat human flesh

Rishis—sages, well-versed in the Vedas

Samskaras—the seeds of our past thoughts and actions

Sankalpa—a sacred vow

Sarasvati—goddess of knowledge and creativity, inspiration of poets

Sarasvati River—sacred river

Shakti—divine cosmic feminine energy

Shikharas—towers as part of temple architecture in North India

Shri Devi—an early term for Lakshmi, the female counterpart of Vishnu or Narayan. The female aspect of the cosmic power that maintains equilibrium or balance in all of the manifest worlds.

Surya Dev—the fully awakened, illumined consciousness that manifests as light, symbolized as the cosmic energy of the sun

Svarga—one of the seven higher planes, heaven, paradise for the devas

Tapasya—spiritual practice

Tulsi—holy basil

Vedas—ancient hymns, directly revealed to the rishis

Yagna—fire ceremony

China

Chang'e—goddess of the moon, celebrated at Mid-Autumn Festival

Dao—The Way

Dao De Jing (Tao Te Ching)—"Classic of the Way of Power," the poetic literature of Daoist philosophy

China (continued)

Daoism (Taoism)—Chinese philosophy based on writings of Lao-tzu in 6th century BCE

Eastern Han Dynasty—ruled from 25 CE to 220 CE

Hanning—independent theocratic state in what is now Sichuan, China; founded by Zhang Lu in 194 CE

Inner Cultivation—Daoist meditation

Laozi—Lao Tzu, literally, old master

Nanya—mother

Qi—life force, central principle in Daoism and Chinese traditional medicine

Tang Empire—the imperial dynasty of China that ruled from 618 to 907 CE,

a golden age of arts and culture

Tianzhu—India

Wu wei—non-doing. The key to following the Dao.

ABOUT THE AUTHOR

DENA MERRIAM is an author, storyteller and the Founder and Convener of the Global Peace Initiative of Women (GPIW), which seeks to bring spiritual resources to address critical global challenges, such as conflict, social justice, and ecological scarring of the earth. Over the years she has worked to bring greater gender balance and balance between the Abrahamic and Dharma-based religious traditions for a more inclusive interfaith movement.

Merriam served as Vice Chair of the Millennium World Peace Summit of Religious and Spiritual Leaders, held at the United Nation in New York in the year 2000. She subsequently convened a meeting of women religious and spiritual leaders at the Palais des Nations in Geneva, and from that gathering founded the Global Peace Initiative of Women in 2002. Among GPIW's many programs is the organization of a session on the inner dimensions of climate change at the annual UN Climate Summits. In 2008, Merriam was one of the founding members of the Contemplative Alliance, which later became a program of GPIW and which explores how meditation and contemplative practices are reshaping the spiritual landscape of our societies.